# COMIC BOOKS 101

## The *HISTORY, METHODS* and *MADNESS*

**CHRIS RYALL** and **SCOTT TIPTON**

**IMPACT**
CINCINNATI, OHIO
www.impact-books.com

Other fine IMPACT Books are available from your local bookstore, art supply store, online supplier or visit our website at www.fwmedia.com.

13  12  11  10  09     5  4  3  2  1

DISTRIBUTED IN CANADA BY FRASER DIRECT
100 Armstrong Avenue
Georgetown, ON, Canada  L7G 5S4
Tel: (905) 877-4411

DISTRIBUTED IN THE U.K. AND EUROPE BY DAVID & CHARLES
Brunel House, Newton Abbot, Devon, TQ12 4PU, England
Tel: (+44) 1626 323200, Fax: (+44) 1626 323319
Email: postmaster@davidandcharles.co.uk

DISTRIBUTED IN AUSTRALIA BY CAPRICORN LINK
P.O. Box 704, S. Windsor NSW, 2756 Australia
Tel: (02) 4577-3555

**Library of Congress Cataloging in Publication Data**

Ryall, Chris.
  Comic books 101 : the history, methods and madness / by Chris Ryall and Scott Tipton. -- 1st ed.
      p. cm.
  Includes index.
  ISBN 978-1-60061-187-2 (pbk. : alk. paper)
  1. Comic books, strips, etc.--History and criticism.  I. Tipton, Scott.  II. Title.  III. Title: Comic books one hundred one.  IV. Title: Comic books one hundred and one.
  PN6710.R93 2009
  741.5'9--dc22                                                  2008044966

Edited by Sarah Laichas
Designed by Wendy Dunning
Cover art by Gabriel Rodriguez
Production coordinated by Matt Wagner

## ACKNOWLEDGMENTS

To Jenny, Julie and Lucy, and our families for the enabling, love, patience and support

To Sarah Laichas, our editor, for making us and the book look so good, and to F+W's Wendy Dunning and Pam Wissman for the opportunity to look good in the first place

To Bernadette Baker-Baughman and Gretchen Stelter for believing in and championing the project

To Tom Morris and Matt Morris for the initial push

To Kevin Smith and Ming Chen for being there at the start

To Ted Adams and Darlene Anderson for the guidance, support and leadership

To Mark Engblom, David Messina and Nick Roche for the "Toon Chris and Scott art"

Special thanks to Gabriel Rodriguez for the cover illustration, Charlie Kirchoff, Tom B. Long and Leonard O'Grady for the interior colors, Clive Barker, Joe Casey, Carr D'Angelo, Paul Dini, Harlan Ellison, Mark Evanier, Joe Hill, Joshua Jabcuga, Stan Lee, Brian Lynch, Jud Meyers, Gene Simmons, David Tipton, J.C. Vaughn, Mark Waid and Marv Wolfman for their invaluable contributions

**CHRIS SAYS**

And to Scott, my first friend in comics, my partner on the website where this book got its start and a friend for whom I'd take a gamma bomb blast any day.

**SCOTT SAYS**

And to Chris, who asked me to start this whole *Comics 101* thing years ago. If I knew then what I know now . . . well, I wouldn't change a thing.

## DEDICATION

For our mothers, Patricia Ryall and Diane Tipton, who were taken from us three days apart in the fall of 2007, but left us with a lifetime of comic-book encouragement and love.

# TABLE OF CONTENTS

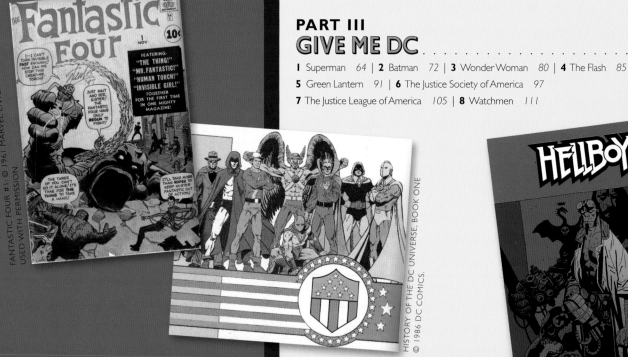

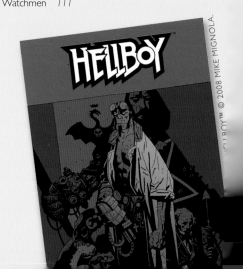

FROM THE COLLECTION OF MARK EVANIER.

BLACK MAGIC #17 © 1952 CRESTWOOD PRIZE GROUP.

## GREETINGS, FELLOW COMICPHILES!

**Stan "The Man" Lee**

Man, do I wish there had been a volume like *Comic Books 101* when I was first getting started in comics. It sure would have made life easier for me. But, since Capricious Chris Ryall and the Professor Scott Tipton decided to get themselves born too late to write their book decades ago when I could have used it, I had to learn about comics the hard way. I hadda work for 'em!

But after you read this amusing, entertaining, interesting and just plain fun collection of practically everything there is to know about comics, you'll be able to sound like a real pro the next time you're at any of the ever-burgeoning comic cons that are springing up faster than you can say, "Don't forget the hyphen in Spider-Man's name!"

To me, one of the greatest things about this terrific tome is the fact that it's all-inclusive. It touches on the history of all comics in general (even though I'd naturally have preferred it to be exclusively devoted to Marvel and, ahem, yours truly!). But hey, I can't win 'em all!

And Chris and Scott cover just about anyone and everyone you'd really want to read about. Think I'm exaggerating? OK, how's this for just enough names to whet your appetite—Jack Kirby, Will Eisner, Bob Kane, Steve Ditko, and Jerry Siegel and Joe Shuster? And they're only the tip of the iceberg, only a tiny sample of the comic-book greats you'll soon be reading about if I ever finish this inspired introduction.

I don't know how they do it, but Chris and Scott don't seem to leave anything out. Wouldja believe they even explore (so that you won't have to) the advent of comic books in the late 1930s—and even before that, they glom onto newspaper strip collections that actually led to the creation of comic books. By the time you finish reading this exemplary edition, you'll probably be qualified to teach a comic-book course yourself at any of the nation's leading universities.

Or, to put it another way, it's essentially a one-stop primer for any comic-book newcomer who wonders why Spider-Man can't challenge Batman or why the Justice League and the Avengers don't battle it out once and for all.

But let's not forget all of Hollywood's great superhero movies. On the pages that follow, you're about to breathlessly behold the source material that led to the greatest superhero movies of our time, and you'll see how some of the most prominent filmmakers manage to give us the most spectacular superhero movies in the known galaxy!

But now, I have a matter of the gravest import to discuss with you. I've been agonizing about it for years and need someone to share this heavy burden with. It has to do with the words "comic book." I say "words," which is plural, because everyone spells it "comic book," as if it really is two words. But verily, I say to thee, a "comic book" implies a funny or "comical" book. That's why I've been on a one-man crusade to have it called "comicbook"—one word! That makes it a generic word, which has come to mean a book featuring stories composed of words and illustrations, rather than a "funny" book. This is the only subject Chris Ryall and Scott Tipton haven't yet covered, but admit it—haven't I given them a great idea for a sequel?

OK, now that we've covered all these weighty matters together, it's time for me to turn you loose and let you attend the first chapter of *Comic Books 101*. Read it carefully, hear? There may be an exam.

Excelsior!

## CHRIS RYALL

When *Superman vs. The Amazing Spider-Man* was released as an oversized Treasury Edition comic book back in 1976, it was maybe the biggest event of my life. Sure, the entirety of my existence only dated back about 2,500 days, but still. I innately knew that these two costumed superheroes couldn't just team up —it was impossible, it was unprecedented, it was … well, it was just so amazingly cool.

It got me thinking. If their pairing was that monumental an event—and it was, according to my older brother Ken, who had four years on me and therefore knew all there was to know— why didn't it happen more often? Why didn't DC's Batman take on Marvel's Doctor Strange? Why wasn't there a flirtation going on between Wonder Woman and Iron Man's playboy alter ego, Tony Stark? These team-ups were potentially comics gold—why weren't more people mining it?

Conversely, my younger sister Carrie had a Treasury Edition of her own to appreciate—an adaptation of *The Wizard Of Oz*, also produced through a joint venture between the country's two largest comic-book publishers, Marvel and DC Comics. Again, a quality production that made one wonder why these two powerhouses didn't pair up more often. Why were they selfish with their characters? What other characters were out there that could potentially be paired up?

These questions assaulted my young brain. So we've written a book to explain it to then-me. More important, it will also explain these things and so much more to you. Whether you're new to comics and curious about which superhero movies are worth your time or you've been a fan for a while and are curious about a character's history, this book was designed with you in mind. Need to know when Marvel, DC and so many other publishers got their start? Curious about the bondage-laced origins of Wonder Woman? Want the truth about the comic-book trials from the '50s or curious about how many millions Superman's creators raked in for creating such an icon? It's all covered here: the good, the bad guys and the ugly truth behind the Superman creators' actual treatment. And much more.

We've taken our lifetime of comics reading— sorry, I mean research!—and crafted a book that introduces you to the creators, characters and concepts that make up the crazy four-color industry that's as much a part of our blood as cosmic rays are a part of the Richards family's (read on, that will soon make sense even to the neophytes among you). The books Scott cites in his intro that follows were largely the same background I had growing up, so it makes sense that we'd combine forces and pass on what we know. Our own version of *Superman vs. Spider-Man,* as it were, for

your edification and enjoyment.
Comics are a hobby that offers
something for everyone, and our
goal is to help interested parties
of all ages and interests find
their area of passion here. So
thank you for your interest, and
welcome to *Comic Books 101*.

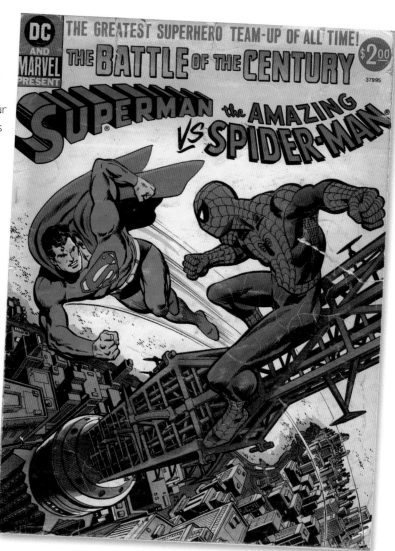

## SCOTT TIPTON

For Li'l Scott, it was all about the Megos. When I was little, the popular toys of the time were eight-inch-tall plastic superhero dolls from a toy company called Mego. Mego was selling superheroes like hotcakes back in the 1970s, and they were putting out as many DC and Marvel heroes as the market would bear. My parents indulged my superhero mania, and as I'd play with the Megos, my father would occasionally drop a nugget or two of superhero knowledge.

"You know, Captain America used to have a sidekick named Bucky."

"When I was a kid, the Human Torch wasn't in the Fantastic Four, and he had a kid named Toro that flew around with him."

I'd hear these things, and try to get my head around the fact that superheroes had a *history*, that they weren't just created that day for my amusement, but had been around for years, long enough to have captured my father's imagination as a kid, just the same way they had mine.

I had to know more.

Luckily, my folks recognized my thirst for superhero knowledge, and soon the books began showing up at the house. *Superman* and *Batman: From the 30s to the 70s*, giant hardbound collections of Superman and Batman comics from the past five decades. And best of all, *Origins of Marvel Comics*, Stan Lee's account of the early days of Marvel and the creation of all its most popular characters.

I inhaled those books. I read them so often that today they're practically in liquid form. Those books virtually imprinted on my DNA. And yet I still wanted more.

Off to the library, to special-request all the rest of Stan's *Origins* books, and other finds like DC's *Secret Origins of the DC Super-Heroes*. Those led me to other discoveries. Walt Kelly's *Pogo*. Carl Barks' *Uncle Scrooge*. And the hours spent in the library's reference section poring through Maurice Horn's *The World Encyclopedia of Comics* (those damned librarians would never let me take that one home).

All of which brings us to today. A lifetime's worth of comic-book minutiae trapped inside my head, and now, finally, a place to put it to good use. For readers just getting introduced to the world of comic books, if we can convey not just the information we've spent a lifetime accumulating, but also our enthusiasm and affection for this great American art form, it'll all be worth it.

Then again, when I look over and see my Mego Spider-Man still behind the wheel of his Spider-Car, or pick up my dog-eared, Scotch-taped copy of *Origins of Marvel Comics*, I realize: It was always worth it. Every minute.

Welcome to *Comic Books 101*.

# PART I

# THE WAY IT BEGAN

Wherein your intrepid instructors begin their march through the entirety of the comic-book universe; this grand entrance includes an exploration of the origins of the comic book, a sideways glance at the various ages of comics and a run-through of the giants by whose hands was this industry built.

# Newspaper Strips vs. Comic Books

## Black, white and spread all over

Telling a story by combining words and pictures is nothing new. In fact, it's centuries old. But comic books likely never would have come into existence were it not for the filler that ran on the back pages of newspapers a hundred years ago.

### STRIP SEARCH

In the early 1900s, some of the most vibrant, mature storytelling available was found in newspaper comic strips, though this might seem hard to believe now. Today, comic strips are being relegated to an ever-shrinking space in a decreasing number of newspapers. Yet it was this golden age of newspaper strips that begat comic books in much the same way the Titans of myth birthed the pantheon of Greek gods who would eventually eclipse them in authority and power. To understand the importance and differences of both formats, let's start at the beginning.

The advancement of comic strips as an art form began with the launch of the newspaper strip *The Yellow Kid* by R.F. Outcault. This comic strip was introduced in the pages of the largest newspaper in the country, Joseph Pulitzer's *New York World* in 1895. *The Yellow Kid* is generally accepted as the first newspaper strip, and was the first successful weekly comic strip that actually led to increased circulation for a paper. *The Yellow Kid* also gave rise to the term "yellow journalism" and was the first strip to be successfully merchandised, too.

The late 1890s and early 1900s were a heady time for newspapers. A bitter rivalry existed between publishing magnate Pulitzer and his chief competitor, William Randolph Hearst. Two years after its launch in Pulitzer's paper, Outcault took *The Yellow Kid* to Hearst's *New York Journal*. Hearst had recently started a Sunday supplement and he featured *Kid* alongside Rudolph Dirks's popular *The Katzenjammer Kids*, a strip heavily influenced by an 1865 German comic strip, *Max und Moritz*.

The race for the next great comic strip was on. This competition led to the launch of other notable strips: Outcault's *Buster Brown*, George McManus's *The Newlyweds*, Winsor McCay's brilliant epic *Little Nemo in Slumberland* and Bud Fisher's wildly successful *Mutt & Jeff*.

Early comic strips were large, running the width of a newspaper page. Sunday strips were even more impressively sized—tabloid-sized newspapers ran some strips across the entire page, nearly a square foot of space per strip. In these halcyon days, strips were scattered throughout the paper, but once papers created a dedicated comics page, their real estate would be drastically reduced.

The advent of sophisticated adventure strips like Edgar Rice Burroughs's *Tarzan*, Lee Falk's *Mandrake the Magician*, Harold Gray's *Little Orphan Annie*, Chester Gould's *Dick Tracy* and Milton Caniff's *Terry and the Pirates* paved the way for the creation of the comic book. These action strips, launched in the period just before World War I to the start of World War II all feature ongoing, serialized tales of action and adventure. Lee Falk's *The Phantom* even featured a costumed adventurer—a popular archetype in pulp novels but a new invention for newspaper strips.

## FAMOUSLY FIRST

It was 1929 when the comic-book industry was launched in a rather humble fashion. Dell Publishing's *The Funnies* kicked things off with what amounted to little more than a folded, stapled collection of newspaper strips inserted inside a tabloid newspaper. Then in 1935, *Famous Funnies: A Carnival of Comics* was distributed at Woolworth's department stores, becoming the first separate comic book to be distributed. Regardless of which comic book came first, the true birth of American comics as it applies to *Comic Books 101* starts and ends with the debut of DC Comics' *Action Comics*.

## GETTING IN ON THE ACTION

*Action Comics #1*, dated June 1938, forever changed the face of comic books. The lead strip in the anthology was a caped superhero named Superman. Superman's creators, Jerry Siegel and Joe Shuster, pitched their initial concept, The Superman, to newspapers for years, finding themselves rebuffed at every turn. While newspaper strips were now showcasing stories of costumed adventurers like The Shadow and Flash Gordon, the idea of a costumed, super-powered character held no appeal to newspaper editors. It was from such humble beginnings and rejections that a new fantasy genre was born.

Superman the comic-book character proved so successful that *Superman* the newspaper strip launched less than a year after the comic's debut, an ironic turn for Siegel and Shuster. The newspaper strip ran for nearly three decades, and featured all-new stories, even introducing future comic-book favorites like Mr. Mxyzptlk. The comic strip was originally created and produced by Siegel and Shuster, too, until their increasing comic-book duties—and wartime responsibilities—precluded their ability to keep up with the added workload.

## THE LITTLE DIFFERENCES

Newspaper strips and comic books share many traits of visual language, such as the use of word balloons and captions placed within an image's panel borders. So what, then, makes them different? It's got to be more than just the staples, right?

### CHRIS SAYS

At the same time Dell released *Famous Funnies*, a competitor called National Allied Publications released a comic book called *New Fun*. This was the first comic to offer all-new content, and many cite it as being the first true comic book. Of course, some European historians cite their comics *The Adventures of Mr. Obadiah Oldbuck* or *Max und Moritz* as being the very first. In comics, as with so many other areas of history, most "firsts" are up for debate, and opinions vary. That's what makes it all so fun.

For one thing, the sheer scope of the story is dictated by the format. A daily comic strip needs to impart very little story, just enough to keep the reader engaged so he wants to read more the next day. Before the days of ongoing adventure stories, strips featured gags that could be read and absorbed in their entirety each day. Characters were not tied to any continuity, and the strip was all about delivering the day's punch line, not telling an extended storyline.

Milton Caniff's *Terry and the Pirates* is an early example of a serialized adventure strip in newspapers.

Once strips like *Dick Tracy* introduced ongoing stories, the format and readers' expectations evolved. Strips needed to ensure that the reader was interested enough to come back to the story the following day, and the day after that. As such, ongoing newspaper strips began to rely heavily on daily cliffhangers.

Sundays could be confusing for readers of these serialized strips. For a while, Sunday strips featured a separate, standalone storyline. The reader could be engrossed in the ongoing weekly adventures of, say, *Terry and the Pirates*, but come Sunday, the strip told an unrelated story, in an attempt to accommodate the many Sunday-only subscribers. Soon enough, however, Sunday strips began to tie in with the weekly plot, telling a longer, more coherent storyline to capture the reader's attention week in and week out.

Comic books, meanwhile, could take their time telling stories that lasted months, juggling numerous plotlines and characters. Perhaps even more importantly, the comics' larger size offered the artists greater flexibility for what they could do with the visuals.

Though comic books have been subject to extreme censorship throughout their history, newspaper-strip creators of the day faced more restrictions and inflexible standards than comic-book writers and artists because of the wider audience of newspaper syndicates.

The price of newspaper strips (free to anyone buying the paper) versus comic books (which started at a dime and now cost in the three- to four-dollar range for a typical monthly comic) also differentiated the two formats. Newspaper distribution has always been much higher than that of even the most popular comic book, so anyone wanting free comic strips has been readily able to find them.

Though newspaper strips birthed some of the most original, innovative and mature examples of adventure tales that the public had ever seen, it was truly the publication of original comic-book content that gave birth to the superhero. And so began the revolution.

With the introduction of serialized stories, newspapers began to rely heavily on daily cliffhangers.

# The Rise of National Comics

## *National pride*

*New Fun* was the first comic book to offer original content. A few years later, *Action Comics* gave birth to the world's first comic-book superhero, Superman. The connection? Both of these comics were released by National Allied Publications, the precursor to DC Comics.

National was founded by Major Malcolm Wheeler-Nicholson, a pulp magazine writer. *New Fun*, National's debut title of 1934 (dated 1935), featured early, pre-Superman work by Jerry Siegel and Joe Shuster and caught people's attention by offering all-new content. National's second title, *New Comics*, wasn't as fortunate, but the series survived initially low sales and was renamed *Adventure Comics*. It went on to be one of the longest-running titles in comic-book history.

Despite some early success, National struggled to find its place in the burgeoning comic-book industry. In 1937, the cash-strapped company launched a third series, *Detective Comics*, a title whose initials would become synonymous with the company. At the same time, Wheeler-Nicholson's financial problems prompted him to sell part of the company to his printer and distributor, Harry Donenfeld. The two, along with Donenfeld's accountant, Jack Liebowitz, launched a new company, Detective Comics, Inc., and Wheeler-Nicholson was ousted shortly thereafter.

The timing of this move makes Wheeler-Nicholson little more than a footnote in comic-book history. Soon after he was forced out, the company launched its fourth title, *Action Comics*, which introduced Superman to the world. A year later, *Detective Comics* #27 (May 1939) introduced Batman, another immense success story Wheeler-Nicholson was not around to experience.

Liebowitz, meanwhile, owned another comics company, All-American Publications, in partnership with a paper salesman, Max Gaines. All-American was home to such popular superhero characters as the Atom, the Flash, Green Lantern, Hawkman and Wonder Woman. In a rare cooperative venture, characters from National and All-American came together in *All Star Comics* series as the Justice Society of America. And by 1944, things would get even more conjoined.

National Allied Publications and Detective Comics, Inc. merged in 1944, forming National Comics, which then absorbed All-American Publications. Max Gaines allowed Liebowitz to buy out his concern, leaving him free to found yet another publisher, EC Comics.

The newly reorganized National (now formally known as National Periodical Publications) was left with a stable of beloved characters that, according to Liebowitz, were often

DC quickly branded itself with the name of its most popular creation.

copied. Liebowitz actively pursued copyright violations by other companies. In fact, it was Liebowitz's suit against another publisher, Fawcett Publications, and its character Captain Marvel—at the time the most popular character in comics—that ultimately drove Fawcett out of comics. But more on that later.

National unofficially referred to itself as DC Comics long before formally changing its name. For years, readers strongly identified with the Superman/DC Comics logo emblazoned on each of National's comics. Eventually the company made the name change official.

Thanks to the strength of the company's three most popular characters, Superman, Batman and Wonder Woman (as well as some dabbling in other genres such as war and romance), DC Comics survived the ebb and flow of the industry as other superheroes fell out of fashion. The Big Three cleverly adapted with the times enough to keep the company profitable, thus ushering in the Golden Age of comics.

## GUEST LECTURER

SIMMONS COMICS GROUP
www.SIMMONSCOMICS.com

### GENE SIMMONS, KISS bassist, god of thunder and founder of Simmons Comics Group

**THE FIRST ISSUE I EVER READ**

I was an immigrant and came to the Land of Dreams. Even though I couldn't speak a word of English and had never seen a TV set in my life, I was drawn to comic books. The first book I picked up was the one on top of a pile my friend had, *World's Finest*, with Superman, Batman and Robin. I was floored. People wore costumes. They flew through the air. They fought for justice, freedom and (yes!) the American way.

It wasn't long until I joyfully discovered the Kirby/Ditko/Lee monster books of Atlas Comics and then fell headlong in love with Marvel's astonishing output of heroes I could relate to—with zits, with girl problems, with anger management issues. I remember *breathlessly* waiting at my local candy store for the new shipments every Tuesday and Thursday.

A testament to America is that a little immigrant boy who loved comics could one day become an actual superhero himself in the pages of Marvel's *KISS* comics. And to be given the opportunity to create my own heroes for my own masthead—Simmons Comics Group with IDW Publishing—is more than even I could ever have hoped for. God bless America.

# The Golden Age

*Turn back the page to the Golden Age*

The Golden and Silver ages are somewhat arbitrary divisions in the history of mainstream American comic-book publishing. Comic-book writer and editor Roy Thomas is fond of saying, "The Golden Age of comics is eight," meaning the age at which he, and many others, discovered and fell in love with the funnybooks—though that is not what most people mean by the phrase. The divisions between eras were first defined by the folks who published comic-book price guides, and most of the comics community is in agreement as to where the divisions begin and end, at least in the early years of comics.

## THE START OF THE GOLDEN AGE

For most, the Golden Age of comics begins in June 1938 with the appearance of Superman in *Action Comics* #1. The arrival of Superman set off a superhero craze, and to a larger extent, a comic-book craze, that went on for more than two decades. At the Golden Age's height, there were numerous mainstream comic-book publishers, all doing extremely good business. In today's market, a circulation of 100,000 copies

**PLATINUM AGE (or Pre-Golden Age):**

*Late 1890s–1937*
Period of newspaper strips' birth. This isn't an era you'll hear much about any longer.

*Notable Comics:* None. (Tabloid- and magazine-sized reprints of existing comic strips.)

## ROCK OF AGES

| 1700 | 1800 | 1900 | 1910 | 1920 | 1930 |

**VICTORIAN AGE**

*Late 18th–Late 19th century*
The first era mentioned in the context of the creation of comic books.

*Notable Comics:* None.

**GOLDEN AGE:** *1938–Mid-1950s*
The first notable era of comics as we know them. Begins with the 1938 launch of *Action Comics* #1 with the first appearance of Superman. Extends to the beginning of the Cold War era following World War II.

*Notable Comics:*
*Action Comics* #1 (DC Comics, 1938)
*Detective Comics* #27 (DC Comics, 1939)
*Marvel Comics* #1 (Timely Comics, 1939)
*Whiz Comics* #1 (Fawcett Comics, 1940)
*All Star Comics* #3 (DC Comics, 1940)

is considered wildly successful. It is staggering to look back on Fawcett's Captain Marvel comics (you know, *Shazam!*) regularly seeing sales numbers in the millions. And that, friends, is the Golden Age. Even after superheroes fell out of fashion in the late 1940s, the comic-book machine stayed in full gear with romance, western, horror, crime and "funny animal" comics all finding various levels of success at the newsstands.

## THE SILVER AGE

Most people set the beginning of the Silver Age at October 1956, with DC's publication of *Showcase* #4, which revived the Flash, a revamp of one of National's more popular superheroes from the 1940s. The success of the Flash led to similar resurrections of characters such as Green Lantern, Hawkman and the Atom. Once these characters were teamed up with superhero perennials Superman, Batman and

---

**SILVER AGE:** *Mid-1950s–Early 1970s*
The Silver Age kicks off with the 1956 release of DC Comics' *Showcase* #4, which re-invented the Flash. Bad press, self-censorship and lack of distribution put the kibosh on the more adult comics of the 1950s, and publishers re-introduce many Golden Age characters to a new audience, ushering in a superhero-comic resurgence.

*Notable Comics:*
*Showcase* #4 (DC Comics, 1956)
*The Brave and the Bold* #28 (DC Comics, 1960)
*Fantastic Four* #1 (Marvel Comics, 1961)
*Amazing Fantasy* #15 (Marvel Comics, 1962)
*The Avengers* #4 (Marvel Comics, 1964)

**MODERN AGE:** *Early 1980s–Present*
The current era of comics, sometimes referred to as the Copper, Plastic, Tin or Iron Age. Comics typify darker superhero titles, a return to adult content and the most widely diverse superhero comics. Era best exemplified by *Watchmen* and *Batman: The Dark Knight Returns*, released in the 1980s.

*Notable Comics:*
*The Uncanny X-Men* #137 (Marvel Comics, 1980)
*Crisis on Infinite Earths* #1 (DC Comics, 1985)
*Batman: The Dark Knight Returns* (DC Comics, 1986)
*Watchmen* (DC Comics, 1986)
*The Sandman* #1 (DC Comics, 1989)
*Spawn* #1 (Image Comics, 1992)

---

| 1950 | 1960 | 1970 | 1980 | 1990 | 2000 |

---

**ATOM AGE:** *Late 1940s–Mid-1950s*
The public's interest in superhero comics gives way to romance comics, science fiction and horror tales made famous by EC Comics. The juvenile delinquency hearings in the mid-1950s end the sale of horror comics and result in the creation of the Comics Code Authority.

*Notable Comics:*
*Tales From the Crypt* #1 (EC Comics, 1950)
*Shock SuspenStories* #1 (EC Comics, 1952)

**BRONZE AGE:** *Early 1970s–Early 1980s*
Comics see a slight darkening in tone, reflective of the Vietnam-era climate. Stories cover real-world issues, such as drug abuse and politics, and overall, superhero comics become more realistic.

*Notable Comics:*
*Conan the Barbarian* (Marvel Comics, 1970)
*The Amazing Spider-Man* #96–98 (Marvel Comics, 1971)
*Green Lantern/Green Arrow* #85 (DC Comics, 1971)
*New Gods* #1 (DC Comics, 1971)
*The Amazing Spider-Man* #121–122, 129 (Marvel Comics, 1973)
*Giant-Size X-Men* #1 (Marvel Comics, 1975)
*Howard the Duck* #1 (Marvel Comics, 1976)
*New Teen Titans* #1 (DC Comics, 1980)
*Daredevil* #168 (Marvel Comics, 1981)

Wonder Woman (who had never gone away) in the pages of *Justice League of America*, a full superhero renaissance was in bloom. DC's spike in sales caught the eye of its downtown rivals at Atlas Comics. Atlas would soon take on the now familiar moniker of Marvel.

Inspired by the success of the Justice League, Marvel editor-in-chief Stan Lee turned his attention to superheroes in a big way. He partnered with artists Jack Kirby and Steve Ditko, and produced nearly every character that Marvel would come to be famous for—the Fantastic Four, the Hulk, Spider-Man, Thor, Doctor Strange, the Silver Surfer, the X-Men, Iron Man and the Avengers. In addition to creating great characters and stories, Stan, Jack and Steve pioneered a new and different house style. It combined realism with an almost soap-opera-like emphasis on the personal lives of their heroes, and an editorial voice that respected the reader and refused to condescend. Moreover, Lee's insistence on frequent guest appearances of characters throughout the publishing line gave the reader a genuine sense that anything could happen in this new Marvel Universe, and it made missing out on issues unthinkable. The Marvel style soon revolutionized comics. DC's Flash may have kicked off the Silver Age, but Marvel owned it.

Here's where it gets tricky. No one is in total agreement as to when the Silver Age ends, nor to what to call the time period that follows. Some comic historians like to peg the ending at *The Amazing Spider-Man* #121 in 1973, with the murder of longtime supporting character and Spidey's love interest, Gwen Stacy, citing it as the moment they lost their personal innocence regarding comic books. A bit sappy, but as good a definition as any, and a marker of the time period when Stan Lee quit writing, and even editing, most of the Marvel titles. (To this day, Stan swears he wasn't even in town when the decision to off poor Gwen was made, and that he found out when he read the published book for the first time.) Others like to place the end of the Silver Age at 1978, when the "DC Implosion" resulted in the cancellation of an armload of DC titles. Still others stretch the Silver Age all the way until the 1980s, when Marvel was revitalized with Frank Miller's *Daredevil* work, Chris Claremont's *The Uncanny X-Men* was firing on all cylinders and John Byrne was doing the best work of his career on *Fantastic Four*.

## THE BRONZE AGE

Some comics-types call the 1970s and '80s the Bronze Age, slavishly keeping with the gold-silver pattern. Others refer to the 1980s as the Mylar Age because bagging comics in Mylar plastic bags became popular among collectors. For a while in the 1990s, some zealous fans started declaring it the Image Age, after Image Comics, when comics like Todd McFarlane's *Spawn* and Jim Lee's *WildC.A.T.s* were breaking sales records left and right. If you ask us, there's the Golden Age and the Silver Age, and then there's everything else.

## A marvelous beginning

It's hard to imagine that the company responsible for creating Captain America could ever be relegated to the sidelines in the history of comic books, yet that's what happened with Timely Comics.

Timely was originally known as Red Circle Comics when publisher Martin Goodman launched the company in 1939. Goodman's past experience had been in pulp magazines, but in 1939, he met a salesman for Funnies, Inc., an organization of comic-book artists looking to publish their own works that needed financial help getting off the ground. Goodman helped them launch their first title, *Marvel Comics* (October 1939), under a new banner, Timely Publications.

This first issue is historic for two reasons beyond its prescient name: it introduced the Human Torch, creator Carl Burgos's flaming android superhero that would have a great impact on a young creator named Stan Lee; it also gave life to the Sub-Mariner, a water-based antihero created by master draughtsman Bill Everett. (Another superhero featured in the issue, Paul Gustavson's character the Angel, wasn't as impactful.)

This debut issue sold well, moving more than 100,000 copies in its two printings. Its success convinced Goodman to hire new employees to grow his fledgling company.

He brought on Funnies, Inc. staff writer and editor Joe Simon, who in turn hired two of his frequent collaborators, artists Jack Kirby and Syd Shores.

Timely launched a half-dozen new titles in its first two years, but nothing that set the world on fire like *Marvel Comics* (one, *Red Raven Comics*, was inexplicably cancelled after just one issue and before any sales information was ever received). The company's long-term success wasn't assured by any means, and things could have gone very differently were it not for the foresight of Everett and Burgos. They recognized that the Human Torch and the Sub-Mariner represented two opposite primal elements, fire and water, so they paired the two together in one comic. Characters crossing over into each other's stories was unheard of at the time, which is why the idea was such an instant success.

### THE BIRTH OF CAPTAIN AMERICA

The Human Torch series launched soon after, and Goodman wanted more. He tasked Joe Simon with the creation of new superheroes, and Simon and his partner, Jack Kirby, set out to do just that. Simon and Kirby were Jewish, as were many of Timely's creators, so all had concerns with the political situation in Germany at the time. Many Timely characters had

Timely Comics logo circa 1939.

already fought Nazi soldiers within the pages of their stories, and Simon and Kirby followed suit with their latest creation, a superhero who played up the burgeoning nationalism running rampant in America.

*Captain America Comics* #1 launched in the early months of 1941. Though America would enter World War II less than a year later, the threat Hitler posed was already well-known. Kirby's cover image (with inks by Simon) depicted this new red, white and blue-clad hero punching Hitler in the face (see cover image on page 118). The cover struck just the right note of patriotism and heroics. Captain America and his teenage sidekick, Bucky, were soon punching out Axis members on a monthly basis.

There had been other patriotic heroes before, but Captain America quickly surpassed them in popularity. One such character, The Shield, published by MLJ Comics, precursor to Archie Comics, shared a few similarities with Cap. MLJ threatened to sue Goodman and Timely for infringement, and Goodman settled the suit in a manner that would make his character even stronger—he changed the design of Cap's shield from its traditional shield-shaped design to the round design the character carries today.

Goodman chased his hit with more patriotic-themed characters, but none resonated the way Captain America did. Still, the company's sales and its staff continued to expand, and Goodman brought on his wife's cousin, young Stanley Lieber, to help. Lieber soon moved to writing backup features for the comics, and adopted the nom de plume that would stick for the rest of his life—Stan Lee.

Simon and Kirby had a financial dispute with Goodman regarding Cap's high sales, leading them to begin moonlighting for Timely's competitor, National. They were fired from Timely after someone reported the news back to Goodman. Fingers were pointed at Stan Lee, a charge he denied. However it went down, it left young Lee to take over as the company's editor-in-chief.

When America entered World War II in December 1941, many comic creators were drafted. Lee himself volunteered for Army service. With so many of his superhero creators off fighting, Goodman began publishing humor comics created by new talents like Basil Wolverton. Vince Fago filled in as editor-in-chief and shifted the company toward "funny animal" comics. Despite the changes, and the paper-rationing that had begun to affect other publishers, Timely continued to prosper. Captain America was even given his own Republic movie serial in 1944. But soon, the public's appetite for superhero comics began to fade, and with the end of the war and the loss of many postwar jobs, the desire to spend hard-earned money to read about patriotic superheroes also began to diminish.

## POSTWAR CHANGES

Stan Lee's postwar return as editor saw some new innovations on Timely's part—westerns, romance comics and superhero teams. Yet these titles faced stiff competition from more shocking horror comics as well as the advent of television, and none would find an audience.

To combat the country's changing moods, Goodman published an increasingly diverse slate of titles, distributed through his own company, Atlas. He adopted the Atlas logo on his comics, effectively changing Timely Comics to Atlas Comics. Later, some distribution problems led Goodman to rapidly decrease the company's output. As Atlas debated its murky future, Jack Kirby returned to the fold. Kirby, with Stan Lee and some new artists such as Don Heck and Steve Ditko, pioneered many monster titles and westerns, some of which were emblazoned with a circular "MC" (Marvel Comics) logo on its covers. And some even prospered for a time. But no one could foresee how the industry would change as a result of the political climate of the 1950s. The Marvel Age of comics would eventually surface, but not yet.

# Fawcett Comics

## Holy moley

Fawcett Publications was founded by the colorful Wilford Hamilton Fawcett (or "Captain Billy," as he was known). Captain Billy was a veteran of the Spanish-American War, a police reporter and a hotelier to the stars. He launched Fawcett in 1919 when his crude war-story pamphlets found a huge audience in disabled veterans.

Fawcett began publishing comics in 1940 and had immense success with its Captain Marvel character created by writer Bill Parker and artist C.C. Beck. Captain Marvel shared some similarities with Superman—both invulnerable strongmen wearing tights and a cape—but there were plenty of differences, too. His alter ego was a young boy, Billy Batson, who spoke a magic word—*Shazam!*—to be transformed into the caped hero Captain Marvel. The character's popularity quickly won him his own title, *Captain Marvel Adventures*, and led to the expansion of the Marvel family in the form of new characters Captain Marvel Jr., Mary Marvel and, uh, Hoppy the Marvel Bunny. In the mid-1940s, Captain Marvel's title even outsold *Superman*.

### SUPERMAN VS. CAPTAIN MARVEL

As you can imagine, competitor National Comics wasn't overly enamored with this new character that looked derivative of its Superman character and was also outselling him. The lawsuit-happy National threatened legal action against Fawcett.

Fawcett's owners knew that National had a strong case against them, so they initially elected to stop publishing Captain Marvel's adventures. But because the character was too important to the company, they had to fight back. The case took years to get to trial. When it did, it came out that National had mistakenly never fully copyrighted Superman. The judge ruled that, similarities or differences aside, National's copyright to Superman was not protected. Unfortunately for Fawcett, the judge also ruled that Captain Marvel was illegally copied from Superman.

The news got worse. National appealed the decision (even while it seemed to crib from Captain Marvel, giving Superman the ability to fly instead of just "leaping tall buildings in a single bound"), and in the early 1950s, the decision was reversed. By this time, superhero titles were beginning to fall out of favor for horror comics, and Fawcett deemed Captain Marvel no longer important enough to fight over. It settled with National, and stopped publishing the character for good.

As Captain Marvel went, so went Fawcett Comics. The publisher cancelled all its superhero titles and laid off all its creators. Many

The Fawcett logo, circa 1948. Fawcett wasn't one to hide its light under a bushel.

of its characters were later sold to another new publisher, Charlton Comics. But Captain Marvel's story wasn't completely over. The character lay dormant for two decades. In that time, the trademark lapsed, and Marvel Comics launched a character with the same name. In 1972, DC Comics acquired the rights to Fawcett's character, but since Marvel had secured the trademark for the "Captain Marvel" name, DC's new titles had to be launched under the name *Shazam!* This got very confusing to us kids, especially to those of us who also watched the 1970s live-action Saturday-morning show that was also called *Shazam!* but featured a character called Captain Marvel. Today he's probably known more by the name SHAZAM! than by Captain Marvel.

Fawcett published a few comics into the 1960s, mostly newspaper strip reprints, and then pulled the plug for good. It's tragically ironic for Fawcett that it's best-known for a character that ended up in the hands of the company responsible for its demise.

### SCOTT SAYS

I've always felt that it was the ingenious child-to-man transformation concept that made Captain Marvel instantly popular, to the point that it outsold nearly every comic on the stands throughout the 1940s. The central concept was one that every kid could get into. First off, the origin was fiendishly appealing: you could never be Superman, since it was pretty clear you weren't from Krypton. And sure, you could be Batman if you devoted decades of your life to study and training, but who wants to do that? But Captain Marvel? Hey, all it took was shouting a magic word, and instantly you're a grown-up (and therefore you couldn't possibly have any problems, right?), super-strong, super-smart, super-brave and you could fly. Oh, and whenever you wanted you could turn back into a kid again. Talk about wish fulfillment.

Most of the Marvel Family stories were written by Otto Binder, who had a knack for churning out month after month of appealing, straightforward adventure stories with more than a hint of whimsy, which matched perfectly with the cartoony, humorous art of C.C. Beck. The result was a dreamlike romp that combined the fantastic non-logic of fairy tales with the action and adventure of the comic books of the era. And with monthly sales that at times topped one million copies, there must have been plenty who enjoyed the formula.

# 6 Dell and Disney
## Gains and losses

Dell Comics was there at the beginning. It was Dell's *Famous Funnies* comic that kicked off the trend of publishing new material in comic-book form (see chapter one). And for nearly half a century, it was one of the most successful publishers in the country.

Despite the prevalence of superhero comics in the late 1930s, Dell followed a different path. In 1938, Dell changed its approach to comic-book publishing, choosing to operate differently from other publishers. After going it alone for nearly a decade, the company partnered with Western Publishing (a large publisher of licensed comics and children's

Golden Books, among other things). Western would produce and package comic books based on its licensed properties—most targeted at a younger audience than other comics of the day—and Dell would foot the bill and distribute the comics.

One of Western's largest licenses at the time was the stable of Walt Disney characters. Another was Warner Bros.' Looney Tunes. Dell's new releases, *Walt Disney's Comics and Stories* and *Looney Tunes & Merrie Melodies Comics*, were huge hits with children. The company followed up those efforts with comics based on Walter Lantz's animated creations (Woody Woodpecker, Andy Panda, Chilly Willy and others) and even *Our Gang* comics, featuring the Little Rascals.

Dell also launched *Four Color Comics*, an anthology that tried out different characters as its lead story. This title was also very popular, and many of the characters featured in its pages—Popeye and various other Disney characters—spun off into their own books. *Four Color* was published as often as twice weekly for a time, and ran for an amazing 1,300 issues.

The arrangement with Western ended in the early 1960s, when Western spun off its licensed characters into a separate publish-

UNCLE SCROOGE #13 © 1956 DISNEY ENTERPRISES. PUBLISHED BY DELL COMICS. ART BY CARL BARKS. COLOR BY PETER LEDGER.

ing line, Gold Key Comics. Dell found itself at a crossroads. With so many of its popular licensed titles belonging to Western, the company decided to delve into creating original properties and licensing some properties of its own (although TV properties like *Bewitched*, *Ghost Stories* and *Combat* would never quite replace popular titles like the Disney and Looney Tunes titles).

The timing of Western's withdrawal didn't do Dell any favors. By the start of the 1960s, the comic-book industry had stared down its greatest crisis and come out the other side as a superhero-dominated industry. Faced with DC's popularity and the resurgent Marvel Comics, Dell's non-caped comics failed to find the same audience it once had. The company held on for another decade, surviving into the early 1970s before finally realizing it no longer had a place in this new, superheroic world.

## DELL'S CREATIVE RENAISSANCE

Licensed titles rarely receive the same respect in the comics industry as original creations. As a result, Dell's preponderance of licensed titles, as well as its struggle to find a foothold in the last decade of its existence, erroneously led many to dismiss the company's importance in comparison to EC Comics, DC and Marvel. In fact, Dell is one of the unsung champions of the early days of comic books and a cornerstone of the industry. Dell had a big role in the formation of the comic book itself as well as a roster of some of the most acclaimed artists who ever put pencil to paper in the creation of a comic.

**CARL BARKS**—One of the biggest names ever to work for Dell. He began his artistic career as an illustrator for Disney's animated shorts, then left to strike out on his own. Western immediately hired him to work on Donald Duck comics, and he took the feisty-but-unintelligible Donald Duck character and gave him a true personality, a family and an entire town in the pages of the comics. Barks's comics were filled with such clean lines, sterling beauty, humor and heart that his "funny animal" comics had more resonance than most featuring human characters.

**WALT KELLY**—A former Disney animator, Kelly is most known as the creator of *Pogo*. He was prolific during his time at Dell, working on many titles, including *Our Gang* and Dell's Disney titles.

**RUSS MANNING**—The creator of *Magnus, Robot Fighter* and namesake of a comic-book award worked for Dell before working on many titles for Gold Key.

**ALEX TOTH**—Acclaimed comic-book artist and animator for Hanna-Barbera, Toth worked for DC Comics before being employed by Dell for a number of years.

**DAN SPIEGLE**—After working for Dell, this veteran cartoonist went on to spend decades working for DC Comics.

**JOHN BUSCEMA**—Best known for his work on Marvel's *The Silver Surfer*, *Conan the Barbarian* and *The Avengers*, Buscema produced many pages for Dell.

# EC Comics and the Comics Code Authority
## Reduction of the innocent

The history of comics can be divided into two basic eras: pre-1950s and post-1950s. Many comics companies' success depended on the outcome of the period in between. So what happened in the 1950s and how did it change everything? The answer is best explained through a look at EC Comics.

EC Comics deserves a special place in the pantheon of comic-book publishers that have helped build the industry into what it is today. It is inexorably tied to a debate that arose over the role of comics in juvenile delinquency and the establishment of a governing body, the Comics Code Authority. Many of its accomplishments are given short shrift in comparison to the controversy.

### A TALE CALCULATED TO DRIVE YOU... MAD

Authority figures have long thought that children are impressionable and should be protected, and the advent of accessible pop-culture elements such as radio, television and, of course, comic books only exacerbated that thinking.

Comic books confounded the establishment from the start. Contrary to the older reader base that buys comics today, the buyers in the 1930s and '40s were primarily preteens, numbering more than a million strong at the time. That impressive sales figure was a particular source of consternation for many adults, especially teachers and librarians, who hated the idea of comics taking kids' attention away from more scholarly pursuits such as reading books. Dime novels and the pulps that came before were bad enough, but now comic books were enticing young readers with colorful characters and fantastic tales of wonder, too. Obviously, they reasoned, something had to be done.

That something was eventually an investigation into the possible corrupting influence of comic books by a Senate subcommittee and the development of the damaging Comics Code Authority institution. This all led to the demise of one of the most creative and influential comic-book companies in the industry's history, EC Comics, which would have come as quite a surprise to company founder M.C. Gaines, who launched EC as Educational Comics in the 1940s.

### THE LIGHTER SIDE

When *Famous Funnies* became one of the first bound-up, magazine-sized newspaper-strip collections distributed through newsstands, the idea was originated by Maxwell Charles ("M.C.") Gaines, a paper salesman. Gaines, born in 1896, was a comic-book visionary, perhaps the most important figure in all of American comics, and responsible for helping launch the industry in the 1930s.

Even today's accepted format of comics (folded, saddle-stitched newsprint pages) originated with Gaines, who at the time worked for the Eastern Color Printing Company. Eastern Color printed many Sunday comic-strip supplements for newspapers. Gaines helped pioneer the idea of folding the supplements in half, doubling the page count and producing an individual magazine-sized publication of comic strips. He offered comic-book reprints of this nature as a premium for companies such as Procter & Gamble, which turned into a profitable affair. Gaines assumed that if it worked for companies, the public would likely be willing to spend a dime for such magazines on the newsstands, too.

Gaines was responsible for other groundbreaking contributions to comics, too. The public rarely hears his name in connection with the creation of Superman, but he was largely responsible for the strips getting picked up by National Comics. In the late 1930s, he left Eastern Color to work for a comic-strip syndicate that had just turned down a new creation by writer Jerry Siegel and artist Joe Shuster. National Comics' publisher, Harry Donenfeld, asked Gaines if he had any suitable material for a new comic he was launching in 1938, *Action Comics*. Gaines wasn't crazy about Siegel and Shuster's character Superman, but his assistant, Sheldon Mayer, was. Mayer persuaded Gaines to show the strip to Donenfeld, who immediately saw the character's potential with his audience of young readers. History was made.

A year later, Gaines was hired by National Comics to create a new publishing house, All-American Publications, working alongside Donenfeld's partner, Jack Liebowitz. The company's first publication, *All-American Comics,* launched some of the world's most successful superhero characters under Gaines, among them Green Lantern, the Flash, Hawkman, the Atom and Wonder Woman. But despite these successes, Gaines and Liebowitz argued constantly until 1944, when Gaines was bought out.

It's fortunate for the industry that he was. In 1945, the socially conscious Gaines started up Educational Comics. He recognized the power of the medium to reach children, so he continued to publish comics based on history and the Bible, something he'd started doing at All-American. But Educational Comics (known as EC Comics) would also go on to publish humor strips and even attempt to duplicate Gaines's earlier hits with superheroes, with limited success. Low sales began to afflict many of EC's sales, and by 1947, the company was near bankruptcy.

Gaines's pioneering spirit had always allowed him to move toward bigger and better things in comics, and it's possible he could have done so again with EC Comics. However, fate played a different hand, and Gaines exited the world in a manner worthy of the many characters he helped create in 1947. He died in a heroic, tragic boating accident in Lake Placid, New York. A speedboat rammed the craft that held Gaines, a friend and the friend's son. Gaines managed to save the young boy's life at the cost of his own.

In the tumultuous time following his death, EC Comics was turned over to Gaines's twenty-five-year-old son, William "Bill" Gaines. This is where EC's story truly begins.

## MAD, BAD AND DANGEROUS TO KNOW

Toward the end of M.C. Gaines's time at EC Comics, he had re-branded its humor comics with an "Entertaining Comics" logo. When Bill Gaines took over the company upon his father's demise, he continued to advertise "Educational Comics" in the ad pages of his publications, but publishing "Entertaining Comics" was his focus.

Bill Gaines had every intention of applying his recent chemistry degree to a life of teaching until his father's death forced him to reconsider. Thrust into a new role in which he had no experience and no real interest, the younger Gaines nevertheless had an eye for talent and a willingness to let the talent create without restriction.

Within three years' time, the resulting comics Gaines published had transformed EC Comics into a powerhouse, one of the most successful comics publishers in history. Gone were stories based simply on the Bible and history. Instead, Gaines began publishing a wide array of horror, science fiction and war series. These comics were notable for advancing the medium in multiple ways:

- **They put a premium on both writing and art**. Gaines and his editors, Al Feldstein and Harvey Kurtzman, developed comics that attracted some of the biggest names in the 1950s comic-book world, including Johnny Craig, Jack Davis, Frank Frazetta, Joe Kubert, Joe Orlando, John Severin and his sister Marie Severin, Al Williamson, Wally Wood and many others. Feldstein himself was an acclaimed artist who also wrote for and edited nearly every EC publication.

- **They promoted the comic-book artist as much as the comic itself**. In the 1950s, with very few exceptions, creator names were not added to comic books. EC Comics changed that; it had its talented writers sign their names to their works and hyped the artists to the public. In today's world of superstar artists, this doesn't seem unique, but at the time, it caused a sea change in comic-book credits. EC Comics talked directly to the readers through editorial pages, forming

EC's comics and its logo became more entertaining under Bill Gaines.

relationships and fostering loyalty among its fanbase, and it used this outlet to make stars out of its stable of talent.

- **They expanded the marketplace.** Comic books had largely been seen as children's publications, with preteen readers numbering into the millions. Adult readers were rare, but EC's more adult-oriented fare—horror, crime, science fiction and war comics—drew an older reader base while still entertaining young readers with solid stories and beautiful art.

However, as much as EC Comics was a boon to the industry, it also sowed the seeds for the company's downfall. EC Comics under Bill Gaines had gained prominence by publishing titles like *Weird Science*, *Tales From the Crypt*, *Shock SuspenStories*, *Crime SuspenStories*, *Two-Fisted Tales* and *The Vault of Horror*. But these comics weren't just gratuitously titled stories designed to shock and titillate. Rather, the war comics pioneered by Kurtzman looked at the futility of war; the horror comics' darkly humorous tales featured bad characters getting their comeuppance, often in shocking "twist" endings; and the science fiction comics held a mirror up to society with explorations of weighty themes like racism and imperialism. These truly innovative publications were enabled by the creatively free and encouraging platform provided by Gaines.

EC Comics followed these successes by branching out further, into satire, in the form of Harvey Kurtzman's *Mad* comic book.

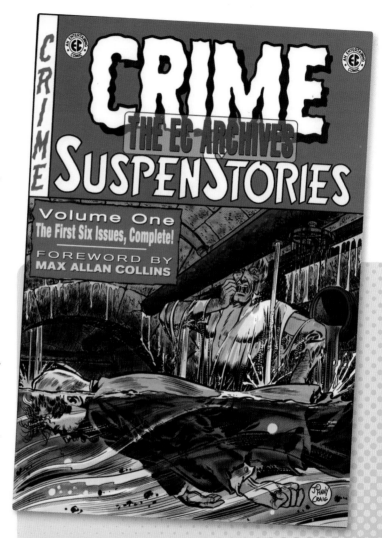

A half-century after being shut down, EC Comics is finally getting proper respect for its pioneering work with these deluxe archive editions.

EC ARCHIVES: CRIME SUSPENSTORIES, VOL. 1 © 2007 WILLIAM M. GAINES, AGENT, INC. PUBLISHED BY GEMSTONE PUBLISHING. ART BY JOHNNY CRAIG.

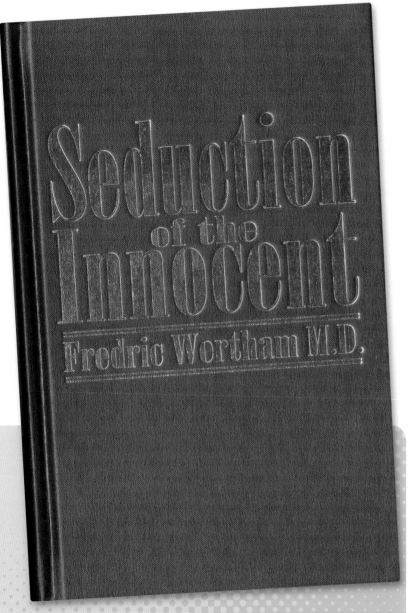

Fredric Wertham's 1954 book, exhibit A in the case against comics.

PUBLISHED BY OPEN ROAD BOOKS © 1954.

Launched in 1952, the comic book was written almost entirely by Kurtzman and featured movie and comic-book parodies illustrated by Jack Davis, Will Elder, Russ Heath, Wally Wood and Basil Wolverton. The comic book was a wild success, running for twenty-three issues as a comic before being converted to a magazine that survives to this day.

For the most part, EC Comics thrived under the younger Gaines's guidance. EC Comics was on top of the world in 1950. However, the company would be beset by problems and driven from existence within four years.

## A MAD LOOK AT ... CENSORSHIP

EC's more adult publications did succeed in expanding the marketplace, but to the world at large, comics were considered kids' stuff. And to the moralizing adults who feared comics' effect on children, gunplay, severed heads, rotting corpses, women in peril and other such staples depicted in crime and horror comics would not stand.

In the past, there had been rumblings over the need to censor comics. But now, church and civic groups focused on comics' effect on juvenile delinquency. The Red Scare was receding into the background, so a hungry press picked up on the story, giving censorship for comic books credence. The publication of psychiatrist Fredric Wertham's 1954 book, *Seduction of the Innocent*, brought the debate fully to life.

The book was a detailed but sensationalistic (and undocumented) look at the more extreme elements within the pages of crime and horror comics. Wertham's public stature outweighed his lack of real evidence, and the book led to an investigation of comic books by the Senate Subcommittee on Juvenile Delinquency. The hearings lasted three days, and in that time, twenty-two witnesses were called and thirty-three pieces of evidence presented. At the end of the three days, the comic-book industry had adopted a self-regulatory code that persisted thoughout the next forty years. The committee's final report stopped short of blaming comics for juvenile crime, but it recommended that comic-book publishers tone down their material. They formed the Comics Code Authority, which banned violent images and even specific words, all of which were prevalent in EC's comics. The code also dictated that criminals always get their comeuppance in the end. For superhero comics, this was always the expected outcome. For EC's comics, which featured more realistic, ambiguous endings, this was a terminal conclusion.

## SNAPPY ANSWERS TO STUPID QUESTIONS

The two central figures in the Senate hearings were Wertham and Gaines. Wertham, a respected psychiatrist, had impressive credentials and was viewed as an expert in the fields of both comics and juvenile delinquency. Gaines, by contrast, was the most outspoken of the four publishers who testified, but his matter-of-fact denials about questions of poor taste in comics fell flat and did him no favors during the hearings. He repeatedly stated that he felt comics were harmless entertainment, not necessarily good for kids but not harmful, either.

Gaines was publicly lambasted. His famous exchange with a senator over whether or not a *Crime SuspenStories* cover featuring a severed head was done in good taste (he replied that it was in good taste—for a horror comic) was the most publicly damning bit of coverage to come out of the hearings. Public sentiment turned against Gaines seemingly overnight as newspaper and television broadcast the "severed-head exchange" for all to see and hear. Gaines, and by proxy the comics industry, was seen as an amoral profiteer out to make a living at the expense of children's welfare. Wertham was largely passed over by the media despite the fact that his book consisted largely of conjecture and opinion, and that he misrepresented some of the comic stories he excoriated during the hearings.

Gaines left the hearings in shock, knowing that he had done more damage than good. Still, he fought to keep his comics free from censorship. While he was forced to

The Comics Code Authority seal, as designed by Ira Schnapp in 1954.

cancel many of his comics because their very titles contained now-banned words, he refused to join the Comics Code Authority. This stance was fatal to EC Comics. By now, many distributors refused to touch comics that didn't carry the Code stamp of approval on their covers. EC Comics persevered for a time despite constant haranguing by Code authorities, then published its last comic book in 1956.

Gaines tried other ventures, but none panned out. His one remaining bright spot was *Mad* magazine, which sold well throughout the hearings and beyond, and has outlived Gaines and is still being published in the twenty-first century. In 2006, Gemstone Publishing undertook the monumental task of producing newly recolored, hardcover reprints of all the EC material. New generations can now see these trailblazing, creatively stunning stories in their full glory.

Following EC's demise, publishers continued to adhere to the Comics Code with only a few notable exceptions. In 1971, the Department of Health, Education and Welfare approached Marvel's editor-in-chief Stan Lee to produce a comic book about drug abuse. However, depictions of drug use of any kind were outlawed by the Code. Lee published the comics (*The Amazing Spider-Man* #96–98) without the Code.

The advent of comic-book specialty stores in the 1980s decreased the industry's dependency on newsstand distribution, which allowed for the advent of more Code-free comics offered by smaller publishers. Finally, in 2001, the Code's relevance reached its nadir, when Marvel Comics officially withdrew from the Comics Code Authority and instead instituted its own ratings system. Today, DC Comics' children's line and Archie Comics are the only publishers still submitting their comics for Code approval.

Through it all, the comic-book industry managed to live up to the standards set by many of its four-color heroes: every time it was knocked out and left for dead, it managed to right itself and live to fight another day. Though the loss of EC Comics is not easily measured, it is profoundly felt. Still, the larger industry survived and even prospered, and the ashes of this unfortunate moment in comic-book history paved the way for the Silver Age of comics.

# Marvel and DC

## The big two

For comic-book neophytes, the notion that there are two big comic-book publishers can be hard to grasp. For the most part, the American comic-book market has been more or less dominated by these two publishers for much of its existence, and certainly for the last five decades.

### SO, DC AND MARVEL. WHO PUBLISHES WHAT?

Television has made this one pretty easy to answer. If you ever watched *Super Friends* as a kid, then you're familiar with the bulk of DC's lineup: Superman, Batman and Robin, Wonder Woman, Aquaman, Flash, Green Lantern, Green Arrow, Hawkman, the Atom.

If it's a recognizable superhero and it wasn't on *Super Friends*, then odds are we're talking about a Marvel character: Spider-Man, the Incredible Hulk, the Fantastic Four, Captain America, the X-Men, Daredevil, the Mighty Thor, Iron Man.

Granted, there are a few comic-book characters who aren't DC or Marvel who have broken through to the mainstream in the last few years, such as Spawn and Hellboy, but for the most part, it's one or the other. It's a happy coincidence that the two biggest comic-book icons in existence, Superman and Spider-Man, belong to separate companies; it makes things easier to identify. Just remember: Supes = DC, and Spidey = Marvel.

### WHAT ABOUT PLASTIC MAN? WHO OWNS HIM?

Plastic Man, the creation of the great Jack Cole, was first published in the 1940s by an entirely different outfit called Quality Comics. Quality also boasted its own stable of superheroes, such as Uncle Sam, the Blackhawks, Phantom Lady, Black Condor, the Ray, Doll Man, Firebrand and (Scott's personal favorite) the Human Bomb. After Quality Comics ceased publishing comics in the late 1950s, DC purchased all the characters and incorporated them into its own line of comics, which is why nowadays you can see Plastic Man hanging out with Superman and Batman in the pages of *Justice League of America* (*JLA*). In fact, DC has made a habit out of buying up stables of superheroes from defunct publishers—they later did it again with the acquisition of Captain Marvel and the related *Shazam!* characters from Fawcett, and still again with Charlton Comics' assortment of hero-types, including Blue Beetle, Captain Atom, the Question, Nightshade and the Peacemaker.

The Big Two logos.

## DC OR MARVEL—WHICH ONE CAME FIRST?

Well, they've both been around in one form or another since the 1930s. Back then, DC was known as National Periodical Publications, or National Comics (although the DC symbol still appeared on all its covers before the imprint took its name from its longest-running and most popular series, *Detective Comics*). In those days, National's most popular characters were Superman, Batman and Wonder Woman, with characters such as Flash, Green Lantern and Hawkman running a close second. As for Marvel, back then it operated under the name of Timely Comics, and it had its own first string of superheroes that sold many a comic book: Captain America and Bucky, the Human Torch and Toro, and Prince Namor, the Sub-Mariner.

## HOLD UP. BUCKY? TORO?

Oh, yeah. After the runaway success of adding Robin the Boy Wonder to the already popular Batman, kid sidekicks popped up all over the place. Captain America had Bucky, the Human Torch had Toro, there was the Sandman and Sandy, the Green Arrow and Speedy, Captain Marvel and Captain Marvel, Jr., and plenty more. National even tried to reverse the trend with the Star-Spangled Kid and Stripesy, a kid hero with an adult sidekick. The fact that you're not hearing about *Star-Spangled Kid: The Movie* should tell you how successful the experiment was.

## WERE DC AND MARVEL ALWAYS THE BIGGEST COMPANIES?

No, not by a long shot. While National was always the 800-pound gorilla with Superman and Batman, Timely was never in the same league. Sure, Captain America, the Torch and Sub-Mariner were popular, but not Superman-popular. And for a while, National was living in the shadow of Fawcett Comics, whose Captain Marvel family of books sold at unprecedented numbers. That is, until National sued them so relentlessly that they eventually got out of the comics business altogether (see chapter five).

National Comics stayed one of the biggest kids on the block through the 1950s and '60s (alongside Dell Comics, which had a corner on the humor and "funny animal" market, at one time publishing comics simultaneously for both the Disney and Warner Bros. properties, as well as dozens of other cartoon characters), until editor/writer Stan Lee and artists/storytellers Jack Kirby and Steve Ditko and their revolutionary Marvel Comics came along and slowly began chipping away at National's decades-long dominance.

## WHO WRITES (AND DRAWS) FOR WHOM?

The nature of the business is such that talent is always jumping from one publisher to another, seeking the best deal, the most creative freedom, you name it. It was like that at the outset, and today is no exception. However, there are a few names that demand attention.

On the DC side, the company owes its decades of success to six people: Jerry Siegel and Joe Shuster, who created Superman; Bob Kane and Bill Finger, the creators of Batman; and William Moulton Marston and H.G. Peter, the originators of Wonder Woman. Although countless writers, artists and editors have contributed greatly to DC's works over the decades, without these three landmark characters, DC most likely would not be publishing today.

As for Marvel, the most important names to know are the Holy Trinity of Marvel Comics: Stan Lee, Jack Kirby and Steve Ditko. Everybody working at the House that Stan, Jack and Steve Built is treading in their colossal footsteps. While new and exciting stories continue to be told involving the characters these three men created, it's important to remember whose original creations you are enjoying. The new coat of paint on the house may be flashy, but it's the structure that makes it stand up.

## SO WHICH IS BETTER, DC OR MARVEL?

Hey, we can't answer that for you; no one can. It all depends on your personal tastes, not to mention the creative outputs of each company in any given month or year. Take your humble narrators as examples: As kids, it was Marvel all the way. In junior high, DC was getting most of our (then very limited) comic-buying dollar. Marvel got back in the game in a big way in high school, then lost out again to DC during our college years.

To make a modern-day, sweeping generalization, DC has more of an eye toward the history and lineage of its characters, and Marvel depends more on topical themes and big, event-type, companywide storylines. Of course, in the mercurial comic-book business such broad analyses can change quickly and often. Your mileage may vary.

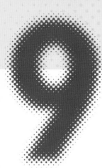

# Image Comics

## Image is everything

In 1991, Marvel Comics dominated the comic-book world. It was selling copies hand over gloved fist. A year earlier, the first issue of a new *Spider-Man* series written and drawn by creator Todd McFarlane sold more than two million copies. A brand-new *X-Men* series written by *X*-stalwart Chris Claremont and new superstar artist Jim Lee sold a staggering eight million copies. To this day, it remains the best-selling comic book of all time.

In both cases, these issues delivered huge sales numbers in part by offering multiple covers and other gimmicks that enticed fans and speculators to buy multiple copies. Mostly, the astronomical numbers were because fan-favorite creators worked on the titles. As such, the creators expected to share in the wealth they were helping bring to their publisher. Unfortunately, the publisher didn't see things the same way.

What happened next rocked the comic-book world at the time. Ultimately, it made the industry stronger and even nudged the Big Two from their comfortable perch high above the rest.

Todd McFarlane and Jim Lee were not the only creators attracting huge fan bases and producing astounding sales numbers for Marvel. Other top artists like Rob Liefeld, Marc Silvestri, Erik Larsen, Jim Valentino and Whilce Portacio also had developed strong followings.

Their art was bringing all kinds of attention to their comics, and they knew it.

In the early 1990s, the big publishers typically paid talent a page rate as well as small royalties on a book's performance; however, creators did not share in revenue that resulted from merchandise featuring their art, or see a sliding scale of increased percentages if a book sold huge numbers. They didn't retain any ownership over any new characters they created for a company, either.

These inflexible deals did not sit well with the creators. The artists banded together and approached Marvel's president, demanding a higher percentage of royalties for their efforts and greater ownership over their creations. The publisher refused to be strong-armed.

### CREATORS' RIGHTS

In early 1992, these same seven creators left the comfort of the Big Two and announced the formation of a new company, Image Comics. The company was founded on the promise of protecting creators' rights—everyone would maintain ownership over his creations, and each creator would run his own "studio," producing his own books while leaving the others to do the same without interference.

Formed by artists, the new company needed more than just clever ideas and great art for a proper launch. It needed the things that an established publisher could offer—business assistance, marketing, production and distribution. Malibu Comics, a small but moderately successful publisher, agreed to help, leaving Image creators free to create content and characters.

This "third-party revolution" began with great fanfare. Some of the early titles these creators developed, such as Todd McFarlane's *Spawn*, Jim Lee's *WildC.A.T.s*, Rob Liefeld's *Youngblood* and Erik Larsen's *The Savage Dragon*, sold in numbers that rivaled Marvel and DC. Unlimited by corporate dictates or editorial red pens, the creators' innovative styles were fully brought to bear on their own creations. This meant the books looked amazing, but were also subject to some valid criticism.

The books were written and drawn by artists, not writers, so storytelling and character development took a backseat to the stunning visuals. Moreover, even with Malibu's aid, the sheer effort needed to run a new company, manage multiple studios and deal with the publishing end of Image Comics took its toll on the creators. They were called on to handle more and more of the business side of comics, and as a result, some of the titles were hindered by lateness. Some Image creators began to

disagree on how to run the company, and accusations of poaching from each other's talent pools caused rifts and ultimately a split between some of the owners.

Creators and studios have left, and others have come aboard, but through all the changes, the company's efforts to offer creators and freelancers full creative control and ownership over their creations has continued unabated. Comic creators have more creative freedom now, and even Marvel and DC have set up some programs allowing creators to earn greater royalties and even maintain ownership over some characters.

Image as a company remains one of the top four publishers in the industry, and the wide array of choices it offers has forever expanded the medium, paving the way for other publishers and innovative creators. This increase of creative options has led to more interesting choices for consumers, which is the substance that this initially style-driven publisher helped deliver.

# Indies and Small Press

## Satisfying your indie jones

Even longtime superhero fans find their tastes developing, and they hunger for more diverse, personal comics. If this happens to you, where should you look? Everywhere.

Post-1950s, comic books played it safe for decades. Superhero comics remained the order of the day, although there were flirtations with romance, westerns and neutered crime comics. It was generally assumed that people would read comics until they outgrew them and moved on to things like novels, magazines and other adultlike diversions. It took a visionary creator like Will Eisner to realize that there didn't need to be a cutoff age for comic-book readers, and that comics could be adult diversions, too.

Eisner's seminal graphic novel, *A Contract With God*—often credited as the very first graphic novel—delivered on the potential of the entire medium, demonstrating in stunning fashion that comics could be more than genre fare. Comics could present sobering subject matter and resonant themes, and tell personal stories as effectively as any prose novel.

Before Eisner delivered *Contract*, the avant-garde *underground comix* movement of the 1960s told stories that were far from superhero tales. They never had the reach of traditional comics and were relegated to the sidelines of the industry. Around this time,

another acclaimed creator, Art Spiegelman, would move far beyond his own underground roots with his work on *Maus*. Spiegelman's *Maus*, a deeply moving tale of his father's experiences in a Nazi concentration camp (which portrayed the Nazis as cats and the Jews as mice), would go on to win a Pulitzer Prize Special Citation in 1992—the first time a graphic novel was recognized by the Pulitzer Prize committee.

While many publishers, including Marvel and DC, have dabbled in producing smaller, more personal comics, a handful of publishers have made great strides in advancing confessional comics. The following is a brief overview of these publishers and their projects, notable for their efforts to publish material that treats comic books as seriously as other forms of literature.

### FANTAGRAPHICS BOOKS

A discussion of confessional comics must start with Fantagraphics Books, a Seattle-based publisher that entered the market in 1976. The publisher, referred to by *Utne Reader* as "the premiere gathering place, publisher and promoter of the era's most exciting and multi-faceted form of literature," has been pushing the

**FANTAGRAPHICS BOOKS**

idea of comics-as-literature since its inception. The home to the critical trade magazine *The Comics Journal*, Fantagraphics has been ranked as one of the five most influential publishers in the history of comics. Its fare extends from autobiographical graphic novels to premiere reprints of classic comic strips like *Peanuts* and *Popeye* to independent-minded tales that hearken back to the publisher's underground roots and many other acclaimed and awarded works such as Dan Clowes's *Ghost World* and Chris Ware's *Jimmy Corrigan, the Smartest Kid on Earth*.

## KITCHEN SINK PRESS
Cartoonist Denis Kitchen founded Kitchen Sink Press in 1969, and ran it for three decades. In that time, his company evolved from the home to underground comix produced by such luminaries as R. Crumb, Skip Williamson and Art Spiegelman to a publisher of works by classic cartoonists Milton Caniff, Frank Frazetta and R.F. Outcault. He also forged a friendship and relationship with Will Eisner and published nearly two dozen of Eisner's graphic novels.

## TOP SHELF PRODUCTIONS
Top Shelf has been around since the late 1990s. In a decade of existence, it has published many acclaimed graphic novels from alternative creators, largely helping to push forward indie and confessional comics. Top Shelf has been rewarded with numerous awards and accolades, and its works often top

many year-end "best of" lists. Top Shelf's roster is filled with esteemed creators such as Alan Moore (*Lost Girls*), Craig Thompson (*Blankets*), Alex Robinson (*Box Office Poison*) and Andy Runton (*Owly*), among many other critics' favorites.

## ONI PRESS
Oni Press was formed in 1997, and it too set out to publish stories that covered subject

matter not often featured in comics from the bigger publishers. Its fare ranges from politically charged dramas by successful novelist Greg Rucka (*Whiteout, Queen & Country*) to quirky series such as Bryan Lee O'Malley's charming *Scott Pilgrim* books and beyond.

# 11 Manga

## *Japanese comics*

Some comics fans will tell you, "I don't read comic books. I only read *manga*."

Let's clear this up for them and for you right now: *manga* is the Japanese word for *comics*. Whether you read those books or superhero comics, we're all simply comics fans. There's no tiered system of importance, despite the need of some folks to qualify their interest in the medium.

But while manga is used to refer to comics that originate in Japan (or other countries like Korea and China, which produce their own forms of manga), it does hold some distinctions over traditional American comics.

### CHRIS SAYS

My first trip to Japan in 2000 was a jarring experience when I hit up a comic-book shop. The store, selling only manga, was packed with people—school-age girls, punky teenagers, businessmen in suits, and the elderly—not common sightings in most comics shops I've frequented. Manga readers across all ages and economic standings seemed to openly embrace the art form to a degree that I don't see here. That's changed now that manga and graphic novels occupy dedicated shelf space at mass-market bookstores, but at the time, it felt like, well, being in a foreign country. One I wanted to visit again and again.

Manga is primarily printed only in black and white. Traditional manga is printed right to left, reading backwards compared to American comics. American publishers have at times printed the pages in left-to-right format, but readers tend to prefer the authentic formatting, so the majority of manga reprinted in the U.S. adheres to the right-to-left style.

There are certain conventions to manga art and lettering, too. Manga art is very distinctive—characters have overly large eyes, very small mouths, and exaggerated expressions. Laughter is expressed by a character's mouth overwhelming other facial features; crying is typified by an excess of tears flying off the face; and storm clouds over a head and cheeks flushed with rage denote anger. The lettering is the same—word balloons are huge and often contain only one or two extra-large words and a plethora of exclamation points. Every word or gesture in many manga tales is larger than life and gives the art an immediately recognizable appearance.

Manga subject matter covers a range wider than most other comics: horror and fantasy are popular genres, as they are in comics the world over, but if you're interested in basketball manga, it exists. Business manga? Check. Pornographic manga, romance tales, political stories, true-life historical dramas? All available in volume after volume of manga.

American publishers have produced their own versions of manga, aping the style and flow of Japanese books. So far, these "Amerimanga" books have not caught on to the same degree as translated Japanese manga. This is partly because fans tend to prefer authenticity over simulations. The main reason why new manga hasn't caught on is the fact that decades of superior Japanese manga is now available in the American market. Talented manga creators are innumerable (see the sidebar on the next page for a brief starting point).

## MANGA CLASSIFICATIONS

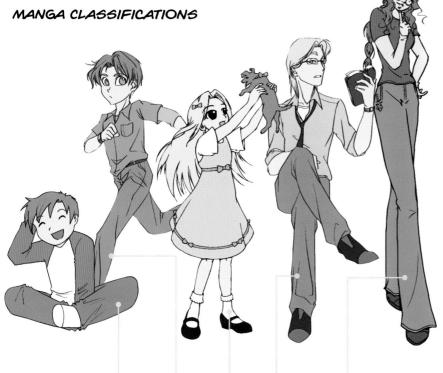

| Manga Type | kodomo | shonen | shojo | seinen | josei |
|---|---|---|---|---|---|
| Intended Audience | children | boys | girls | adult males | adult females |

see the sidebar on the next page for a brief starting point

### CHRIS SAYS

It can be daunting to know where to begin if you want to check out manga. *Lone Wolf and Cub* is my favorite, but Kaiji Kawaguchi's *Eagle: The Making of an Asian-American President* is a close second. It details the 2000 U.S. presidential election, only with a Japanese-American candidate running for the first time. It simplifies the electoral process enough to make the story accessible and not like a textbook, and it features a healthy dose of sex, political corruption and intrigue—it's *seinen* manga, for sure—to make for a truly captivating thriller over its 2,500 pages.

# A BRIEF INTRO TO MANGA CREATORS

## OSAMA TEZUKA

Tezuka is probably the most important, influential Japanese comic creator, the architect of the medium as it exists today. Tezuka is said to have created more than 150,000 pages of manga, with *Astro Boy* and *Phoenix* among his most popular. Tezuka, a non-practicing medical doctor, infused his works with a great humanity and respect for life.

## KAZUO UMEZU

Umezu is considered the godfather of horror manga, thanks to works such as *Reptilia* and *The Drifting Classroom*.

## HIDEYUKI KIKUCHI

Kikuchi is a writer of pulps and novels, and his popular novel series *Vampire Hunter D* led to an acclaimed series of manga books and animated movies (*anime*), as well as video games and other merchandise.

## KAZUO KOIKE AND GOSEKI KOJIMA

The seminal work from writer Koike and artist Kojima is *Lone Wolf and Cub*. The twenty-eight-volume series influenced acclaimed American creators Frank Miller (most notably in his *Ronin* series) and Max Allan Collins (whose *Road to Perdition* was an Americanized retelling of *Lone Wolf*), among many others. The long-running series inspired six movies and a television series in Japan. The creators considered it gekiga ("dramatic pictures"), not manga, although now the two terms are typically used interchangeably.

## KATSUHIRO OTOMO

Otomo's *Akira* is a standard-setting cyberpunk series that led to one of the most popular animated movies (*anime*) ever.

## NAOKO TAKEUCHI

Takeuchi's *Sailor Moon* is one of the more popular manga series of the past two decades. The series, which also became a long-running anime, is noted for its revitalization of the magic-girl genre.

## KEIKO TAKEMIYA

Takemiya is the most famous female shojo manga creator. She got her start working on *COM* magazine in the late 1960s, when the magazine was edited by Osamu Tezuka.

## MASASHI KISHIMOTO

Kishimoto's *Naruto*, a manga and anime series featuring a teenage ninja, debuted in 1997 and quickly became one of the best-selling mangas in both Japan and America.

## MASAMUNE SHIROW

Shirow's futuristic *Ghost in the Shell* was one of the more direct influences on the Wachowski brothers' *Matrix* movie trilogy.

# Collapse and Recovery

## The rise and fall and rise again

Would a comic book sealed in a polybag containing a glow-in-the-dark holographic cover, a numbered trading card and a temporary tattoo be enough to entice you to pick up a comic you might otherwise avoid? If you answered "yes" to this question, it's likely the year 1991.

In the early '90s, artists ruled the comic-book industry. Always a vital component to the visual medium, the comic-book artist became the propelling force of the industry in the final decade of the twentieth century, driving the marketing machine full-bore. Marvel and DC found success with some bigger titles through the offering of limited, variant covers, and they exploited this fact in a big way. While these comics sold huge numbers, they also had the less desirable effect of creating false demand for a title. Did the first issue of superstar artist Jim Lee's *X-Men* sell eight million copies because of its great writing and amazing art, or did it put up high numbers as a result of its six different covers? The answer is likely both.

The problems grew from there, though they didn't happen right away. At first, publishers thought that if a first issue sold well with six covers, then producing a variant issue with a chromium foil-stamped image would perform the same. Followed by a glow-in-the-dark cover and then a sketch-art cover. Fans liked these variants, and soon trick covers were driving the bus, and, to extend the metaphor a bit further, soon crashed into a wall. Storytelling and character development took a back seat to flashy covers. Marvel and DC looked for the next gimmick to entice readers into buying multiple copies of an issue.

### THE FALL

The core audience that was invested in the characters felt increasingly unimportant as it watched hopeful investors fill the comics shops to buy multiple copies as investments, driving up back-issue prices as a result.

Some of these speculators who inflated sales numbers so greatly had shifted from buying limited baseball-card sets in the late 1980s to this new hopeful cash cow. However, one factor that people buying seventy-five copies of, say, *Superman* #75 (the infamous "Death of Superman" issue) didn't take into account was that, in the long run, a comic with a print run in the millions would be hard-pressed to ever become valuable. Old comic books are worth a lot of money because a limited number of good copies exist. Demand exceeds supply.

As it happens in speculator-driven markets, the bottom fell out, the speculators bowed out and the industry was left in a shambles. Many smaller publishers and some distributors and retailers disappeared as sales shrank. A title that once sold a million copies was now selling a hundred thousand copies—not the sort of decline that many small businesses are equipped to withstand, and serious repercussions would be felt for years to come. Although some titles today put up occasional sales numbers of 250,000 copies, the days of a million-seller were left behind.

### RISING FROM THE ASHES

Surviving publishers took steps to rectify the damage, placing a greater focus on writers. Marvel's and DC's renewed emphasis on writing in the wake of the crash came at the same time the market for smaller-press, independent-minded graphic novels helped comics recapture some of its cachet. While not huge sellers compared to superhero titles, these kinds of books gave the industry the credibility it lacked and a means to reach out to more sophisticated audiences (and to readers who had tired of the gimmicky superhero comics in the first place).

This is why Neil Gaiman's *Sandman* book, a title that crept into stores to little fanfare in 1991, was so heralded—the writing is intelligent and resonant, and the art sublime and impactful. Reprints still top best-seller lists more than fifteen years after its launch. Meanwhile, modern-day comic conventions are filled with boxes of other comics from the same year—many of them still sealed in their original polybags and with their bonus trading cards intact—and now available for a quarter a copy.

The formula is simple—good writing plus good artwork equals sales, or at least the best chance for a book to find an audience. Some lessons are learned the hard way, and this was a difficult one well-learned. Which is fitting for an industry that gave us the refrain "with great power comes great responsibility."

# PART II

# BREAKING IT DOWN

*Wherein the construction of a comic book is analyzed—pages are broken down, creators' roles defined—the ultimate difference between comic books and graphic novels gives way to a list every comic-book fan should absorb.*

## 1

# Anatomy of a Comic Book

## *The power of the printing press*

A comic book is defined by Merriam-Webster as "a magazine containing sequences of comic strips—usually hyphenated in attributive use." Simple enough. But in the sixty-odd years since the definition was put forth, some things have changed a bit, requiring some expansion and clarification.

Comic books have had an uphill climb to critical acceptance largely because of the connotations of the word "comic." It doesn't help newcomers that the term "comic books" is often shortened to "com-ics," a term that may conjure images of both funny newspaper strips and stand-up comedians. In essence, comic books are neither comics nor books, but are composed of elements of both.

### PARTS OF A WHOLE

Comic books are made up of bound, stapled pages. The pages come off the printing press in *spreads*—a front page and back page that are printed together then folded in half. These folded spreads, known to the printer as a *signature*, are placed over a *saddle*—in the early days it actually was a saddle—and stapled along the spine by a saddle-stitch stapler. This may seem like not-so-exciting information, but it is important to understand when discussing the different formats of comic books and their thicker counterparts, *graphic novels*. In the 1950s and '60s, comic books with thicker page counts, usually eighty pages or more, were differentiated as "Specials," "Annuals," or the more obvious "80-Page Giants." These books had a true spine, but were still considered comic books. Only in the past two decades or so have longer-form comic books started to be referred to as graphic novels, a term defined and explained later in this section.

IDW Publishing's *30 Days Of Night* was originally released as a three-issue miniseries and then collected into one graphic novel.

## THE COVER

The Chinese proverb that states, "a picture is worth a thousand words," applies to a visual medium like comic books in general, but even more so to their covers.

The cover of a comic book works hard to grab readers. The image must be striking and intriguing, beckoning the reader to want to read more. But because comic books have far shorter page lengths than novels and are serialized in nature, it's important not to give away any big moment in the comic. Cliffhangers are best left for the end of an issue, not spoiled on the cover.

With a comic-book cover, you will typically find the logo of the comic situated in the top quarter of the page. This is more of a guide than a rule. Comics used to be sold on waterfall-like newsstand racks, so it was important to be able to see the title from underneath other comics and magazines. Artists occasionally will change the placement of the logo, or in some cases depict a character blocking it or shattering it to add more impact. Unlike novels, comics appear every month with the same title so sometimes drastic steps are necessary to call attention to a title.

In the 1950s, publishers—we're looking at you, DC Comics—started a trend of producing covers that had nothing to do with the interior story. They showed images of shocking weddings or unexpected team-ups or even more bizarre imagery, all sleight of hand intended to lure the reader in. It got so prevalent that when a shocking image actually did apply to the

In this impactful cover, the Mighty Thor and his logo have both seen better days.

story, the caption "Not a hoax! Not an imaginary story!" was added to the cover.

Exclamatory expressions and word balloons were used on covers more prevalently than they are today. The publishers wanted to leave nothing to chance. Create a good piece of art, add to it some captivating dialogue and likely draw in the potential customer. And if that's not enough, add a blurb to help further hype the issue ("This issue: someone dies!"). When you're a kid, and you see these colorful characters, and read some interesting dialogue, and get teased that the issue features a momentous development, too—well, they've got you.

Covers also carry other relevant information: the price, the publisher's logo and, until the bigger publishers finally did away with it, the "Approved by the Comics Code Authority" stamp. In recent years, they've also contained UPC bar codes—an eyesore when placed on top of comic-book cover art, but necessary for retailers to ring up and track sales.

## THE NUMBERS GAME

The final element on the comic book's cover is the issue number, a topic unto itself. You'd think it would be easy—issue #2 follows #1, and so on. However, this simple matter got complicated a couple of decades ago. In the mid-1980s, DC's *Crisis on Infinite Earths* series led to the relaunch of titles like *Superman, Justice League* and *Wonder Woman*. Titles that had been running consistently for nearly a half-century, with numbering into the 400s and beyond, were now starting over with a new issue #1. Marvel did the same thing a few years later, with its *Heroes Reborn* series, ending long-running series like *Fantastic Four, Captain America* and *The Avengers* and restarting them from scratch.

The reason for this is that new first issues, especially those featuring popular characters, always see a spike in sales. So, when a comic's numbering runs into the hundreds, it can be good business sense to relaunch the title with a new #1.

However, comic-book fans take issue numbering very seriously. If they've been collecting a title for years, and have amassed a run of continuous issues into the hundreds, a new #1 just breaks this streak and causes consternation (long-time comics fans can be rather vocal about their likes and dislikes). As a result, Marvel and DC made a concession to fans, keeping the new numbering but also adding a smaller number to the cover stating what number the comic would be had a new series not started. So a new issue #3 might also be shown as being issue #465.

Confusing? Welcome to the world of comic-book collecting.

### CHRIS SAYS

When I was young, the cover was also the place where a publisher exercised advance damage control. In the 1970s, a blurb on the cover that stated, "Still only 35¢!" was a sure indication that a nickel or dime price increase was coming in the next few months. To me it translated, "Your allowance is on borrowed time! Next month or the month after, we're coming for even more of it."

# The Comic-Book Page
## *Breaking it down*

Reading comics can be tricky, especially if you've never experienced them through the malleable eyes of a kid. Just as a foreign film with subtitles requires a different viewing approach, comic books ask more of the reader than a typical prose novel or magazine.

Let's assume the cover of a comic has beckoned and you've given in and bought the sucker. Now what? Opening the comic, you are typically faced with an ad on the inside front cover. The story itself begins on the right-facing page, the *splash page*, where the comic book's page numbering begins. Same as any magazine. Simple.

## THE SPLASH PAGE

The first page of the story, especially in superhero comic books, is the splash page. The complete page is usually one large, eye-catching image that kicks off the story. It also can lead in to an even more eye-catching art spread that fills the entirety of pages 2 and 3.

The splash page commonly contains two other elements beyond eye-catching artwork: the subtitle for the issue (if there is one) and the issue's creator credits. We say "commonly" because on occasion, the title of an issue is held until a crucial opening scene is complete, much as you'd see in, say, a James Bond movie. And sometimes, to really make

an impression on the reader, or just to prevent a secret from being spoiled at the start, the title will be held until the final page of an issue. One of the best examples of this is *The Amazing Spider-Man* #121 (June 1973), which thankfully held the issue's title, "The Night Gwen Stacy Died," until the shocking final-page cliff-hanger.

The splash page of *The Amazing Spider-Man* #121. When Gwen Stacy died in this shocking reveal, so did much of comics' innocence.

## THE COMIC-BOOK PAGE

Comic-book pages are made up of multiple panels, the same as a newspaper strip, and arranged to be read in sequential order, top-left to bottom-right on each page. Training your eye to pay heed to both the words and the visuals in each panel can take some practice. Unlike most newspaper strips, comic-book storytelling consists of more than just a visual that services the dialogue. The visuals might show one thing while the words say another, or the words and visuals may purposely contradict each other to make a larger point. Some nuances of the story can be lost if the reader fails to process the two on their own merits, understanding how they connect to the larger story. A tendency for new comic-book readers is to read the words on the page first, and then go back and look at the images. But only when each panel is taken in all at once does the story truly come alive.

Word balloons can bring a scene to life as explosively as the art itself.

## WORD BALLOONS

A word balloon is the speech bubble in which a character's dialogue appears. Most comics do what has always been done—place the balloon above or near the speaking character's head and lead a pointed balloon tail down near the speaker's mouth. Different comic books have played with this format a bit. *Spawn* tried something new when it launched in the early 1990s—placing the words atop a straight line and using another line to represent what would be the balloon's tail—but the use of word balloons remains one of comic books' oldest and most familiar conventions.

Within the balloon, the words can be of varying sizes, or given added emphasis through **bolding** and *italics* or even outlining. Punctuation, broken letters, colored words and different balloon shapes are other common word styles.

## THOUGHT BUBBLES

In addition to speech balloons, a unique element to comic-book storytelling is the thought bubble. It appears as a cloud shape with a trail of bubbles leading to the person thinking the thoughts. Though out of vogue in today's comics, the thought bubble was an effective way for a writer to show a character's thoughts and reveal his personality.

## CAPTIONS

When comic books started becoming more adult-oriented in the mid-1980s, word balloons gave way to caption boxes that contained a character's inner monologue, the same way voice-over is used in film. This accomplishes the same basic purpose of the thought balloon, but is considered by writers a more sophisticated way to let the reader peer inside a character's head. As with word balloons, any convention can become a crutch if used too often. This may explain why "archaic" thought balloons are making a comeback and captions are now used more sparingly.

Caption boxes are also used to establish time and place, to spell out for the reader details that might not be conveyed through art or word balloons. These kinds of captions present omniscient facts and details about specific settings.

In EC comics of the 1950s, captions also served as art direction for the artist, which is why many EC comics feature large caption boxes explaining exactly what is happening in a scene, coupled with art doing exactly the same.

## LETTERS PAGE

Periodicals have long offered pages dedicated to letters to the editor, and comics are no different. Before the advent of the Internet, letters pages were a great way to accomplish multiple goals, including:

- **Building loyalty.** The printing of letters makes readers feel more invested in the comic book. Readers who write in obviously care enough about the creative team or characters to offer their opinions; they also stick around to see if their letters are

What would a hard-boiled horror-noir tale be without the private dick's interior monologue captions?

DEAD SHE SAID #1. © 2008 IDW PUBLISHING AND STEVE NILES. PUBLISHED BY IDW PUBLISHING. ART BY BERNIE WRIGHTSON. COLOR BY GRANT GOLEASH.

The suit. This would be its first field-test, but really, they told him, it would be no different than a space suit or deep-sea outfit. It'd protect him from the pressure, the heat, and... other things.

It would also help Dack keep his mental faculties, a handy thing when entering a realm full of untrustworthy demons and the damned.

It was only later that Dack would realize how wrong theologians and poets were. For now, he could only sit in silence. He knew she was right. He also knew he had no choice.

Well, this is its first field-test, but in practice, it worked perfectly.

No debt is worth your life, Dack. But I know I can't stop you.

"Practice." Yes, practice means a lot in this case. Since we know nothing about Hell other than what theologians or poets have written.

Dack's training was intended to build his body...

...and his mind. Great religious scholars taught Dack all there was to know about Hell, which amounted to hearsay and speculation, nothing more.

The suit is functioning at 90% capacity. The depths won't be a problem for him.

Dante Alighieri was right. Hell consists of nine circles—with the greater sinners being found the deeper you go.

Probably.

The escapee from Hell was from the first circle—a virtuous pagan.

If one man from the first circle of Hell escaped, more could follow. Someone had to go before Hell on Earth became a very real thing.

His body temperature is 120 degrees. All the time.

He's legitimate.

The escapee was a first circler, babe—same as the unbaptized. Essentially there because of a clerical error, that's all. Harmless.

But I'll be careful. I love you.

"Circle 7," written by Chris for *Gene Simmons House of Horrors*, used captions that paid homage to the EC Comics of the 1950s.

printed months later, or if their suggestions are taken to heart and reflected in later issues.

- **Speaking directly to the readers.** Editors, and in many cases the creators themselves, will reply to the mail they receive, and this personal interaction with creators engenders a close relationship with the readers.

- **Promotion**. In lettercol (short for letter column) replies to letters, editors can hype upcoming storylines and other titles.

In the case of Marvel Comics under Stan Lee, all three things were accomplished on a monthly basis. Stan's conversational manner of speaking to fans brought them closer to the company. The formation of fan clubs was a logical outgrowth of this, and soon every "Marvel zombie" was eager to join the Merry Marvel Marching Society (M.M.M.S.) and band together in support of Marvel's titles.

In recent years, the proliferation of message boards and fan forums has resulted in even more direct interaction with some creators, but at the expense of many letters pages. Fans can post on message boards the same day an issue is released and can often engage the creators themselves. Still, some of today's writers recognize the value of letters columns and have brought them back in successful ways. Brian Michael Bendis (*Powers*), Robert Kirkman (*The Walking Dead* and *Invincible*) and Eric Powell (*The Goon*) have all built loyal readerships through engaging lettercols.

## CHRIS SAYS

Letters pages have always been a big part of my overall comic-book experience. I recall writing a long, rambling missive regarding *Fantastic Four #208* when I was eight years old. It never got printed, nor did it deserve to be, but it did land me one of Marvel's famed "No-Prizes," a blank envelope that contained literally no prize.

Many established comics pros first caught the attention of editors through their letters, too. Roy Thomas, Mark Gruenwald, Mark Waid, Kurt Busiek, Beau Smith and even your esteemed co-writer of this book were printed numerous times before ever going pro. You always remember the whens and wheres, too: I was first printed in an old issue of *Swamp Thing* and again years later in an issue of Brian Michael Bendis's *Fortune and Glory*.

**Chris's First Letter:**
*Swamp Thing #118, 1992*

Even worse than seeing old photos of my bad haircuts is re-reading my old lettercol ramblings.

## SCOTT SAYS

Yours truly was also a letterhack back in the day, with letters printed in *The West Coast Avengers*, *The Incredible Hulk*, *Secret Origins*, *Solo Avengers* and *Captain America*, just to name a few. Back in junior high school, I remember it being a great feeling to open that comic book and see my letter in the back; it instilled a feeling of community within the comic book biz that I think is sadly missing these days. My lettercol contributions also led to my friendship with Marvel editor Mark Gruenwald. But we'll get back to that later.

**Scott's Letter:** *Solo Avengers #6, 1988*

For the record, I typed "Dr. Druid" in the letter at left when I wrote it, not "Dr. David." Yes, I typed my letters to the editor. I was that big a geek, and I'm that old.

---

So, Nancy, welcome aboard, as I welcome myself aboard. The only other thing I would like to know is, being a fan of the Stephen King/Dean R. Koontz-type horror novels, I would really like to read some of yours. I just can't seem to find them anywhere out here! Oh, well. I'll keep looking, you folks keep doing what you do, and do your best to keep Tom and Kim on board, as well.

See you next time,
Chris Ryall

Welcome aboard from us too, Chris. Nancy's new novel, In the Blood, should be out by now, and her other books should still be in print, so happy hunting. As for Swampy, as you mentioned, WHO'S WHO #15 contains a lot of information; so do the three Swamp Thing trade paperbacks available: SWAMP THING: DARK GENESIS, SAGA OF THE SWAMP THING, and SWAMP THING: LOVE AND DEATH.

\* \* \* \* \*

Hey, Stuart,
First, let me just tell you I'm a big fan of all DC's horror comics. I've been with SANDMAN and SHADE since the beginning, and HELLBLAZER for about two years. After fifteen-odd years of collecting comics, the super-hero stuff is starting to get a little, say, repetitive, so these titles are perfect. The only problem was, I needed *more!* I then remembered, hey, SWAMP THING has a new writer, and is supposedly back-to-basics horror. I had always resisted Bon Gumbo in the past, because I felt there was too much history behind him, and I would be hopelessly lost. Luckily, I changed my mind and bought the annual and STs 114-114 last week. Incredible! The stories throughout have been great! Horror just as it should be: normal (?) people in extraordinary situations. Nancy Collins has given a great supporting cast life (who is new and who ain't, I don't know, but it doesn't matter). The annual was great and terrible all at once, as it should be, yet there is also an underlying sense of macabre humor in her stories (Swamp Thing for governor? I love it!) which all horror titles need.

All of her stories have been great, and the most recent, #114 and Dark Conrad, was no exception. John Constantine was very well written for someone so new to comics, but aren't any of his ancestors normal?

There's still a lot I don't know about ST's history, such as how he could have had Tefé, let alone why he's in the...uh...shape he is, and a lot more. (Thank God for next month's WHO'S WHO.) But half the fun is being along for a new ride, discovering things as I go. And I *will* be along!

\* \* \* \* \*

This month in HELLBLAZER #52: "Royal Blood," a major new storyline, begins. A series of grisly murders leads Constantine to an exclusive British club...and to the highest levels of society. Hard-hitting horror by Garth Ennis and William Simpson.

ALSO THIS MONTH: SANDMAN #36 is the extra-sized climax of "A Game of You," by Neil Gaiman, Shawn McManus, Bryan Talbot, and Stan Woch... SHADE THE CHANGING MAN #22 features a special dream-trip back to Meta, written by Peter Milligan and drawn by special guest artist Brendan McCarthy... ANIMAL MAN #46 is a good starting point for new readers of that title; it's a flashback to teenage Buddy Baker's vision of his future life as Animal Man, written by Tom Veitch with art by Steve Pugh...and in DOOM PATROL #54, Grant Morrison, Richard Case, and Stan Woch present Rebis's startling transformation on the moon. All fine reading! Yeah!

And NEXT ISSUE: The Bad Man ...Swamp Thing...Les Perdu... and the introduction of a very important new character. Sound intriguing? Nancy, Scot, Kim, and I will all be here; hope to see you, too.
—Stuart

---

Dear Mark,
Now *this* is what a Marvel comic should be like! Action, adventure, and drama without being depressing and bleak like all those mutant books. Maybe I'm from the old generation, but I like a book that lets you put it down feeling good.

Anyway, enough complaining. Do you know what this book reminds me of? Those classic split-books from the sixties, right down to the funny repetetive credits (Edited with a two-by-four." I love it!) The Hawkeye feature has kept up to its high standards on both script and art, although there were a couple of points I pondered over. Why didn't Hawk just take Mocky with him to Paris? It's not like she couldn't take care of herself. Shouldn't Hawkeye's arrows have notches at the end? I realize it's a nit-pick, but there are a few of us out here who still wonder about these things.

The Moon Knight feature was well done, but a bit premature, I thought. There are many Avengers who've never even had their own feature once, much less two books. I'm confused about one thing, though. Does Moon Knight have multiple copies of each weapon, or what? I thought the Black Knight shattered most of them while in Death's Realm in the WCA Annual. I just wonder which way it happened, that's all.

Suggestions for future issues? Of course, one for my main man Doctor Pym is a must, and it'd be neat to see how the Avengers would react to the Beast's new look. A Scott Lang Ant-Man story would be nice, as would a Hellcat feature. How about the return of Moondragon? Sure, she's just a pile of compost now, but you could work from that. What the heck, why not a Jarvis solo story too? I miss ol' Jarv, when's he coming back? A couple of people I definitely don't want to see in these pages right away are the Wasp, Tigra, and Dr. David. Wasp and Tigra have had plenty of exposure over the last year, and I think Dr. David is a dink. But I won't get into that again...

Well, SOLO AVENGERS #3 makes it 3 for 3, guys. Nice going, and keep it up.
Scott Tipton

You got it, Scott! As for Moon Knight's weaponry, our guess is that it was restored to its unbroken state when the Avengers were returned to life. Either that, or MK took his local blacksmith's shop for

# The Roles of Creators

## *Giving credit where it's due*

"What do you mean, it takes more than one person to create a comic book?"

Comic creators have often been asked this question by a friend or family member. The idea that an assembled team is needed to produce comic books seems to surprise anyone new to the industry. Perhaps this is because comic books to the uninitiated are thought to be the same as newspaper strips, and strips are by and large created by one person. *Peanuts*? No one but Charles Schulz ever put a line on the page or a word in a balloon for that strip. But with only a few very skillful exceptions, nearly all comic books are put together by a committee. Even those gifted cartoonists who both write and draw their own stories usually make use of various support staff, be it inkers, letterers or colorists, not to mention the services provided by a publisher, such as production and editorial work. So, before we go into the hows of getting a comic book produced, let's define a few terms.

### WRITER

Generally, the person credited as writer is responsible for the direction of the story (or *script*), the structure of the narrative, and the creation and cultivation of character through dialogue. Occasionally you'll see the role broken down even further, into plotter and scripter. The *plotter* generates the narrative thrust and twists and turns of the storyline, while the *scripter* provides the actual words that appear in the story, dialogue and captions. In this way, comic-book scripts are not so different from screenplays or teleplays. In comics, the camera or stage direction takes the form of *panel direction*, descriptions that inform the artist what to draw and where.

The writer serves as the director for the production, moving the action along from panel to panel and page to page. Comic-book scriptwriting presents some challenges that differ from screenplays. Each panel must convey only one action, and the words and images need to complement each other, rather than just using words to describe the art.

Shocking reveals and genuine scares or laughs can also be tricky to present on the printed page—a quick flip-through of the comic can spoil what was designed for dramatic impact.

### PENCILLER

Traditionally, the art in comic books is first rendered in pencil, usually on heavy, white bristol board. If an artist is credited solely as *penciller*, it means that another artist came in later to ink, or "finish," the work. However, this is not an indication of the degree of the penciller's involvement. Depending on the level of detail of the writer's instructions, the penciller is often entirely responsible for determining the panel-to-panel breakdowns, which can visually make or break a comic-book story. If the penciller is not able to clearly and concisely convey the action in the story through the poses of the figures, the facial expressions and the continuity between the panels, the best dialogue in the world won't make it a good story.

## INKER

Occasionally referred to as the *finisher*, the *inker* comes in after the penciller and inks over the penciller's lines in heavy black ink, so the page can be cleanly reproduced. While the inker was memorably and derisively referred to as "a tracer" in Kevin Smith's film *Chasing Amy*, the role of the inker is far more important than that. Some pencillers provide very little detail, leaving the final look of the figures and backgrounds in the hands of the inker. (In the case that a penciller only provides rough sketches and the inker provides most of the finished art, you'll see the penciller credited with merely *breakdowns*.)

The inker is far more pivotal to the process than most readers realize. A good inker can save some very wobbly pencilling, while a bad inker can drown a penciller's delicate, detailed linework in a sea of smudgy black. Opinions vary about what makes a good inker, but you know it when you see it. There's no fooling the eye, even to those who are new to comics.

## COLORIST

When the comic-book art has been pencilled and inked, it's turned over to the *colorist*, who assigns a color code to each figure or area, and is responsible for the consistency of those colors from panel to panel and throughout the book. In recent years technology has revolutionized the coloring process in comic books—digital coloring with computers offers a vast palette of colors and shadings compared to the original "four-color" days of the 1930s and '40s.

As comic-book art has become more sophisticated in recent years, and with digital coloring offering more and more special effects, the sheer act of coloring a comic-book page can be too laborious for one person. Many colorists now employ *flatters* to help them out. A flatter is a person who lays down a first layer of color on the art, using *flat colors*, colors with no shading, gradient or highlights. Once the page has been filled with flats and colors have been assigned to all figures and backgrounds, the colorist adds the finishing layers of colors and special effects in a fraction of the time it would otherwise take.

## LETTERER

It's one of those things no one ever thinks about, but someone has to inscribe all the words that appear in the speech balloons, thought bubbles and caption boxes. That's the job of the *letterer*, or at least it used to be. In recent years, many publishers have turned to computerized lettering fonts, so not much lettering is done by hand, which is a shame. While computerized lettering is no doubt faster and cheaper, there's a certain artistic delicacy that comes with the human touch. Letterers such as Tom Orzechowski (*The Uncanny X-Men*), John Workman (*The Mighty Thor*) or Todd Klein (*The Sandman*) are able to convey emotion and inflection through their scripts in ways that can't be achieved with standard fonts. A letterer typically handles all captions, sound effects and speech balloons on the page, although an artist occasionally draws in the sound effects during the art stage. The letterer employs different fonts, bolding and italics for inflection, and varies the size of the words in the balloons, or the very shape of the balloons themselves, to convey volume, emotion and tone.

## EDITOR

Generally, the role of the editor remains the same as it would on most publications: the assignment and trafficking of work, copy-editing, troubleshooting and general quality control. However, especially at Marvel and DC Comics, the editor's role takes on a more creative aspect. Often the editor will dictate the creative direction of a given series, and will replace the creative personnel if they are unable or unwilling to meet certain requests. Sometimes this can result in a more focused, consistent level of quality, and sometimes this can result in uninspired, miserable comics in which writers and artists struggle to fulfill the whims of a capricious editor. (On occasion,

EVERYBODY'S DEAD #3
By Brian Lynch and Dave Crosland

PAGE SIX

Panel 1

Patio. CLOSE UP on Greta, who looks confused.

1. GRETA
Right, soooo…
2.
…do you have any idea what's going on?

Panel 2

Kristen, in a change of clothes, is leaning against the patio rails, angry and stewing. She's not even looking at Greta.

3. KRISTEN
In a nutshell, Jack won't give me a ride bak to my sorority house. I want to see my sisters, I swear I'm gonna dump him, it's not like I can't do better.
4.
Plus there's some weird kind of people-eating going on or whatever.

Panel 3

Kristen walks away, dialing her cell phone. Greta looks back towards the house.

5. GRETA
So you don't have a car?

6. KRISTEN
I do—it's a Prius and it's adorable. Go ask someone else, I'm busy.

7. GRETA
'kay. I like your hair.

Panel 4

A Junk Yard. Let's call it PAT'S JUNK. Piles of tires, rotted cars Junk. The Driver's car that picked up Westerberg and Aurora has CRASHED into the fence of the junkyard. They're inside, but we can't see them. At most, they're very far away.

8. DRIVER
I wasn't like this yesterday!

**1** **WRITING**
Brian Lynch's script for his zombie comedy *Everybody's Dead* directs the action even while dialoguing the characters.

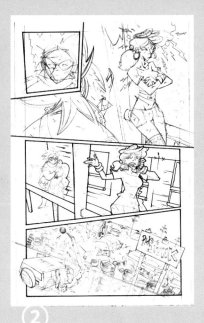

## 2 PENCILLING

Artist Dave Crosland's initial sketch interprets the script in his own inimitable style.

## 3 INKING

Crosland then tightens all his lines by inking the pencils and preparing the page for the colorist.

## 4 COLORING

Leonard O'Grady digitally lays down the color palette.

## 5 LETTERING

Digital lettering is then added as a separate layer, finishing off the page.

both can happen at once: 1950s Superman editor Mort Weisinger helped create and cultivate much of the Superman mythology that carried the series through decades of success, but to this day, tales abound of his unpleasant treatment of his writers and artists.)

## THE MARVEL METHOD: A MATTER OF STYLE

*"I've always felt that the Marvel Method strips were true collaborations between artist and writer in the most literal sense."*
—Marvel Comics founder Stan Lee

There are many different methods of writing a comic-book script. Some, as discussed on page 56, adhere closely to the structure of a screenplay or teleplay—writers create scripts with detailed descriptions of the visuals and dialogue. Others offer only plot points, leaving more of the visual storytelling to the artist. There is also the so-called Marvel Method, pioneered by Marvel Comics writer and editor Stan Lee.

The Marvel Method developed as much out of necessity as it did creativity. In the mid-1960s, Stan Lee was the writer and editor of numerous popular monthly properties. Most of the artists who drew these comics were freelancers who pulled no salary and were paid only for the pages they produced. When an artist finished one comic, he was anxious for the next script to maintain a steady income, but often Stan was busy scripting issues for other series and other artists. Something had to give if he was to keep everyone employed and steadily working.

Marvel's primary artists at the time, Jack Kirby, Steve Ditko and others, had worked with Stan for a while, and he was comfortable with their storytelling skills. Rather than make them wait for the next full script to come in, he would verbally describe to them the plot of the next issue. He'd give them the issue's key points and allow them to run with it. As Stan explains it, the artists "were more than fabulous illustrators, they were creative innovators in the full sense of that term. None of them really needed a complete script. As long as they knew what the main concept was, they were able to lay out their panels as well—and often far better—than I could describe."

After the artists completed their pages, Stan would add in dialogue and captions and request the occasional artistic change. He preferred this method because it was easier for him to provide dialogue for characters if he could see their poses and expressions. Collaborating with artists in this manner often led to the creation of new characters and took the stories in unexpected directions.

This unique style isn't used as frequently nowadays. For the Marvel Method to be successful, the writer and artist must have a familiarity with each other's style, and the artist needs to have a solid sense of how best to convey drama through visual composition. Many artists prefer to work from a full script to avoid guesswork, but it varies from person to person.

# Comic Books vs. Graphic Novels
## *Getting graphic*

When the vampire film *30 Days of Night* was marketed for release in October 2007, the film's posters were adorned with the tagline "based on the graphic novel." Other comics-based movies—*Sin City* and *300*—were promoted the same way. This designation is not completely accurate because all of these projects actually originated as comic books.

If you go into any mass-market bookstore, you'll find an abundance of graphic novels, including *30 Days of Night*, *Sin City* and *300*. So it's easy to see why those unfamiliar with the comic-book industry hear the term "graphic novel" and think this means something different from "comic book." After all, the only comic books you're likely to find in these same bookstores are along the lines of *Archie* and *The Simpsons*. So if the two are not interchangeable terms, what's the difference between the two, anyway?

In chapter one of this section, we defined a comic book as "a magazine containing sequences of comic strips." In its simplest comparative definition, a "graphic novel" is "a book containing sequences of comic strips." However, at times, the term "graphic novel" may also be used to imply more sophisticated and higher-quality material than what's offered in a comic book.

The term "graphic novel" has been used to describe longer-form comic books since an Amateur Press Association newsletter published the term in the late 1960s. However, its official entry into the popular lexicon is attributed to the back-cover text of Will Eisner's *A Contract With God* from 1978. Eisner did acknowledge that the term was used prior to the publication of his book, but he also stated, "I had not known at the time that someone had used that term before."

Some might wonder why there's such debate or confusion over the origination of such a simple term as "graphic novel." To which we can only add, hey, we're comic-book fans, obsessing over details is what we do.

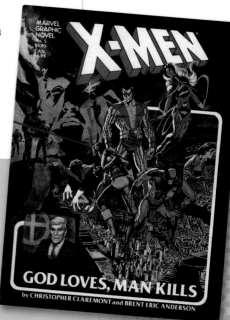

Marvel started a line of oversized, long-form comics under the imprint Marvel Graphic Novel. *X-Men: God Loves, Man Kills* inspired a plot point in the second *X-Men* movie.

COVER, X-MEN: GOD LOVES, MAN KILLS: © 1982 MARVEL ENTERTAINMENT, INC. USED WITH PERMISSION. ART BY BRENT ERIC ANDERSON.

# 25 ESSENTIAL GRAPHIC NOVELS

A list of essential graphic novels is a good spot for debate, since tastes vary so much. So consider this a starting place regardless of how you define the term "graphic novel." Our list contains comics of all shapes and sizes—book-length fictional stories, bound-up collections and more.

30 Days of Night by Steve Niles and Ben Templesmith (IDW Publishing, 2002)

The Amazing Spider-Man Omnibus by Stan Lee and Steve Ditko (Marvel Comics, 1963)

Astro City: Life in the Big City by Kurt Busiek and Brent Anderson (Image Comics, 1997)

Batman: The Dark Knight Returns by Frank Miller (DC Comics, 1986)

Batman: Year One by Frank Miller and David Mazzucchelli (DC Comics, 1987)

Berlin: City of Stones by Jason Lutes (Drawn and Quarterly, 2000)

Bone by Jeff Smith (Cartoon Books, 2004)

Box Office Poison by Alex Robinson (Top Shelf, 2000)

Camelot 3000 by Mike W. Barr and Brian Bolland (DC Comics, 1985)

A Contract With God by Will Eisner (Baronet Books/DC, 1978)

Daredevil: Born Again by Frank Miller and David Mazzucchelli (Marvel Comics, 1986)

David Boring by Daniel Clowes (Pantheon Books, 2000)

DC: The New Frontier by Darwyn Cooke (DC Comics, 2004)

The Fantastic Four Omnibus by Stan Lee and Jack Kirby (Marvel Comics, 1961)

From Hell by Alan Moore and Eddie Campbell (Top Shelf, 1999)

Jimmy Corrigan, the Smartest Kid on Earth by Chris Ware (Pantheon Books, 2000)

Kingdom Come by Mark Waid and Alex Ross (DC Comics, 1996)

Marvels by Kurt Busiek and Alex Ross (Marvel Comics, 1994)

Maus by Art Spiegelman (Pantheon Books, 1986)

Persepolis by Marjane Satrapi (Pantheon Books, 2003)

Pride of Baghdad by Brian K. Vaughan and Niko Henrichon (DC/Vertigo, 2006)

The Sandman by Neil Gaiman and others (DC/Vertigo, 1996)

Top 10: The Forty-Niners by Alan Moore and Gene Ha (DC/Wildstorm/America's Best Comics, 2006)

V for Vendetta by Alan Moore and David Lloyd (DC Comics, 1988)

Watchmen by Alan Moore and Dave Gibbons (DC Comics, 1986)

No matter the term's true origin, Eisner's book helped show other creators, if not the world at large, that comics were capable of telling serious and literate stories just as any novel. It accomplished this in these ways:

1. **Subject matter.** *Contract*'s meditation on Jewish tenement life was novel-length in size and adult in scope. Eisner once said of *Contract*, "I can't claim to have invented the wheel, but I felt I was in a position to change the direction of comics."

2. **Respect.** Although *Contract* didn't cause a sea change in public perception about comics, it did offer an example of work that created distance between the goofy-superhero stigma of comics. Now, mass-market stores give graphic novels their own dedicated sections, whereas comics are lumped in under hobby magazines.

3. **Vanity.** Calling a book a graphic novel immediately gives it more importance than if labeled by the word "comic." It's a novel, see? And it helps sell a movie to the public to say "based on an award-winning graphic novel," rather than "this story started as a comic book."

In recent years, most of the confusion between the terms is because many times, comic books and graphic novels feature the same content. Today's business model is to release most comic books in thirty-two-page format, and then release collections of complete storylines in bound-up graphic novels.

# PART III

# GIVE ME DC

Wherein a rocket from Krypton brings with it an entire universe of costumed heroes and heroines, an array of whom are defined, discussed and detailed here.

# Superman

## Truth and justice

Seen through the eyes of today, Superman can seem old-fashioned, almost cliché. The garish tights and the cape, the unshakable moral certainty, the whole notion of "truth, justice and the American way." But when writer Jerry Siegel and artist Joe Shuster introduced Superman to the world back in 1938, he was a revelation, an all-new kind of literary character that would become so popular so fast that scores of imitators would appear practically overnight. And while the tale of Superman's creators is less than heartwarming (see page 184), the character remains as popular and inspirational as ever.

### IN THE BEGINNING

Let's look at Superman's origins, as described in the expanded origin sequence from *Superman* #1 (1939). The issue consists mostly of reprints from Superman appearances from the previous year's *Action Comics*. We begin with a rocket ship from Krypton hurtling toward Earth, saving the child contained within from the planet's explosion. (Later, when Siegel and Shuster got their long-desired *Superman* syndicated newspaper strip, Superman was given his Kryptonian name, Kal-L, and his parents were given the names Jor-L and Lora. The names were later refined to Jor-El, Lara and Kal-El.)

The rocket makes it to Earth and is discovered by the Kents. (Although Mr. Kent refers to his wife as "Mary," later versions of the story, such as George Lowther's 1942 novel *The Adventures of Superman*, christen them Eben and Sarah Kent. Eventually, the comic books settled on the now-familiar Jonathan and Martha Kent.) The Kents turn the infant over to a local orphanage, which the super-strong infant nearly wrecks before the Kents return, seeking to adopt the child. The orphanage gladly hands over the child, whom the Kents name Clark.

As Clark grows, he discovers the scope of his abilities, and "that he could hurtle skyscrapers... leap an eighth of a mile... raise tremendous weights... run faster than a steamline train... and nothing less than a bursting shell could penetrate his skin!" All of these abilities would multiply in leaps and bounds over the next few years, along with some entirely new powers. Upon the death of his foster parents, Clark resolves to use his abilities to benefit mankind, and assumes the guise of Superman, "champion of the oppressed."

Several other familiar story elements debut in Superman's first appearance in *Action Comics* #1, albeit under slightly different names. Clark tries to get a job as a reporter at the *Daily Star*, but is rebuffed by the editor. Clark wants the job so he can be "in a better position to help people" as Superman, so when he overhears a tip about a lynching at the county jail, he zips to the scene, stops the lynching as Superman, then reports the story as Clark Kent. This lands him the reporter's job and sets a pattern that is followed in the Superman strips for decades. Eventually, the *Daily Star* is renamed the *Daily Planet*, and the editor, originally named George Taylor, is renamed Perry White, following the lead of the long-running *Superman* radio show.

Also introduced in the first issue is Clark's fellow reporter Lois Lane, and the Clark-Lois-Superman love triangle is established. A disinterested Lois agrees to go out with Clark, only to dump him when he fails to stand up to a masher who puts the moves on Lois (of course, we know he was only pretending to be weak to disguise his secret identity). When the hood chases down Lois's car and kidnaps her, Clark, having changed to Superman, smashes the thug's car (in the famous scene from the cover of *Action Comics* #1) and returns the now-smitten Lois to safety.

## EVER-CHANGING SUPERPOWERS

Superman's powers grow and change dramatically over the years. Whereas Superman is only super-tough and super-strong in the 1930s, by the mid-1940s, artillery shells bounce off his chest with ease. By the 1950s, Superman can withstand the blast of an atom bomb. By the 1970s, Superman is so strong he can, if need be, alter the Earth's orbit by pushing on it.

In the beginning, Superman merely leaps prodigiously from place to place, but by the 1940s, he is able to fly around in full defiance of gravity (the transition from leaps to flight was another by-product of the radio show, which used a loud wind-tunnel sound effect to express his flight). Eventually, Superman's ability to fly increases to the point that he is able to surpass the speed of light and break the time barrier, allowing him to time travel.

More powers develop along the way. X-ray vision first shows up in the 1940s, followed closely by heat vision and microscopic vision. Things get a bit silly by the 1950s, with the addition of powers like freeze breath and even, get this, "super-ventriloquism," which comes in handy for the many times he needs to dupe Lois Lane into thinking Superman and Clark Kent are in the same place at the same time. Superman also becomes super-intelligent. A photographic memory and total recall, super-scientific know-how, and the ability to read and speak every known language on Earth are all added to his already incredible range of powers.

**BLACK:** splits a Kryptonian into two separate entities

**GOLD:** causes permanent power-loss for Kryptonians, although a 2008 issue of *Action Comics* posited the power-loss only lasted fifteen seconds

**BLUE:** causes pain, power loss and eventual death for Bizarro Superman; created by the same duplicator ray that created Bizarros, this has no effect on the average Kryptonian

**JEWEL:** amplifies the psychic abilities of Kryptonians trapped in the Phantom Zone

# THE COLORS OF KRYPTONITE

**WHITE:** kills all plant life

**GREEN:** most common form, it causes pain, power loss and eventual death for Kryptonians

**RED:** causes temporary and unpredictable physical and mental changes in Kryptonians, such as shrinking, growing, sleepwalking, hallucinations and loss of control of powers; created when Green K passes through a crimson cloud in deep space

## WHAT DO YOU MEAN, WEAKNESS?

Superman obviously needs an Achilles' heel, and for decades, there were only two: magic (on the rare occasions when he would run into wizards and sorcerers) and Kryptonite, those emerald-colored chunks of mineral from Superman's home planet that emit radiation lethal to Kryptonians.

Kryptonite first appeared on the *Superman* daily radio show in 1943, when it was used to put Superman into a weakened, near-death state for weeks at a time, allowing actor Bud Collyer to take off for a week's vacation. However, in recent years, unused script and art by Jerry Siegel and Joe Shuster has surfaced introducing "K-Metal," which is, for all intents and purposes, Kryptonite. The story, which predates Kryptonite's radio introduction by three years, was never published because the story also featured Clark revealing his secret identity to Lois (a baffling move that would've removed one of the most popular themes of the series). It is unknown whether or not the radio writers came up with the Kryptonite concept on their own, or were perhaps handed it by the editors at National Comics.

The standard, run-of-the-mill Kryptonite, or Green K, can put Superman into a near-coma with close exposure and eventually kill him. Soon, Superman writers in need of new plot devices introduced all kinds of varieties of the deadly mineral, a veritable rainbow of Kryptonite.

## LOIS LANE AND OTHER LOVELY LADIES

When it comes to romance for Superman, it's all about Lois Lane. The Lois character is introduced as a bit of a shrill harpy, but is eventually softened into a spunky reporter who has genuine affection for Superman, even if she is eternally attempting to prove that he is really Clark Kent.

The "suspicious Lois" routine is a running theme in the series for years, and Superman utilizes all kinds of ruses to discount Lois's accusations, including inflatable balloons, dummies and the ever-popular Superman robots (by the 1960s, Superman has amassed a small army of robotic duplicates to sit in for him if he needs to be in two places at once). He even gets a little help from trusted friends such as Batman and President John F. Kennedy, who once agreed to pose as Clark Kent during a television tribute to Superman in *Action Comics* #309 (cover date February 1964). By the 1970s, under the pen of writers Cary Bates and Elliot S! Maggin, Superman and Lois enter into the beginning of an actual relationship when he admits his feelings for Lois, and that it is his fear for her safety that is keeping them apart.

But Lois isn't the only woman in Superman's life. In 1945, DC began publishing the adventures of young Clark Kent as Superboy in *More Fun Comics* and *Adventure Comics*, and the teenage Clark develops a romantic interest in redheaded neighbor Lana Lang. Much like Lois, Lana is more obsessed with discovering

Superboy's real identity than having anything to do with Clark. In the 1960s, an adult Lana Lang shows up in Metropolis and becomes an ongoing rival to Lois for Superman's affections.

Our favorite of the Superman girlfriends is Lori Lemaris, because of the sheer goofiness of the storyline. Not familiar with Lori? She is Clark Kent's college girlfriend when he is attending good ol' Metropolis U. They have a brief but serious romance, until family obligations force Lori to leave college and return home. And oh, yeah, she's a mermaid. Yes, "The Girl in Superman's Past!" from *Superman* #129 tells the story of how Clark romances the wheelchair-bound Lori and even proposes marriage before discovering her secret. He does, however, get suspicious when he checks out the trailer she lives in off-campus and discovers no bed, only a tank of salt water.

Yes, Superman does seem to date a lot of women with the initials "L.L." (Just how Lex Luthor fits into this fixation, God only knows.) The trend continues in *Superman* #141 (November 1960), "Superman's Return to Krypton," in which Superman, stranded on his home planet Krypton some twenty-nine years before its destruction, finds work as an assistant to his father and falls in love with Lyla Lerrol, Krypton's most famous actress.

### THE REST OF THE GANG

Other than Lois, Superman's supporting cast is pretty sparse. There's Clark Kent's boss, *Daily Planet* editor-in-chief Perry White, and the *Planet*'s cub reporter/photographer Jimmy Olsen, and that's pretty much it. The real focus of the series for decades is Superman and Lois; the Perry and Jimmy characters originated in the radio show and were only later incorporated into the comic strip.

Metropolis is nondescript throughout much of the 1940s and 1950s, with its only distinctive landmark being the *Daily Planet* building with its trademark globe at the top. Joe Shuster's hometown, Toronto, served as the original visual basis for Superman's adopted city.

The most significant supporting character introduced to Superman's world first appears in *Action Comics* #252 (May 1959), in "The Supergirl From Krypton!" written

How does Superman open the really big door to the Fortress of Solitude? A really big key, naturally.

by Otto Binder and drawn by Al Plastino. While investigating a rocket crash outside Metropolis, Superman discovers a young girl from Krypton, Kara, clad just like himself. She explains that a large chunk of Krypton remained intact after the planet's destruction, bearing Argo City beneath a protective dome. The Argo City folk had survived because the girl's father, scientist Zor-El, covered the ground with sheets of lead to block the Kryptonite radiation. For years, they thrived; Zor-El married Allura, and they had a daughter, Kara. Unfortunately, when Kara is just a girl, a meteor swarm strikes the city and punctures the lead shielding, slowly killing the Argonian population with K-radiation poisoning. Before they perish, Zor-El builds a rocket to carry Kara safely to Earth, where they have spotted Superman through a telescope. Superman tells Kara his own story of coming to Earth, and they discover that Superman's father, Jor-El, was Zor's brother, making Superman and Kara cousins. Finally, Superman, long an orphan on Earth, has family.

## SUPERMAN'S REFUGE

While Clark Kent no doubt has a place in Metropolis (at 344 Clinton Street, to be exact), he spends most of his downtime at the Fortress of Solitude hidden away in the Arctic. The door to the Fortress is an enormous keyhole that fits a key so heavy, only Superman can lift it. Inside the Fortress are tributes to his Kryptonian parents and his foster parents, as well as museum displays of his friends at the

*Daily Planet*, his friends Batman and Robin, Supergirl and, oddly enough, himself. There's also a trophy room containing mementos of his adventures, a high-powered telescope for observing threats in outer space, an interplanetary zoo, a protective vault containing all known varieties of Kryptonite and a storage room for his Superman robots, and much more.

### SCOTT SAYS

Here's where the story of Superman kinda falls apart for me. Follow along: Fifteen-year-old Kara has just lost her family and everyone she's ever known, and through an amazing twist of fate, Superman turns out to be her cousin, a blood relative, in a foreign and alien world. Superman promises to "take care of you like a big brother, cousin Kara." The overjoyed Supergirl says, "Thanks, cousin Superman! >choke!< You mean I'll come and live with you?" And Superman, the hero of Earth, the model of morality, says no. He just says no.

"Hmm... No, that wouldn't work! You see, I've adopted a secret identity on Earth that might be jeopardized!" You heartless bastard.

Instead, Superman drops Kara off at an orphanage, where she's stuck in a dump of a room with a broken bed and a cracked mirror, and forced to wear a godawful brunette wig with pigtails as Linda Lee. (Yes, more double L's.)

Even as a kid, whenever I'd read a Supergirl story, I'd always wind up thinking, "Man, Superman's a real jerk. Here's poor Kara living with all the orphans, while he's cooling his heels up in his fat pad at the Fortress of Solitude building robots of himself. What a punk."

## SUPER ENEMIES

Though Superman's rogues' gallery of villains isn't quite as extensive as, say, Batman's or Spider-Man's, his list is choice. At the top is the original supervillain, Lex Luthor, whose origins in the series are a little muddy. Pre-dating Luthor is a bald evil-scientist character named the Ultra-Humanite, who transplants his brain into other people's bodies, such as movie actress Delores Winters's, among others, before finally settling into his final body of an albino gorilla. (Gotta love comics.) Luthor's first appearance comes not long after Ultra's. Early on, his assistant is actually the bald one, and Luthor has a head full of red hair. By 1941, however, Luthor becomes his standard bald self.

By the 1950s, Luthor's appearance has changed into that of a portly businessman, but the focus of his power remains his mechanical genius. (He often utilized synthetic Kryptonite of his own invention.) A more lean and mean Luthor is brought about in the 1960s—one of the best Luthor periods—and he's so obsessed with killing Superman that he doesn't even bother changing out of his prison jumpsuit whenever he breaks out of jail.

By the mid-1970s, Luthor wears a purple and green jumpsuit with a truly fabulous disco collar, which, despite being more than a little garish, is one of the cooler supervillain costumes of the time. It's this outfit that TV viewers of that generation associate most closely with Luthor—he wore it on the *Challenge of the Super Friends* episodes as leader of the Legion of Doom.

Despite the hot threads, the Luthor stories of the 1970s tend to involve a cooler-headed, more calculating opponent. In 1983, Lex acquires an extraterrestrial combat suit (designed by George Pérez) that allows him for

### SCOTT SAYS

When John Byrne was preparing to revamp the Superman titles in 1986, longtime *Superman* editor Julius Schwartz was given the chance to publish a grand finale for his run on the titles, and say goodbye to the Superman that readers had known for almost fifty years. When word got out about the project, Alan Moore reportedly told Schwartz, "If you let anybody but me write this, I'll kill you." Considering that Moore was currently in the midst of his groundbreaking work on both *Swamp Thing* and *Watchmen*, it's hard to imagine that Schwartz needed much convincing. The result was something special: "Whatever Happened to the Man of Tomorrow?"

The story is told by a now-married Lois, being interviewed by a *Daily Planet* reporter on the tenth anniversary of Superman's death. Lois tells of how all Superman's enemies came home to roost and how Superman (as well as several of his friends) made the ultimate sacrifice to save the ones Kal-El held most dear.

If this all sounds pretty somber, it is, and it gets worse. However, the story ultimately ends on a happy, hopeful note, and serves as a fitting climax to a story begun in 1938 by two kids from Cleveland. All great stories need an ending, and it's often been said that the continuous nature of mainstream comics characters is what keeps them from truly becoming great. Alan Moore and Curt Swan (in a fitting farewell to his decades on the character) gave us just that. It's hard to point to any single Superman story and say, "This is what the character is all about." Not much comes closer than this.

the first time to go toe-to-toe with Superman. The new suit establishes Luthor as a more vital, intense opponent than seen in years. Unfortunately, the Superman reboot by John Byrne in 1986 would do away with all of it.

Reconceived by Byrne and Marv Wolfman, Luthor is no longer a scientific genius, but a ruthless billionaire magnate whose thirst for power drives him to eliminate Superman. But this never seems like sufficient motivation, and many of the new Luthor plots and schemes ring hollow. The classic Superman-Luthor relationship is unique, especially how it has evolved over decades, and we've never understood the decision to throw that out in favor of a more pedestrian crimelord-type villain.

In recent years, *Superman* writers have tried all sorts of things to spice up the Luthor character: he dies of Kryptonite poisoning from overexposure to his Kryptonite ring then comes back from the dead in a cloned body posing as his own son. He's rejuvenated by the DC Universe's resident version of Satan, and even serves a term as president of the United States. Yes, that's right. In the world according to DC, Luthor for president. Ironically, his election was less controversial than Dubya's.

### SCOTT SAYS

One of my favorite early Luthor appearances comes in 1940, when the red-headed Luthor offers Superman a challenge: his scientific genius vs. Superman's strength. In a fast-paced and funny sequence, Luthor tries to beat Superman at long-distance racing, altitude, weightlifting, sturdiness and even lung capacity. Luthor admits defeat when Superman offers to test Luthor's strength by bashing the scientist's head against his own airplane.

# 2 Batman

## "I shall become a bat"

In 1939, artist Bob Kane and writer Bill Finger were looking for work. After the unprecedented success of Superman, Kane was told by National Comics editor Vin Sullivan that he was looking for another costumed hero character for his series *Detective Comics*. Kane immediately set to work.

Using the Superman-style tights as a basis, Kane came up with his new character, Bat-Man, sporting red tights, a black domino mask, and bat wings inspired by the designs of Leonardo da Vinci's ornithopter, a bat-winged flying device. Kane took his designs to Finger, who suggested changing the mask into a full-head cowl-type hood with bat ears, the wings into a scalloped cape and the red tights to a more moody gray. Finger also suggested the pointed scallops that were eventually added to Batman's gloves.

### BATMAN'S INFLUENCES

Kane and Finger found inspiration from a variety of sources in the creation of the character. According to Les Daniels's book, *Batman: The Complete History*, Kane was inspired by two films—*The Bat Whispers* (1926), about a costumed killer known as the Bat, and the Douglas Fairbanks version of *The Mark of Zorro* (1920). The swordsman Zorro's posing as foppish dilettante Don Diego inspired Batman's wealthy (and wimpy) secret identity. Finger incorporated a dose of swashbuckling derring-do as inspired by D'Artagnan in Alexandre Dumas's *The Three Musketeers*, as well as the detective style of Arthur Conan Doyle's Sherlock Holmes. The pulp hero the Shadow was also an influence—notably his black flowing cloak as well as his double life split between the Shadow and his alter ego, socialite Lamont Cranston.

Batman made his first appearance in *Detective Comics* #27 (May 1939) in "The Case of the Chemical Syndicate." But the story bears a byline by "Rob't Kane," and Kane alone. What's up with that?

### LI'L SCOTT SAYS

Time for a time-travel trip in the Wayback Machine. Set the dials for the year 1975. Li'l Scott has been forcibly called inside from playing in the front yard. Visibly miffed at this development (though not able to verbalize it at age four), Li'l Scott is plunked down in front of the TV while dinner is prepared. It's 4:30 in the afternoon, and the dial is turned to Channel 2. On the screen, Adam West and Burt Ward are duking it out with Cesar Romero and his hapless henchmen (probably named "Tee" and "Hee" or something like that), while giant colored graphics fly across the screen. "Pow!" "Thunk!" "Biff!"

Li'l Scott has been introduced to Batman and things would never be the same.

The omission of Bill Finger from much of the public credit for Batman has been a decades-long sticking point for comics historians. Essentially, Kane was contracted to provide Batman for National, with Finger as his employee. It was common practice in the early days for newspaper comics and comic books to only credit the artist and not his writers or assistants. But considering how much Finger contributed and would continue to contribute to the Batman mythology, the omission remains galling.

Notoriously bad at standing up for himself, Finger was perpetually insecure about his reputation and his ability to land work, in part because of his struggles with writer's block and deadlines. Kane, however, had no such insecurities. Unlike Siegel and Shuster, Kane was a shrewd businessman, and negotiated himself a deal for Batman that ensured the continued appearance of his byline, as well as a much richer contract for future Batman stories than Siegel and Shuster ever had for Superman.

Finger went on to co-create Robin, many of Batman's villains, Gotham City, and much, much more over the course of three decades and hundreds of Batman stories, but he never saw any of the fame or riches that Kane did, and died relatively unknown and penniless. Decades later, though, Kane himself admitted that he should have given Finger a byline.

## IN THE BEGINNING

The first Batman story, "The Case of the Chemical Syndicate," is a fairly standard pulp-style murder mystery, with the Batman investigating a series of murders involving a group of business partners. The story is mostly notable for Kane's simple, rough style of art and the ruthlessness of Batman himself, who knocks the murderer into a vat of acid with few compunctions.

While there's no Batmobile in evidence, Batman does tool around in a large sedan (which, surprisingly, is bright red—so much for stealth). Although the Batman's later penchant for gadgetry and equipment is absent, he does exhibit his trademark quick thinking when he saves one of the business partners from a deadly gas chamber by tying off a gas valve with a handkerchief. The Batman costume itself does not change much, only the small purple gloves and uniquely shaped cowl stand out as early variations. Commissioner Gordon is also introduced in this first story, beginning a long career of being one step behind Batman.

A better example of the early Batman plotline can be found in the story "The Batman Meets Doctor Death," from *Detective Comics* #29 (July 1939). Many of Batman's later story conventions pop up here, including the sinister villain-type, Doctor Death (as opposed to run-of-the-mill hoodlums), and the utility belt. In the utility belt's earliest appearance, Batman loads it up with items for a specific operation, rather than the universally equipped bag of tricks it becomes in later decades.

The story also features something that would become a running theme in the Batman comics: an injury. In sharp contrast to the invulnerability of Superman, Batman takes a bullet in this story, the first of many injuries and wounds that the decidedly mortal Batman would suffer.

The early Batman appearances are entertaining if slightly out of character compared to today. In several stories written by Gardner Fox, the Batman is even more vicious than in his first appearance, carrying a sidearm and using a machine gun to shoot down innocent people who've been turned into zombie creatures, with little more than a "the poor devils are better off this way" as justification for the killings.

## BORN OF TRAGEDY

However, a mere two pages in *Detective Comics* #33 (November 1939) would alter the character forever, elevating Batman from just another pulp hero to a true piece of modern American mythology. Looking to develop Batman's character further and give him some motivation, Bill Finger and Bob Kane constructed a masterful origin sequence, both perfectly logical and emotionally devastating.

By now we all know the story: Thomas Wayne, his wife Martha and their young son Bruce are walking home from a movie when they're accosted by a mugger. When the criminal tries to grab Martha's necklace, Thomas interferes, and the mugger shoots him. When Martha calls out for police, the mugger shoots her as well, then runs away. Young Bruce is left alone on the pavement with the bodies of his murdered parents, and he swears an oath to avenge his parents' death by devoting his life to "warring on all criminals." Jump ahead to an adult Bruce, who has spent the ensuing years in preparation and training, becoming a "master scientist" and training his body "to physical perfection." Ready to begin his war on crime, Wayne ponders how exactly to go about his quest: "Criminals are a superstitious, cowardly lot, so my disguise must be able to strike terror into their hearts." Just then, a huge bat flies in through the open window. "A bat! That's it! It's an omen... I shall become a bat!"

The simplicity of Batman's origin can distract the reader from its psychological underpinnings. It may seem a bit of a genre

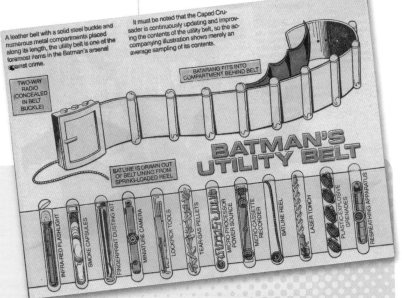

A leather belt with a solid steel buckle and numerous metal compartments placed along its length, the utility belt is one of the foremost items in the Batman's arsenal against crime.

It must be noted that the Caped Crusader is continuously updating and improving the contents of the utility belt, so the accompanying illustration shows merely an average sampling of its contents.

BATARANG FITS INTO COMPARTMENT BEHIND BELT

TWO-WAY RADIO (CONCEALED IN BELT BUCKLE)

BATLINE IS DRAWN OUT OF BELT LINING FROM SPRING-LOADED REEL

## BATMAN'S UTILITY BELT

INFRA-RED FLASHLIGHT
SMOKE CAPSULES
FINGERPRINT DUSTING KIT
MINIATURE CAMERA
LOCKPICK TOOLS
TEAR-GAS PELLETS
MICRO-PROCESSOR POWER SOURCE
MICRO-CASSETTE RECORDER
BATLINE REEL
LASER TORCH
PLASTIC-EXPLOSIVE GRENADES
REBREATHING APPARATUS

The classic yellow capsule utility belt worn for years by the Caped Crusader.

cliché now—his parents were murdered by criminals, so he fights crime— but it was certainly not in 1939. American society was only beginning to see the urbanization of its cities and more common street crime. Moreover, Batman keenly taps into one of the primal fears and insecurities of children: parental abandonment.

Over the years, writers have revisited and revised the origin, but not by much. The one significant story element added in the late 1940s, the identification of Bruce Wayne's parents' gunman as Joe Chill, and his eventual confrontation with an adult Batman, has been wisely edited out of the origin again in recent years. Batman's motivations make more sense if his own personal tragedy remains unresolved.

## SEND IN THE SIDEKICK

The origin story was so effective in cultivating an emotional bond between Batman and young readers that it was used again in 1940, when Kane and Finger added a new character to the series, one that altered the character forever and fundamentally changed the nature of the series: Robin, the Boy Wonder. Although National editors were at first skeptical about a child character in harm's way fighting alongside Batman, sales doubled after Robin's introduction, and they quickly changed their tune.

Robin made his debut in *Detective Comics* #38 (April 1940) in "The Sensational Character Find of 1940... Robin, the Boy Wonder." The story opens when young circus acrobat Dick Grayson overhears the circus owner

being threatened by local gangsters demanding "protection money." Later, at that night's performance of "The Flying Graysons," the trapeze rope snaps and John and Mary Grayson, Dick's parents, fall to their deaths before the eyes of their son, a shocking and deliberate echo of Batman's origin five months earlier.

Dick overhears the gangsters gloating over the "accident," and is about to go to the police when Batman stops him. The whole town is run by the organized crime kingpin, Boss Zucco, and Dick would be killed if he went to the police. When Batman explains that he was the victim of a similar circumstance, Dick insists on joining his crusade, and the duo an oath: "And swear that we two will fight together against crime and corruption and never to swerve from the path of righteousness." Heavy stuff to ask of a ten year old, but considering Dick's recent experience, it works.

After many months of training and preparation, Dick Grayson is ready for action as Robin. His addition permanently changes the dynamic of the comic. The dark moodiness gradually lessens over time, and the days of Batman as a dark vigilante are over.

## WHERE DOES HE GET THOSE WONDERFUL TOYS?

By 1941, Batman and Robin refer to their convertible roadster as the "Batmobile," but it is still fairly indistinct, save for a small bat-shaped hood ornament. Sometimes, though, bats gotta fly, and Batman is no exception. As far back as 1939, Batman makes use of specially designed aircraft, specifically the "Batgyro," a combination plane/helicopter introduced in *Detective Comics* #31.

Within a year, however, the Batgyro is abandoned for a more traditional "Batplane," initially an open-cockpit fighter-plane design. Much like the Batmobile, the Batplane evolves over the years, becoming first what looks like a passenger plane, then shifting to a more streamlined jet fighter.

For greater flexibility, the Batcopter is introduced in the late 1950s, as is a personal favorite: the Whirly-Bats. The Whirly-Bats are collapsible, one-man helicopters, which Batman and Robin keep stored in the Batmobile's trunk, ready to bust out at a moment's notice.

As if all that isn't enough, there is also the Batboat, the Batmissile for suborbital jaunts, and even, yes, the Batmarine, first utilized to keep Batman and Robin underwater and alive while they slowly depressurize, so they don't get the bends—it's a long story.

## GUEST LECTURER

### JUD MEYERS, owner, Earth-2 Comics

#### GOOFIEST SUPERHERO COMIC
*World's Finest* #193 (May 1970). Batman and Superman are stripped of their powers and forced to work in the "deathcamps" of Lubania. Gaunt, unshaven and starving (yet still in costume), they must stop themselves from fighting over scraps of food while painting "down with democracy" propaganda. Good stuff!

## YOU GOTTA BE JOKING
Batman has one of the most famous and well-rounded rogues' galleries in all of comics, but when it comes to Batman villains, there's just one name that tops the list: the Clown Prince of Crime, the Joker.

The Joker first appears in *Batman* #1 (1940), courtesy of writer Bill Finger and artists Bob Kane and Jerry Robinson. Credit for the actual creation of the character has long been a dispute between Kane and Robinson. Robinson claimed that the inspiration came from a pack of playing cards, while Kane claimed to have come up with the character on his own. Finger, who was known for keeping an enormous reference file, rejected Kane's initial sketch for the new villain as too clown-like, and provided the artists with photo stills from the film *The Man Who Laughs* (1928), which starred Conrad Veidt as an English nobleman with an unsettling smile permanently carved into his face. The makeup worn by Veidt was most creepy, and a clear inspiration for the Joker's appearance, particularly the bags under the eyes, the creased brow and distinctive high hairline.

In the Joker's first appearance, he's not quite the wacky loon he later becomes; however, he's as murderous as ever. Though original plans called for the Joker to die in that issue, Kane and Finger must have realized they had a good thing on their hands, and the Joker was swiftly brought back from the dead three months later in *Batman* #4.

What's the key to the Joker's appeal as a villain? Let's face it: clowns are creepy. Furthermore, the escalating humor found in the numerous Joker stories perfectly counter the often serious and grim Batman stories. In addition, the Joker's chaotic nature provides a dark mirror to Batman's own tortured existence. Where as Batman is constrained by the trauma of his past, forced into a life of vengeance by his own memories, the Joker's insanity allows him to do anything his twisted heart desires.

As the years go by, the Joker loses much of his deadly edge, and his murderous extortion plots are gradually replaced by more and more outlandish criminal schemes. The Joker doesn't get an origin until *Detective Comics* #168 (February 1951), "The Man Behind the Red Hood!" Batman is invited to teach a criminology course at State University. (Gotham universities clearly have a less-than-stringent policy regarding faculty.) Professor Batman challenges his students to solve the case even he never cracked—the mystery of the Red Hood, a criminal who terrorized Gotham wearing a metallic red dome with no eye slits. After a series of pursuits, Batman had cornered the Red Hood in the midst of a robbery at the Monarch Playing Card Company. In a last-ditch effort to escape, the Red Hood dove into the plant's catch basin of chemical waste that empties into the river, and his body is never recovered.

When word hits the papers that Professor Batman has reopened the Red Hood case,

# BATMAN'S ROGUES' GALLERY

**THE JOKER** The yang to Batman's yin, the chaos to his order. Sheer insanity to match the Dark Knight's unyielding logic.

**THE RIDDLER** Obsessed with riddles and puzzles, Edward Nigma can't commit a crime without compulsively leaving the Batman a clue.

**THE PENGUIN** With his trademark umbrella and tuxedo, Oswald Cobblepot's humorous appearance belies a deadly and capable criminal interior.

**CATWOMAN** Master jewel thief Selina Kyle always manages to get away with one more rarity: Batman's affections.

**TWO-FACE** Former Gotham D.A. Harvey Dent suffers horrible facial scars after having acid thrown in his face, and becomes obsessed with duality.

**RA'S AL GHUL** An immortal ecoterrorist, Ra's is determined to convince Batman to inherit his empire, or else eliminate him entirely.

**MR. FREEZE** Cursed to life in subzero temperatures by a lab accident, Victor Fries dreams of a Gotham City shrouded in ice.

**POISON IVY** Immune to all poisons and irresistible to men, genius botanist Pamela Isley plots the downfall of humanity and vegetation's triumph.

it doesn't take long for Mr. Hood himself to come out of retirement. After a confrontation with the Red Hood, Batman and Robin analyze a hair left behind by the villain, and they determine the Red Hood's identity: the Joker himself. The Joker explains that he survived the swim through the chemical vats thanks to the oxygen tank built into the hood, but when he emerged, the chemicals had permanently dyed his skin chalk-white, his lips red and his hair green. Taking a cue from the playing card company, he renamed himself the Joker, and embarked upon his new career in crime.

The Joker appeared regularly in Batman comics in the 1940s and 1950s, and we mean *regularly*. With Batman and Robin appearing in *Batman*, *Detective Comics*, *World's Finest* and S*tar Spangled Comics*, the Joker was making almost monthly appearances; that is, until 1956, when the Joker practically disappeared. Why? Former DC editor Mike Gold theorizes that the Joker disappeared with the rise of the Comics Code Authority (see pages 28–34), and that the Joker's clownish appearance was too offensive for either the Code or the now skittish DC editors. Thankfully, the Joker made his return to the pages of *Batman* the following year, but never with the regularity of his appearances in the 1940s and early 1950s. This ended up being a good thing; the Joker in smaller doses made his appearances more meaningful.

Still, by the 1970s, the Joker had become pretty much toothless, in part because of the 1966 *Batman* TV series based on the comic.

The Joker was no longer an insane figure of fear and menace, but rather an outlandish buffoon attempting larger-than-life spectacles of crime. (An elaborate plan to use the Jokermobile to splatter enormous tubes of oil paint all over Wayne Manor? Not exactly Public Enemy No. 1.)

The Joker would soon return to his previous murderous glory, however, thanks to Denny O'Neil and Neal Adams, who had been revamping the Batman comics, working toward restoring the Dark Knight to his moody, noir-ish origins. *Batman* #251 (September 1973) featured "The Joker's Five-Way Revenge!" and starred a truly frightening, intimidating Clown Prince of Crime for the first time in decades. The Joker's on a murder spree, killing five of his former henchmen, to get revenge on whichever one of them betrayed him to the police. He takes utter glee in the murder of his former goons, with none of the harmless whimsy he'd been saddled with in years past—now he is far more dangerous and unpredictable. In one sequence, he agrees to release his final target in exchange for Batman's taking his place in the shark tank, only he immediately reneges and drops the hostage to the tank anyway. Simple rule, Bats. Never, never, never trust the Joker. Neal Adams's stark, slightly more realistic art style was a perfect complement to O'Neil's new and edgier Batman and Joker.

In recent years, DC creatives have ratcheted up his profile by having him murder the second Robin, Jason Todd, and permanently cripple Batgirl. In addition, the Joker also murders Commissioner Gordon's second wife, Sarah, at the climax of the "No Man's Land" storyline. While these heinous crimes do effectively make the Joker Batman's most hated and feared foe, there's a real danger of harming the Batman's character in the process: there comes a point where any reasonable man, even one as morally principled as Bruce Wayne, will strike back with lethal force against anyone who causes so much harm and pain to his extended family. For Batman not to do so somewhat weakens him. Perhaps this is why we prefer the 1990s animated version of the Joker. In the cartoons the Joker does not cross the line and harm any members of Bruce Wayne's family, and it's easier to accept Batman's mercy in allowing him to live.

## GUEST LECTURER

**PAUL DINI**, Emmy Award-winning writer, *Batman: The Animated Series*; *Detective Comics*

### THE FIRST ISSUE OF *DETECTIVE* I EVER READ

That would be *Detective Comics* #365 (July 1967), "The House the Joker Built." I may have glanced through earlier issues of 'Tec at the barbershop or at the drugstore, but #365 was the first issue I remember buying with my own money. As for the plot, Gotham crooks shell out big bucks to watch Joker humiliate Batman and Robin on a special pay-per-view closed-circuit channel. Mr. J proves he is an entertainment visionary by beating HBO and Showtime to the punch by almost fifteen years.

### THE BEST CREATIVE TIME ON THE TITLE

It's awfully hard to beat Steve Englehart's and Marshall Rogers's 'Tec run in the late '70s. Hugo Strange, Silver St. Cloud, the Laughing Fish, unforgettable stories and characters. A perfect distillation of Batman and his world up until that time.

### THE BEST COVER

I have to go with *Detective* #40 (June 1940). Yes, there are more colorful, visually arresting covers, but this early one deftly captures the mixture of the pulp thrills, wish-fulfillment heroism and cheery sadism that defined Batman's debut years.

### THE GOOFIEST STORYLINE/ISSUE

I don't know if it's the goofiest story, but it certainly has the goofiest cover—*Detective* #314 (April 1963), "Murder in Movieland." While investigating a crime on a movie set, Batman and Robin are terrorized by a giant mechanical version of Moby Dick. It isn't often that I personally identify with Batman and his menaces, but when I was a kid, I was traumatized by the same thing. It's probably the only parallel I can draw to the Dark Knight.

# Wonder Woman

## *Enter Diana*

M.C. Gaines was no dummy.

According to Les Daniels's book *Wonder Woman: The Complete History*, Gaines, the publisher of *All-American Comics*, read an admonishing opinion article, "Don't Laugh at the Comics," in the October 25, 1940, issue of *Family Circle* magazine. While it didn't outright attack comic books, it did imply that they weren't exactly good for kids. In the article, prominent psychologist William Moulton Marston suggested that the overwhelming dominance of male heroic figures in superhero comics needed to be balanced by a strong female hero. The savvy Gaines understood that the best way to quiet a critic was to get him on the payroll, so he dispatched his editor, Sheldon Mayer, to meet Marston and get him on board as an advisor.

Little did Gaines and Mayer know that their attempt to get a little positive press would instead net them arguably the third great archetype character in comic books, as well as give one of America's earliest feminists a monthly platform for his most unusual agenda, in the pages of his creation—Wonder Woman.

Mayer had little idea just how dedicated Marston was to the concept of the equality and supremacy of women when they met to discuss his potential advisory position and later his creating a new female hero character for All-American Publications. In the 1930s, Marston, a well-known psychologist of the time and creator of the polygraph lie detector test, had a prediction: the next one hundred years would "see the beginning of an American matriarchy." He theorized that women's superior emotional development would lead them to develop the "ability for worldly success" and eventually "to rule business and the nation."

Marston came back to Mayer with a synopsis for a character called Suprema, the Wonder Woman. His intentions for the character were plain—to introduce a character who would be "tender, submissive, peaceloving as good women are," combining "all the strength of a Superman plus all the allure of a good and beautiful woman." Mayer wisely cut Suprema from the title character's name, sticking with Wonder Woman. Then, over Mayer's objections, Marston chose newspaper artist Harry Peter (credited in the comics as H.G. Peter) to illustrate the feature, claiming merely that "he knew what life is all about." Marston undoubtedly had other motives in mind.

### WOMAN'S WORLD

Wonder Woman made her debut in a backup story in *All Star Comics* #8 (December 1941),

"Introducing Wonder Woman." The comic is credited to Marston's sobriquet, Charles Moulton.

The story opens with a U.S. Army plane crashing on Paradise Island, a mysterious, uncharted isle populated by the Amazons, a tribe of beautiful and scantily clad women. The plane and its injured occupant, Captain Steve Trevor, are discovered by Diana, daughter of Hippolyte, Queen of the Amazons. While Trevor is nursed back to health by the Amazon doctors, the lovestruck Diana asks her mother why she can't attend to the wounded airman, and thus unfolds the story of the Amazons.

In ancient Greece, the Amazons were taken into slavery by Hercules, who defeated Hippolyte in personal combat through trickery. The goddess Aphrodite helped Hippolyte and the Amazons escape and vanquish Hercules and his armies, but in return, the Amazons had to agree to leave the world of man and establish a new world of their own on Paradise Island. If they remained on the island and did not permit themselves to again be deceived by men, then they would remain young, strong and immortal. Aphrodite also decreed that the Amazons wear bracelets fashioned from their captors' chains, "as a reminder that we must always keep aloof from men."

As Hippolyte finishes the story, Aphrodite appears before her and declares that one of the Amazons, the strongest and bravest, must return Steve Trevor to America and remain in the "man's world" to help defend America, "the last citadel of democracy, and of equal rights for women." So, to determine the strongest and bravest, Hippolyte prepares a tournament, but forbids Diana from entering, unable to bear the possibility of her daughter leaving the island. She enters anyway, in disguise, and wins the contest. The masked Amazon is revealed, and Hippolyte has no choice but to name her daughter the winner and award her the uniform and title of Wonder Woman.

Wonder Woman's first adventure continues in *Sensation Comics* #1 (January 1942). The Amazon princess returns the injured Steve Trevor to America in her invisible plane, dropping him off at Walter Reed hospital in Washington, DC. As she is exploring the "Man's World," she finds herself foiling a robbery and her "bullets and bracelets" trick—deflecting gunshots with her bracelets—is noticed by a passing theatrical agent. He puts Diana on stage, enabling her to make some quick cash while Trevor recuperates. Then, in one of those "only in comics" coincidences, Princess Diana runs into a despondent nurse who laments that she lacks the funds to join her fiancé in South America. Because the princess needs a nursing job in order to be near Steve Trevor, and conveniently has a fistful of cash to spare from her theater gig, an arrangement is quickly made. Soon the nurse is off to join her fiancé, never to be seen again, and Princess Diana takes over the nurse's job and identity. The nurse's name? Diana Prince, of course.

## GIRL POWER

Wonder Woman's golden Lasso of Truth would later be introduced, and is perhaps a direct correlation to Marston's real-life invention of the polygraph machine. He gives Wonder Woman the same power he felt he gave the world: the ability to determine truth from lies. The lasso is a weapon of submission that renders opponents helpless, a theme that Marston would return to again and again, such as the final twist revealed in the Wonder Woman concept: that she becomes powerless when bound by a man.

This detail further underlines Marston's feminist agenda in the series, by subtly reinforcing his premise that women in American society must free themselves from male domination if they're ever to be truly strong and independent. It also provides a convenient excuse for Wonder Woman to be tied up, chained, shackled, gagged and otherwise restrained literally hundreds of times over the course of the series, all lovingly illustrated in Peter's pulpy, disturbingly adult style. This, we contend, was the real reason for Marston's insistence on Harry Peter as the *Wonder Woman* artist: to infuse the comic with highly suggestive imagery to help keep the attention of male readers, particularly young adolescent males, who might otherwise hesitate to buy a "girls' comic book." Once Marston had pulled

At least Kryptonite was hard to come by. Wonder Woman's weakness? Being bound by men.

in a large, captive audience with Peter's lurid bondage art, he was able to proselytize his enlightened, feminist agenda.

After the death of William Moulton Marston in 1947, the *Wonder Woman* strip entered a new phase of its publication. No longer single-mindedly focused on issues of gender equality and submission, *Wonder Woman* instead took on a straightforward adventure style, being handled primarily by writer Robert Kanigher and artist Ross Andru. Andru's clean and traditional style departed from that of artist H.G. Peter and more closely resembled DC's general output. A minor revision was made in Wonder Woman's costume, replacing her red-and-white boots with red Greco-Roman-style lace-up sandals.

The only significant change to the character (other than when the series briefly returned to a World War II setting to synchronize with a CBS television series during the 1970s) was when Wonder Woman's costume changed in *Wonder Woman* #288 (February 1982), when the eagle on her chest plate was replaced with a stylized double "W" symbol.

## EXTREME MAKEOVER

By 1985, it was decided that Wonder Woman would be completely revised by the end of DC's epic miniseries *Crisis on Infinite Earths* (intended to simplify and refine DC's complex universe of characters and timelines), and so the old Wonder Woman was wiped from existence, erased as if she'd never existed.

### SCOTT SAYS

Robert Kanigher's stories took a lighthearted, almost fairy-tale approach to the Wonder Woman narrative, one in which logic and continuity often flew right out the window. Kanigher made use of Queen Hippolyte's Magic Sphere with a vengeance. This television-like device introduced in Wonder Woman's first appearance allowed Hippolyte to see any place or time in the world, and Kanigher used it to tell tales of Princess Diana as a girl, and even as a toddler, known as Wonder Girl and Wonder Tot, respectively. The adventures of young Diana often involved innocent flirtations with mythological types such as Bird-Boy and Mer-Boy. Even stranger, sometimes Wonder Woman would travel back in time through the screen of the Magic Sphere to have adventures with Wonder Girl and Wonder Tot, despite the fact that they were all three the same person.

This even resulted in the accidental creation of a new character. When the creative personnel at DC (who apparently were not steady *Wonder Woman* readers) were putting together their new *Teen Titans* series, they took a look at issues of *Wonder Woman* and said, "Hey, there's a Wonder Girl! Put her on the team, too!" They failed to realize that Wonder Woman and Wonder Girl were one and the same. When the mistake was eventually discovered, a backstory was hastily constructed for Wonder Girl, and she became Donna Troy, an orphan rescued by Princess Diana and raised on Paradise Island as Diana's sister.

The problem was that DC hadn't finalized its plans for its new, post-*Crisis* Wonder Woman. In his foreword to the trade paperback collection *Wonder Woman: Gods and Mortals*, writer/artist George Pérez recalls that there had been many proposals submitted for a new Wonder Woman, some that changed everything but her name. The editors at DC, however, were intent that the basic character remain recognizable as Wonder Woman. When Pérez expressed interest in handling the Wonder Woman revamp, all current plans in place were changed, and Pérez came on board as both the artist and writer, with longtime collaborator Len Wein lending a hand on the script.

Of the three major revamps undertaken by DC in the post-*Crisis* days of 1986 (Superman and Batman being the other two), Wonder Woman's was the most successful creatively, and it catapulted the character back to a level of importance and significance that had not been seen in decades. It shook off the detritus of years of neglect, and combined the strongest elements of the original concept with a modern sensibility. Pérez strengthened the series' ties to Greek mythology, using all the Greek names for the deities, renaming Paradise Island Themyscira and even giving Diana more traditionally Greek features. Retained from the original is Steve Trevor's crash-landing and convalescence on Paradise Island, although wisely, this time the creators don't have Diana fall madly in love with the first man she sees. As always, Perez's art on the series is gorgeous, and his redesigns of villains like Ares, as well as new characters like Decay, Deimos and Phobos, gave the series the brand-new spark it had long needed. As for characterization, here Perez gave us a strong, confident and powerful woman, still uncertain about her role in Man's World, innocent yet not naïve.

## A most memorable run

By 1940, the rampant success of Superman was obvious. Publishers were tripping all over themselves to get the next superhero comic out the door. However, creators were cautious. National's successful legal action against Fox Comics had recently ended the derivative Wonder Man feature from Eisner and Iger Studios. So, what to do? Specialize! Before long, every superhero was more than, well, super, and had a distinct and legally defensible niche. Timely Comics introduced the Human Torch and the Sub-Mariner, while National's sister company All-American headlined its new series *Flash Comics* with two of its own—Hawkman and the Flash, the first of the speedster characters in comic books.

The Flash has been a remarkably long-running character, with only a five-year gap in publication since 1940, second only to Superman, Batman and Wonder Woman, who have remained continually on the stands since their inception. The Flash concept is also the best example of one of DC Comics's great strengths: a sense of legacy. The tradition and title of the Flash is passed down from generation to generation through the decades. Let's take a look at the men who have carried the lightning.

### THE FIRST FLASH

The original Flash's first appearance was in *Flash Comics* #1 (January 1940), courtesy of writer Gardner Fox and artist Harry Lampert. We meet Jay Garrick, an "unknown student at Midwestern University" who's getting absolutely nowhere with co-ed Joan Williams because of his lack of skills on the gridiron. After all, she says, "a man of your build and brains could be a star... a scrub is just an old washwoman!!" Ouch. No love for Jay.

In the lab, however, research student Jay is a brilliant scientist who's been studying the gases of "hard water" for three years. Working in the lab late one night, Jay decides to relax with a cigarette. (Comics in the 1940s were a whole different animal.) As he leans back to take a big drag, Jay knocks over the bottles containing the mysterious hard-water fumes, and they quickly render him unconscious.

After weeks in the hospital, Jay eventually recovers, and the doctors discover that the hard water elements have permanently affected his reflexes. The doctor drops some slightly dubious science on Jay: "Science knows that hard water makes a person act much quicker than ordinarily... by an intake of its gases, Jay can walk, talk, run and think swifter than thought!" If you say so, Doc. Jay is now the fastest man alive, and in a burst of self-interest unusual for superhero comics, he uses his newfound abilities to win the state football game and score a date with the scrub-hating Joan. After college, Jay finds himself using his new powers to fight crime; no great motivation or anything, he just feels better about himself using his speed to help humanity.

The Golden Age Flash stories in which Jay Garrick uses his speed to fight common criminals and gangsters were written primarily by Gardner Fox. Original Flash artist Harry Lampert departed after the first two issues, and was replaced by E.E. Hibbard, whose rough, basic style became the trademark of the series. However, when the superhero trend died out in the late 1940s, most of the heroes went with it, and only Superman, Batman and Wonder Woman maintained respectable sales. After a healthy eleven-year race, the Flash's run came to a sudden stop.

## EVERYTHING OLD IS NEW AGAIN

When DC editor Julius Schwartz was looking for a new feature for his anthology series *Showcase*, a revival of the Flash seemed to fit the bill. After all, it had been roughly five years since the last *Flash* comic in 1951, and the general belief at the time was that kids only read comics for about five years, so therefore a whole new audience would be ready for more of the fastest man alive. Schwartz turned the Flash revival over to writer/editor Robert Kanigher and artist Carmine Infantino, who had both worked on the first *Flash* series toward the end of its run. This time, Schwartz instructed them that everything for the new Flash series had to be different—secret identity, origin, costume, the works. In *Showcase* #4 (October 1956), Kanigher and Infantino delivered.

"Mystery of the Human Thunderbolt" opens with police scientist Barry Allen chuckling over an old issue of *Flash Comics*. Back at his lab, Barry is standing in front of a cabinet full of chemicals when a bolt of lightning strikes through an open window, drenching him in chemicals.

Later, Barry heads off to meet his girlfriend, Iris, and watches in horror as a bullet slowly makes its way toward her head. He knocks her out of harm's way, while fully realizing that the combination of the lightning and the chemi-

The Flash of the Golden Age as depicted by the strip's original artist/creator, Harry Lampert.

FLASH COMICS #1 © 1940 DC COMICS. THE FLASH™ & © DC COMICS. ART BY HARRY LAMPERT.

cals have granted him unthinkable reflexes and speed. (The bullet heading for Iris? Just a stray from a getaway by the Turtle Man, the criminal known as "The Slowest Man Alive," and a rather unremarkable villain.)

Inspired by the old *Flash Comics*, Barry resolves to carry on the Flash identity and soon devises a costume for himself made from the same material as a Navy life raft, which can be stored inside a ring and swells to full size with the touch of a button.

Carmine Infantino's re-design of the Flash costume was truly inspired. Streamlined and slick, the lightning bolts on the costume's forearms, belt and boots serve as the perfect visual cues for Infantino's illustration of super-speed. Flash would streak across a panel, and his blurred crimson figure was followed by highlighted, yellow streaks of movement. Infantino's style became the generic model for illustrating speedster characters in comics, and the Flash's costume is one of the few Silver Age designs that has remained unchanged for more than sixty years.

Writer John Broome took over when the new Flash got his own magazine in March 1959 (*The Flash* #105, picking up where the original *Flash Comics* series numbering had left off). Month after month, Broome and Infantino introduced new supervillains, each more outlandish than the last. Flash's rogues' gallery is one of the best in comics, with villains such as Captain Boomerang, the Trickster, Captain Cold and Mirror Master. The genius behind the Flash's mob of villains is

that they all hang out together. They hold competitions to see who can bust out of jail first, have the best heists or devise the best death-trap for the Flash—they even go to the same tailor! Something of a homicidal family.

Many of Barry Allen's adventures involve time travel. In fact, one of John Broome's greatest concepts is the Cosmic Treadmill. Follow along: If the Flash runs at near light-speed, then what happens when he runs in place on a treadmill? Time travel, obviously. Pure scientific gibberish, yet perfectly satisfying comic-book logic. One of Barry Allen's far-future foes is Abra Kadabra, a miscreant from the sixty-fourth century whose technology is so advanced, his antics look like magic to all us twenty-first-century types. Not satisfied with merely killing Barry, Kadabra delights in torturing him, often subjecting his body to bizarre transformations such as a living marionette. Transmutation is something of a running theme in *The Flash*, with Barry Allen being transformed into a mirror, into pure electricity, into a video-game character, and the list goes on and on, so much so that it is eventually explained that Barry Allen has complete control over every molecule in his body, thus allowing him to survive all of these bodily traumas.

The most dreaded of Flash's foes is Eobard Thawne, a.k.a. Professor Zoom, the Reverse-Flash. Another resident of the far future, he bears a centuries-old family grudge against the Allen bloodline. Thawne discovers one of Barry Allen's Flash costumes, and scientifically

# THE FLASH'S ROGUES' GALLERY

**PROFESSOR ZOOM, THE REVERSE FLASH** Obsessed with destroying Barry Allen's life, Professor Zoom's appearances only mean one thing: something bad is about to happen.

**CAPTAIN COLD** Len Snart uses his patented "cold gun" for crime, but more often gets distracted by Barry Allen and winds up on ice.

**MIRROR MASTER** Flash has to beware all reflective surfaces—he never knows when this murderous crook could emerge from the mirror.

**GORILLA GRODD** Exiled from the secret Gorilla City, this super-intelligent ape plots to use his mental powers for conquest.

**CAPTAIN BOOMERANG** Master of the trick boomerang, Digger Harkness repeatedly bedevils the Flash. And like his namesake, he always comes back.

**THE TRICKSTER** Circus acrobat turned practical-joking supervillain James Jesse uses "air shoes" of his own invention in his battles with the Flash.

**WEATHER WIZARD** Thanks to a wand invented by his scientist brother, Mark Mardon can control the weather, sending plenty of dark clouds the Flash's way.

**ABRA KADABRA** A sixty-fourth-century magician who uses his future technology in ways that look like magic. Did we mention he turned Flash into a puppet?

treats it to extract the residue of Flash's powers, transferring them to whoever wears the costume. Now just as fast as the Flash, Zoom uses his historical knowledge of Barry Allen's life to torment him, appearing during the happiest moments of his life and trying to snatch the joy away. After numerous tries, Zoom finally succeeds, and murders Iris, Barry Allen's wife. (Yes, the Flash was a happily married superhero, another of John Broome's innovations.) Barry Allen mourns, grieves and moves on, eventually meeting someone else, a young woman named Fiona Webb. Barry and Fiona's relationship grows over time, and on their wedding day, you can probably imagine who shows up. Only this time, Barry plays for keeps and breaks Zoom's neck in the struggle.

The Flash's murder of Professor Zoom sets off a lengthy storyline in which the Flash stands trial for manslaughter. The series ends with *The Flash* #350 (October 1985), when Barry Allen leaves the twentieth century forever to live with his miraculously resurrected wife, Iris, in the far-future world of the thirtieth century. Unfortunately, Barry and Iris enjoy only a few weeks of renewed marital bliss before DC's epic miniseries *Crisis on Infinite Earths* hits, and, well, it doesn't end well for the second Flash. After twenty-nine years of publication, Barry Allen is dead. The Flash, however, is destined to keep running.

## THIRD TIME'S A CHARM

Back in 1960, Broome and Infantino had introduced Wally West, Iris's nephew and the world's biggest Flash fan. While on a tour of his "friend" Barry Allen's laboratory, the Flash shows Wally how he got his powers, even rearranging the contents of the chemical cabinet exactly as they were when the lightning struck. By blind, sheer, stinking, plot-device coincidence, another lightning bolt hurtles through the window and strikes the cabinet exactly as it had before, drenching Wally in the same chemical mixture. Wally gains the same super-speed powers as Barry, who quickly gives the youngster his own costume and ring and dubs him Kid Flash.

Kid Flash is active throughout the next three decades, eventually changing from a copy of Barry's uniform to his own unique and much cooler costume. He appears in the pages of *The Flash* and alongside other teen sidekicks Robin, Wonder Girl, Aqualad and Speedy in various *Teen Titans* series.

With the death of Barry Allen in *Crisis*, Wally gives up his Kid Flash identity and takes on the costume and name of his departed mentor. With the first issue of his own series, *The Flash* (Vol. 2) in 1987, Wally struggles to fill Barry's shoes. But the defining period in Wally West's career as the Flash is during Mark Waid's lengthy run as writer.

Waid focused the series on the legacy of the Flash. In Waid's mind, Wally was the first teen sidekick to "fulfill the promise" and actually replace his mentor. Waid slowly added every major speedster character in the DC Universe to Wally's supporting cast, including the semi-retired Jay Garrick, Golden Ager Johnny Quick

and his daughter Jesse, and Max Mercury, a mysterious speed guru. Max Mercury introduces Wally to the Speed Force, an energy field beyond the speed of light that all speedsters tap into, knowingly or not. As Wally taps into the Speed Force, his speed increases dramatically, and reaches levels of velocity previously matched by only Barry Allen. Waid also introduced Impulse, a.k.a. Bart Allen, Barry's grandson from the thirtieth century. Bart would have his own brief run as the Flash in 2007, but a negative reception from the fans and poor sales led to his untimely demise and the return of Wally West.

Waid's *Flash* run lasted nearly a hundred issues, starting with #62 (May 1992), and stands as the best treatment of the Wally West character, second only to Broome/Infantino as far as *Flash* comics go. Several of the story arcs are available in trade paperback, including Waid's retelling of Wally's origin and early career, "Born to Run," as well as "The Return of Barry Allen" and "Terminal Velocity," the introduction of the Speed Force. The "Terminal Velocity" trade also includes the story "Flashing Back," a touching time-travel tale of ten-year-old Wally West and his meeting with a stranger from the future. Very good stuff.

## MARK WAID, writer, *The Flash*

### THE FIRST ISSUE OF *THE FLASH* I EVER READ

*Flash* #163 (August 1966)—editor Julius Schwartz's favorite cover of all time. Flash holds his hand out to us and commands us to "STOP!" and read the issue— his life *depends* on it! Got *my* attention!

### THE BEST CREATIVE TIME ON THE TITLE

The first four or five years, from about 1959 to 1964 or thereabouts. Artist Carmine Infantino was at his peak, showing us vistas and super-speed tricks we'd never seen in comics before, bringing his legendary sense of design and storytelling to every page.

### THE BEST COVER

Despite what Julie said, I think it's *The Flash* #174 (November 1967), the "giant logo" cover. Maybe the best comic book cover of all time, certainly one of the best 1960s covers. It's bold, it's dramatic and it pops from across the room—the three things you want most in a cover.

### THE BEST STORYLINE/ISSUE

*The Flash* #173 (September 1967), "Doomward Flight of the Flashes." It had none of the Flash's characteristic rogues' gallery villains, but did have all the other characteristic elements that made the Flash exciting and original, such as Kid Flash and the Golden Age Flash and a weird science-fiction adventure on another planet. Plus, the story is genuinely good.

### THE GOOFIEST STORYLINE/ISSUE

When talking about 1960s *Flash* comics, how can anyone not say *Flash* #167 (February 1967), "The Real Origin of The Flash!" An impish, clumsy, scatterbrained wizard from another dimension comes to Earth and claims to be responsible for the freak accident that gave the Flash his speed. Wow. Way to undercut the whole tone of the series. As someone who's unintentionally written more than his share of bad stories, I have to be careful about throwing stones, but . . . wow.

# Green Lantern

## In brightest day, in blackest night

Lots of superheroes are self-explanatory: Batman, Superman, Spider-Man. You kind of get the idea right from the get-go. Others require a little more elucidation. Case in point: just what the blankety-blank is a Green Lantern?

As the story goes, struggling artist Martin Nodell approached National Comics editor Sheldon Mayer in the winter of 1940 looking for work. Mayer informed the artist that they were looking to expand their line of superhero comics, and if Nodell had any good ideas, they were willing to listen. Encouraged by the meeting, on the way home Nodell was inspired by a delay at the subway station, and by the green lantern the trainman waved to indicate that the tracks were all clear.

Nodell utilized the green lantern in the character he was devising, one whose greatest power would be his own willpower. Nodell soon returned to Mayer's office with his new character concept, the Green Lantern. Mayer approved, and brought in Batman writer Bill Finger to provide the scripts for Nodell's stories. The two clicked immediately, and the Green Lantern made his debut in the pages of *All-American Comics* #16 (July 1940).

In his first appearance, entitled "The Green Lantern," readers meet engineer Alan Scott, whose company is selected to construct a trestle bridge for the government. One of Scott's competitors does not take kindly to the selection, and sabotages the bridge, destroying it just as Scott takes a train across the bridge on a test run. All aboard the train are killed except for Scott, who was clutching an emerald-colored train lantern at the time of the crash. Suddenly, the lantern flares brightly, and in a burst of exposition begins to explain its origins to the dazed engineer.

Hundreds of years ago, the lantern explains, a meteor fell to Earth, landing in provincial China and "speaking" to those who witness its fall. "Three times shall I flame green! First – to bring death! Second – to bring life! Third – to bring power!"

The meteor is carved into the shape of a lamp by a local sorcerer, who is then murdered by fearful villagers. And just as the meteor promised, the lamp comes to light, killing the murdering villagers. The lamp changes hands many times over the passing decades, eventually landing in the workshop of an asylum, where a patient reworks the metal into a modern train lantern. When the patient sparks the lantern, the green flame comes alive again and cures the patient's mental illness, bringing life.

Now, in the hands of Alan Scott, the lantern will bring power. At the lantern's instruction, Scott carves off a piece of its metal to construct a ring, which will channel the lantern's power.

Artist Martin Nodell, creator of Green Lantern, revisited his creation in a 1994 con sketch for Professor Tipton.

The ring must be touched to the lantern once every twenty-four hours to recharge its power. As Scott uses the ring's power to go after the saboteurs, he discovers that the ring allows him to fly, pass through physical objects, generate a force field to protect him from danger, and create physical manifestations of his will—its only limitation is the imagination and willpower of its wielder. Alan Scott also discovers that the ring is incapable of affecting anything made of wood, and therefore its force field cannot protect him from attacks made with wooden objects.

After bringing the saboteurs to justice, Scott resolves to continue to battle the forces of evil: "I must make myself a dreaded figure. I must make a costume that is so bizarre that once I am seen I will never be forgotten." Scott then dons a poofy red shirt, green tights, red-and-yellow lace-up boots and a purple cape with a high Dracula collar. Mission accomplished, dude. In addition, while Alan Scott recharges his ring, he also recites a solemn oath:

> *"And I shall shed my light over dark evil, for the dark things cannot stand the light, the light of the Green Lantern!"*

The Green Lantern was an immediate hit. He soon appeared not only in *All-American*, but also in the anthology title *Comics Cavalcade*, as a member of the Justice Society of America over in *All Star Comics*, and eventually in his own title, *Green Lantern Quarterly*.

Yet despite the fanciful mystic trappings of his origin, Green Lantern's adventures in the 1940s were very much down-to-earth, and focused more on urban crimes like kidnapping and racketeering. When the superhero craze died down in the late 1940s, Green Lantern slipped into limbo like most of National's mystery men.

## THE SAME, BUT A LITTLE DIFFERENT

By 1959, DC Comics editor Julius Schwartz was looking to follow up the success of his Flash revival, and chose Green Lantern for his second subject. As with the Flash, Schwartz opted for a streamlined, science-fiction approach, and placed his new assignment in the hands of writer John Broome and artist Gil Kane.

As reconceived by Broome and Kane in the pages of *Showcase* #22 (September 1959), the new Green Lantern was daredevil test pilot Hal Jordan. The story, "S.O.S. Green Lantern," opens with the crash landing of an alien spacecraft, piloted by Abin Sur, who lies dying within. Abin Sur is a member of the Green Lantern Corps, an intergalactic organization of space policemen organized by the Guardians of the Universe, a race of immortals with great intelligence and mental power. In his final moments, Abin Sur commands his power ring to seek a deserving Earthman to carry on as his replacement, one entirely without fear.

At that very moment, at Ferris Aircraft in Coast City, California, pilot Hal Jordan is suddenly enveloped in a green glow and whisked through the air at amazing speed, touching down at the site of Abin Sur's grounded craft. The dying alien explains to Jordan that he has been chosen to take his place in the Green Lantern Corps, protecting this sector of the universe. He gives Jordan a power ring and the battery of power, which have the power to do anything that the wearer imagines, based only on his willpower. To charge the ring it must be touched to the power battery every twenty-four hours, but because of the impurity of the battery's construction, the ring, and battery will have no effect on anything yellow. With that, Abin Sur is no more, and Hal Jordan is the Earth's new Green Lantern. Like the Green Lantern of the 1940s, Hal Jordan also recites an oath when he charges his ring:

*"In brightest day, in blackest night,*
*No evil shall escape my sight!*
*Let those who worship evil's might*
*Beware my power – Green Lantern's light!"*

## GUEST LECTURER

### JUD MEYERS, owner, Earth-2 Comics

#### ALL-TIME FAVORITE SUPERHERO
Green Lantern. He protects the entire universe, he's only limited by his imagination and belief in himself (meaning he can have any power he can dream up) and he always gets the girl (alien or otherwise). He makes Batman look mean and Superman look downright insecure.

Gil Kane's modern art style was a perfect match for the new Green Lantern. In contrast to the gaudy operatic costume of Alan Scott, Hal Jordan's Green Lantern uniform is sleek, streamlined and downright snazzy. The stories are vastly different from the urban-jungle, street-crime-focused Lantern tales of the 1940s. Instead, the sci-fi trappings of the new GL origin open the door to all kinds of cosmic concepts, such as the Weaponers of Qward, evil scientists from the antimatter universe of Qward determined to get their hands on all of the Green Lantern power batteries.

In time, Hal Jordan meets other members of the Green Lantern Corps, an organization of galactic peacekeepers 3,600 strong. Members include the birdlike Tomar-Re, the crystalline entity Chaselon, the walking vegetable Medphyl, the alien chipmunk Ch'p, the enormous Kilowog of Bolovax Vik (charged with training new recruits) and many, many others. (Nothing's as funny, and at the same time cool, as the rock dude, the veggie-man and the chipmunk charging their rings and reciting the Green Lantern oath.)

The Corps is headquartered on the Guardians' homeworld of Oa, a planet located in the exact center of the universe. The individual members power their batteries from the Central Power Battery on Oa, which is itself fueled by the combined mental energies of the Guardians.

Hal's most tenacious adversary over his career is the renegade Green Lantern Sinestro. Once a revered member of the Corps, Sinestro is seduced by his own power, and sets himself up as dictator of his sector. His actions force the Guardians to strip him of his ring and banish him to the antimatter universe of Qward, where he secures a yellow power ring, the perfect weapon against the Green Lantern Corps.

## THE MORE THE MERRIER

There have been other human Green Lanterns over the years, as well. When the Guardians order Hal Jordan to train an alternate GL in case he should become incapacitated, Hal enlists Detroit architect John Stewart, whom the ring identifies as totally honest and without fear. John subs for Hal Jordan on many occasions, and has had several lengthy stints as Green Lantern from the 1980s until today.

Another famous (or perhaps infamous) Green Lantern of Earth is Guy Gardner. In an interesting twist on the Hal Jordan origin, the Guardians reveal to Hal that there were actually two men on Earth who the ring found worthy of replacing the dying Abin Sur—Hal Jordan was chosen first because he was geographically closer. Curious, Jordan goes to meet the other candidate, schoolteacher Guy Gardner. After he receives a power ring, Guy spends much of the 1980s and 1990s serving in both the Justice League and Green Lantern Corps as a sort of right-wing reactionary loose-cannon GL with an "I-hate-everyone" attitude and one of the most atrocious "bowl-haircuts" in comic-book history. Guy's a hoot.

Another Green Lantern from Earth, Kyle Rayner, has a more complex introduction.

Travel back to 1993, when the biggest news in comics is the death of Superman. At the climax of the storyline, the resurrected Superman is facing off against one of his replacements, the Cyborg Superman. The Cyborg's fiendish scheme depends on the success of his creating two massive engines that will destroy two American cities: Metropolis and Coast City. Superman manages to save Metropolis, but Coast City is not so fortunate. Hal Jordan's hometown is destroyed, and seven million souls killed. Driven insane by the tragedy, Hal first tries to re-create Coast City with his own power ring. When that's not enough, Hal realizes that he needs more power, and he knows just where to get it: Oa.

Hal heads to Oa, murders his friend and trainer Kilowog, dispatches numerous Green Lanterns, kills Sinestro (who the Guardians

The Green Lantern logo.

had enlisted as a last line of defense) and then murders all the Guardians but one, absorbing the almost limitless power of the Central Power Battery in the process. Hal then renames himself Parallax, making the full transformation from hero to villain.

The sole remaining Guardian, Ganthet, manages to get away with the ring that had belonged to Abin Sur and Hal Jordan. He flees to Earth, where he haphazardly passes on the ring to the first person he sees: young artist Kyle Rayner. It is worth noting that the conversion of one of DC's first-string heroes to supervillain status was highly controversial, and somewhat tainted Kyle Rayner's reputation as Hal's successor. It took a few years' worth of good comics to really dissipate the negative opinion.

As for Hal Jordan, after Kyle and Hal's longtime friend Green Arrow thwart his attempt to destroy and then recreate the universe with an intact Coast City (all this taking place in the pages of DC's *Zero Hour* miniseries in 1994), he resurfaces in *The Final Night* (1996), and sacrifices his life to destroy the Sun-Eater, a mysterious creature that was to extinguish the Sun, with Earth and its inhabitants slowly freezing to death.

However, fans would not allow Hal Jordan to rest in peace, and DC was forced to resurrect him, first as Earth's ghostly protector, the Spectre. Later, in the miniseries *Rebirth* (2004) written by fan-favorite Geoff Johns, Johns skillfully returns Hal Jordan to the land of the living, and manages to explain away his villainous acts, making him, once again, a bona fide hero. He has since provided some of DC's best comics in his new *Green Lantern* series, which stars not only Hal Jordan, but also John Stewart, Guy Gardner and Kyle Rayner. In doing so, Johns wisely chooses not to alienate fans of any particular Green Lantern character. Make no mistake, though—Hal Jordan remains front and center, which, in our humble estimation, is as it should be.

## SCOTT SAYS

The random aspect of Kyle Rayner's selection is a big part of what makes him so appealing as a GL. Instead of being chosen as the bravest and best the planet has to offer, Kyle simply stumbles upon the most powerful weapon in the universe and has to find his own way through the responsibilities he now carries. As created by writer Ron Marz and artist Darryl Banks, Kyle could be any one of us. He makes mistakes, he has doubts and he never feels like he's living up to the huge expectations set by his predecessors.

Marz and Banks had a huge task before them to gain comics fans' acceptance of Kyle after the vicious and extremely vocal backlash of the Hal Jordan character assassination, and they pulled it off admirably.

Writer Grant Morrison's portrayal of Kyle in his *JLA* revival also helped a great deal, placing an uncertain Kyle on the same legendary footing as Superman and Batman.

# The Justice Society of America
## *Strength in numbers*

Sometimes it's easy to forget that comics, like everything else, don't exist in a vacuum. Everything that comic-book readers think of as conventions, as benchmarks, even as clichés of the genre had to appear somewhere first. Even something as basic as, say, the team-up.

Before 1941, despite the fact that the newsstands were positively overflowing with the cape-and-mask set, superheroes just did not team up. Never met, never hung out, didn't even refer to one another. After 1941, though, things were very different, and not just in comics. The notion of separately created fictional characters meeting up in a "shared universe" has spread from its comic-book origins to the worlds of prose, television and film. So what happened in 1941? Five words: the Justice Society of America (JSA).

The inception of the Justice Society had the same motivation as most other commercial fiction of the time: profit. By 1941, the superhero business was booming, so much so that many characters were expanding past their original homes in magazines such as *Action* and *Detective*. To help meet demand, Superman and Batman were also given their own solo magazines. For characters that weren't quite popular enough for their own comic books but still had a rabid following, All-American Comics (National's sister company) created an anthology book, *All Star Comics*.

In its first two issues, it featured such first-string heroes as Hawkman, the Flash, Green Lantern and the Spectre as well as less popular ones such as Biff Bronson (love that name) and Red, White and Blue. It was with *All Star Comics* #3 (late 1940–1941) that the revolutionary leap was made—if these characters are in the same book, why not have them meet and interact with one another?

### THE FIRST TEAM-UP

So whose idea was it? Unfortunately, the exact answer has been lost in the sands of time, and the truth falls somewhere within the following three names: All-American Comics publisher M.C. Gaines, *All Star Comics* editor Sheldon Mayer and *All Star Comics* writer Gardner Fox. The rationale behind the team of characters is much less of a mystery—charter membership consisted of All-American's most popular characters: the Flash, Green Lantern, Hawkman, the pint-sized pugilist the Atom, the pulp-style mystery man the Sandman, the ghostly avenger the Spectre, the mystical sorcerer Doctor Fate, and the pharmaceutically enhanced strongman Hourman. Along with official mascot Johnny Thunder (a hapless goof who stumbles through adventures with

The charter membership of the Justice Society, from left to right: the Sandman, the Spectre, the Flash, Hawkman, the Atom, Green Lantern, Hourman and Doctor Fate.

the help of his magic Thunderbolt), this was the roster of the team in its first appearance in *All Star Comics* #3.

The first meeting of the Justice Society was little more than that, a meeting. Johnny Thunder, upset at his exclusion from the newly publicized gathering, crashes the party with the help of his magic Thunderbolt. Johnny wishes he could attend the meeting, and all the members are magically drawn to him, and he gets an invite to the hotel where the Justice Society had planned to have dinner. At the dinner, Johnny recommends that each member tell a story about a recent adventure; each member recounts a seven-page tale, and that's pretty much the extent of the issue. In addition, JSA membership for Superman and Batman is implied when the Flash makes a passing comment that someone has to look after things while the rest of them are at the meeting.

In *All Star Comics* #4, the Justice Society is summoned to FBI headquarters in Washington, DC and given a mission to close down a network of saboteurs working to attack the U.S. from within. Each JSA member is given an envelope containing his orders, and the members go their separate ways to carry out individual missions. This sets up the formula for Justice Society stories for years to come: the team meets up or is otherwise collectively informed of a threat, then the members go their separate ways to investigate the matter, reuniting at story's end to finish off the threat. *JSA* writer Gardner Fox would use this solid structure again and again. It allowed for new solo adventures of the popular characters (drawn by their own signature artists) and gave excited readers something they'd never seen before—their favorite heroes teaming up.

## JSA ROLL CALL

The first membership change for the JSA came in *All Star Comics* #6 (August 1941). When a character became popular enough to earn his own solo magazine, he would be named an honorary member of the JSA, removed from active membership and replaced by a new member. In this case, it was the Flash, and mascot Johnny Thunder was initiated to take his place as a full-time member.

*All Star Comics* #7 (October 1941) is most notable for the appearances of Superman and Batman as JSA members. The new JSA chairman, Green Lantern, challenges the members to each raise $100,000 of relief aid for war orphans in Europe and Asia. Johnny Thunder boasts that he can raise $300,000, to make the group's total an even million. When he fails to fulfill his promise, he falls back on his magic Thunderbolt, who conjures up honorary JSA members Superman, Batman and the Flash, who each pony up the necessary money to meet Green Lantern's intended goal.

The roster soon changes again. *All Star Comics* #8 (December 1941) reveals that Green Lantern has also been granted honorary status, having earned his own self-titled magazine. Also gone is Hourman, though not because he was given his own magazine. Instead, the Man of the Hour is rather ignominiously booted from the team, with only a note stating "a leave of absence is hereby granted to the Hourman." No respect at all.

The first of the two open spaces is taken by Starman, a rich playboy-type who fights evil with the help of a cosmic rod that allows him to fly and fire off bursts of energy. The second spot is filled by Doctor Mid-Nite, the first blind superhero in comics. Having lost his sight in an explosion, he discovers that he can see perfectly in total darkness, prompting him to invent his infrared goggles (enabling him to see in daylight) and blackout bombs (which blind his enemies as he continues to see perfectly).

## THE WAR EFFORT

The war effort takes on even greater emphasis in issue #11 (June 1942). The JSA members decide to enlist in the military and fight on the frontlines, rather than on the homefront and on the occasional FBI special mission. Carter Hall, Wes Dodds, Kent Nelson, Al Pratt and Ted Knight (otherwise known as Hawkman, the Sandman, Doctor Fate, the Atom and Starman) enlist in the army, while Johnny Thunder joins the navy. Dr. Charles McNider (Doctor Mid-Nite) is commissioned to serve in the Army Medical Corps, despite his disability, and the Spectre—well, the Spectre's dead, so he ain't signing up for jack. The ultimate way to beat the draft.

Despite themselves, the JSA members are drawn into action as superheroes while on duty. Then, while visiting his longtime girlfriend Shiera Saunders, Hawkman runs into Diana Prince and lets slip that the JSA has somehow found out that she's really Wonder Woman. By the issue's end, the JSA's military commanders discover the various superheroes in their midst, and argue over whose outfit has the most effective super-soldier. In response, the commanding officer of the U.S. forces in the Pacific pulls the JSAers from each of their units and reforms them into the new Justice Battalion (including new member Wonder Woman). The JSA is back together again, as if anyone really had any doubt.

The JSA supported the war effort in various ways. An example is the "Food for Starving Patriots" story in *All Star Comics* #14 (December 1942), in which the team embarks on a mission to deliver concentrated dehydrated food to European civilians suffering under Nazi occupation. Such war stories often reinforced the concepts of charity and sacrifice instead of just depicting superheroes clobbering buck-toothed caricatures. Even the JSA fan club, the Junior Justice Society of America, promoted such ideals, asking its members to "keep our country united in the face of enemy attempts to make us think we Americans are all different, because we are rich or poor; employer or worker; native or foreign-born; Gentile or Jew; protestant or Catholic." Good advice even six decades later. Who'd have thought we'd still need to be reminded?

## THE INJUSTICE SOCIETY STRIKES

Another comics first came in *All Star Comics* #37 (October 1947), with the first appearance of "The Injustice Society of the World!" The JSA's team of opposites is made up of previous JSA villains such as the Wizard, Brain Wave and Per Degaton; Green Lantern villains the Gambler and Vandal Savage; and Flash antagonist the Thinker. The Injustice Society makes a big splash, setting off five different jailbreaks across the country to recruit troops to its criminal army, declaring martial law and seizing control of a small but sizeable portion of the American Midwest.

And as if that wasn't epic enough, the very next issue sets the JSA against an even greater collaboration of villainy in "History's Crime Wave!" The Justice Society is pitted against the greatest villains in history: Genghis Khan, Attila the Hun, Nero, Goliath, Cesare Borgia and Captain Kidd. Although the historical haters turned out to be impostors (more precisely, the disguises of an insane guard at a wax museum), they manage what no other JSA foe has ever accomplished: the murder of the Justice Society. In one gruesome scene after another, we see our heroes perish, in what appear to be permanent and sometimes grisly deaths. Fortunately, the quick-acting Wonder Woman and prospective new member Black Canary whisk the JSAers to Paradise Island just in time to be resurrected by the amazing Amazon Purple Healing Ray.

The Justice Society makes its final Golden Age appearance in *All Star Comics* #57 (March 1951). There's no grand finale for the father of all superhero teams, either. The following issue simply and unceremoniously changes to *All Star Western*. Readers expecting their regular dose of superhero action are instead treated to the adventures of the Trigger Twins and similar fightin' cowpokes. Hardly a fitting end for such an auspicious series, but not to worry: the Justice Society of America would not be gone for long.

## BACK BY POPULAR DEMAND

By 1962, DC Comics had fully embraced its superhero renaissance. Revived and redesigned versions of the Flash and Green Lantern were tearing up the sales charts, and an updated version of the Justice Society, entitled *Justice League of America*, reunited all of DC's first-string superhero characters (plus the Martian Manhunter, but that's another story) in a single monthly team book. With superheroes selling hot at the newsstand once more, many of DC's old-time fans requested the original heroes of the Golden Age of comics.

Editor Julius Schwartz revived the original Flash Jay Garrick in the pages of *The Flash* #123 (September 1961), "Flash of Two Worlds!" The story, by writer Gardner Fox and artist Carmine Infantino, introduces the "parallel Earths" concept to the DC Universe, which allows the original 1940s versions of characters to exist on a separate parallel Earth—Earth-Two—from their modern-day 1960s counterparts on Earth-One. Once the Earth-One Flash (Barry Allen) meets the

Earth-Two Flash (Jay Garrick), it becomes just a matter of time before the rest of Jay Garrick's teammates come out of retirement and cross over to visit Earth-One. And come out they do in *The Flash* #137 (June 1963), in "Vengeance of the Immortal Villain," again by Fox and Infantino.

Two months later, the JSA returns in a much bigger way in the classic "Crisis on Earth-One!" from *Justice League of America* #21 (August 1963), by writer Gardner Fox and artist Mike Sekowsky. In this adventure, the reunited Justice Society members face off against their old foes the Wizard, the Fiddler and the Icicle, while at the same time, the Justice League of Earth-One is challenged by frequent adversaries Chronos, Felix Faust and Doctor Alchemy. Little do the JSA and JLA know that their enemies are actually working together, using a fairly well-thought-out plan to escape between each other's Earth and enjoy the fruits of their thievery without fear of capture.

However, boredom soon gets the best of them, and the Crime Champions of the two worlds begin to run rampant, challenging each other's foes to combat. When the defeated Justice League is magically trapped in its own headquarters, a tip from the Flash leads the JLA to contact the JSA through a séance, summoning the Justice Society to Earth-One. With a little magical help from

Doctor Fate, the JLA is sent to Earth-Two to battle its own enemies, while the JSA stays on Earth-One to round up its foes.

Together, the united Justice Society and Justice League put an end to the Crime Champions and propose that the two teams stay in touch in case a future need arises for their combined strength. And for nearly every summer for the next twenty-five years the pages of *Justice League of America* would feature a team-up between the Justice Society and the Justice League.

The annual summertime Justice Society appearances were sometimes used as a plot device to revive other Golden Age characters, too, such as the Seven Soldiers of Victory (the Bad News Bears of superhero teams, boasting such lesser-knowns as Green Arrow and Speedy, the Star-Spangled Kid and Stripesy, the Vigilante, the Shining Knight and the Crimson Avenger) and Quality Comics' stable of characters (including Uncle Sam, Phantom Lady and Black Condor), whom DC would later dub the Freedom Fighters. It wasn't until 1976 that the Justice Society would again regain a monthly series all its own in the pages of the newly revived *All Star Comics*, which picked up where the last JSA appearance left off, issue #58, entitled "All Star Super Squad" (January–February 1976), by writer Gerry Conway, artist Ric Estrada and comics legend Wally Wood.

An effort was definitely made here to give the old-timers a shot in the arm with some brash, younger members, focusing in the

**SCOTT SAYS**

Power Girl, in contrast to her fellow JSA characters, was a distinctly 1970s superheroine. She was forever spouting about "women's liberation" and railing against Wildcat for being a chauvinist, all while showing some of the biggest cleavage ever seen on a comic-book rack.

first story on Robin and two new members: the Star-Spangled Kid, freshly brought back from being lost in time since the 1940s and utilizing Starman's cosmic rod so as to make him a more powerful character, and the newly introduced Power Girl, the Earth-Two version of Supergirl, Superman's Kryptonian cousin.

The revived *All Star Comics* had a respectable run, notable mostly for Wally Wood's art and the return of most of the JSA's rogues' gallery, including Vandal Savage, Per Degaton, an all-new Brainwave and Solomon Grundy. The series also utilized the original Earth-Two Superman more than most JSA stories of years past—Wood clearly rendered him in the style of original Superman creator Joe Shuster.

Another lasting creation to come out of the series was the Huntress—Helena Wayne, the daughter of Batman and Catwoman, who made her debut in *All Star Comics #69* (November–December 1977), "United We Stand," by Paul Levitz and artist Joe Staton. The Huntress is the last new member the group would see for quite some time.

## THE JSA RETURNS

After an ugly period in the 1990s when the JSA was first banished to limbo and later led to slaughter, the popularity of James Robinson's *Starman* series and Grant Morrison's use of the JSA in his *JLA* series moved DC to bring the team back in a big way.

Fans became reacquainted with the history of the team through the "Justice Society Returns!" event in 1999, a series of nine comics that featured the JSA back in the 1940s.

Their own title followed in late 1999, *JSA*, written by James Robinson and David S. Goyer, and drawn by Scott Benefiel and Stephen Sadowski. Present are original JSAers Jay Garrick, Alan Scott, Wildcat and Hippolyta (Wonder Woman's mother, retroactively added to the team in a bit of time-travel sleight of hand). Members of the next generation are also added: new Starman Jack Knight, Black Canary (daughter of the original), the new Hourman (an android from the future imbued with the memories of original Hourman Rex Tyler), Atom Smasher (godson of the original Atom Al Pratt), the new Star-Spangled Kid (Courtney Whitmore, stepdaughter of the original Kid's sidekick Stripesy) and Sanderson Hawkins, the now-grown sidekick of the original Sandman (who occasionally fought alongside the JSA as Sandy the Golden Boy). Joining later in the first story arc are the new Hawkgirl and the new Doctor Fate, revealed to be Hector Hall, son of original JSA member Hawkman. When Hall returns to the living, the decision is made to officially reform the Justice Society of America. All eight of the younger members eagerly agree to join up, and Sand Hawkins is elected the JSA's new chairman.

This was the magic element that earlier JSA revivals lacked. While the series should pay respect to the team's history, there also needs to be a balance between admiration for the past and simply dwelling on it. Robinson and

Goyer understood this, and cleverly combined the team's veterans with experienced, younger hands like Black Canary, Jack Knight and Atom Smasher and neophytes still learning the ropes such as Hawkgirl and the Star-Spangled Kid.

This balance gives the *JSA* series a mood separate from any other team books in comics: a feeling of legacy. Before, there was no real interest in accepting new members to carry the torch. Now, not only is respect for the past assumed, it is a requirement to secure a place on the roster. On top of "beating the bad guys," the team serves a valuable purpose—to train tomorrow's heroes and keep the spirit of the Justice Society alive.

# The Justice League of America

## And justice for all

If it worked before, it'll work again.

That was what DC Comics editor Julius Schwartz must have been thinking in late 1959, as he prepared to debut the latest feature in his burgeoning line of superhero titles. He had already successfully revived the Flash and Green Lantern in the anthology book *Showcase*. So what next? The choice for Schwartz was easy—a revival of one of the biggest successes for National Comics in the 1940s, the Justice Society of America. However, Schwartz wasn't crazy about the name. As he explained in the in-house DC fan magazine *Amazing World of DC Comics* #14 (March 1977), "To me, 'Society' meant something you found on Park Avenue. I felt that 'League' was a stronger word, one that the readers could identify with because of baseball leagues."

The revamped team, the Justice League of America (JLA), would solidify DC Comics's full-time return to the superhero business. Its success would not only herald the introduction of scores of superhero titles at DC, but also inspire DC's rival Martin Goodman at Marvel to instruct Stan Lee to create their own superhero team, thereby kick-starting the Marvel Universe.

## JLA ROLL CALL

While the name was changed, the basic concept was not. So who then would be drafted into Schwartz's new JLA? Schwartz's new rising stars, the Flash and Green Lantern, were a given. Wonder Woman still had her own solo magazine, so she was in. Aquaman was nestled into a monthly spot backing up Superboy in *Adventure Comics*, and he got the call. And also J'onn J'onzz, the Martian Manhunter. Who, you ask? J'onn J'onzz, the Pete Best of the Justice League.

J'onn, a.k.a. the Martian Manhunter, was a holdover from the sci-fi craze in comics in the late 1950s. Premiering as a backup feature in *Detective Comics* #225 (November 1955), J'onn is a Martian accidentally teleported to Earth by the well-intentioned if somewhat skittish scientist Professor Mark Erdel, who drops dead from shock at the sight of the newly arrived Martian. Stranded on Earth, J'onn anglicizes his name to the more American-sounding John Jones, and uses his Martian abilities to shape-change into a human. J'onn works as a police detective and uses his Martian powers on the job in superheroic fashion, and there are quite a few of them. Aside from the shape-changing, J'onn is super-strong and can fly, turn invisible and read minds. Plus, there is his ill-defined and infrequently used Martian vision and Martian

Justice League of America: DC's biggest stars. Only the best made the cut.

breath. (J'onn's major fallibility is that he is extremely vulnerable to fire.)

At the time Justice League of America was getting started, J'onn J'onzz had appeared as a six-page feature in *Detective Comics* for more than five years, thus earning him a spot on the team. Unfortunately, the Martian Manhunter would be written out of *JLA* by the time Hanna-Barbera premiered the Saturday-morning TV series *Super Friends,* its animated version of the Justice League, in 1973. Legions of young comics fans would later pick up old Justice League comics and ask, "Who's the bald green guy?"

But what about the two biggest guns in DC's arsenal, Superman and Batman? Initially there was some resistance to the inclusion of the Big Two in Schwartz's new League, namely from Superman editor Mort Weisinger and Batman editor Jack Schiff. They argued that Superman's and Batman's inclusion might overexpose the heroes and negatively affect sales, so the three editors compromised. Superman and Batman would be included as full members with smaller roles in the adventures (they were often busy in outer space or other missions), and would not appear on the cover.

Schwartz diplomatically handled the inevitable questions from fans asking about Superman's and Batman's absence. He wrote in the first JLA letter column that "these two popular heroes appear in so many other DC magazines that we thought it would be more appropriate to play up the other members."

This policy continued throughout the series' first year until DC higher-ups, noticing the absence of the two on the *JLA* covers, intervened. On orders from upstairs, Superman and Batman took part in more adventures and were featured prominently on the covers.

In assembling his creative team, Schwartz brought on Gardner Fox, longtime writer of the original comic-book super-team, the Justice Society of America. Back in the 1940s, Fox had helped established the sturdy formula of the team book, in which the JSA would gather at the beginning of the issue when a threat appeared, break up into solo or smaller-group adventures and then reunite for the grand finale. No need to mess with a good thing. This successful framework would continue for countless JLA stories, both by Fox and his many successors.

For the art, Schwartz selected Mike Sekowsky, whose art is far from flashy but contains a crude brilliance that is a perfect fit for the title—simultaneously futuristic and fairy-tale simple. Sekowsky's figures weren't the most heroically cut—sometimes the Justice League looked more like a bunch of middle-aged businessmen dressed up for a Kiwanis Club masquerade party. His backgrounds were usually sparsely detailed and occasionally his anatomy could get a little, shall we say, creative. Still, Sekowsky's *Justice League of America* looked like nothing else on the rack at the time. The fact that the League members looked less flashy and polished in the pages

of *Justice League of America* compared to their solo books helped to break out the series as its own animal.

## JLA VERSUS A STARFISH. REALLY.

Schwartz scheduled the Justice League for a three-issue tryout in the pages of another of DC's anthology books, *The Brave and the Bold* #28 (March 1960). The Justice League of America face off against the alien threat of Starro the Conqueror in the logically named story, "Starro the Conqueror!"

Schwartz and Fox dispense with an origin story, and instead drop the reader into the action at a point after the League has been in service long enough to have already handed out signal devices and constructed a secret (and, for the time, rather stylish) headquarters. At the start of the story, a friendly puffer fish warns Aquaman of the arrival of a mysterious giant starfish from outer space. The giant starfish—calling himself Starro—has changed three local starfish into duplicates of himself and declared his intention to conquer the planet. Concerned, Aquaman summons his fellow Justice League members to convene at headquarters to discuss the matter (with the glaring exception of Superman and Batman—Superman is off stopping a meteor shower and Batman is

**SCOTT SAYS**

The League's first recorded battle with Starro set off a mysterious trend: most all of the Justice League's recurring opponents had a name ending in the letter O. Starro was followed by Professor Ivo and his android Amazo, after which came Despero, and after that Kanjar Ro. The hidden message here? Gardner Fox liked the letter O. That's all we've got.

**CHRIS SAYS**

I was always a Marvel kid growing up. Sure, DC's Wolfman/Pérez *Teen Titans* and the Levitz/Giffen *Legion of Superheroes* won me over, but for the most part, I had no real interest in big team books like the JLA. Until, that is, writers J.M. DeMatteis and Keith Giffen took over and brought with them the amazingly expressive artist Kevin Maguire. Their *Justice League* work is most often referenced for its well-developed humor and marvelous facial expressions, but it's so much more than that. The book instantly gives life to characters that held no resonance before. The unfortunate death of Blue Beetle nearly two decades after their JLA tenure only meant what it did because their earlier work with the character was so strong. It remains one of the very best comics to come out of the 1980s.

tracking down two suspiciously vague "arch-enemies." (Sounds like an excuse to get out of dinner plans.)

The League members split up to handle Starro's three starfish deputies, and soon the Flash discovers Starro's main power, aside from being, well, a really big starfish—mind control. Starro's deputy has mentally enslaved the entire population of Happy Harbor, except for one person: the teen hipster Snapper Carr, who remains mysteriously immune. After Flash defeats the giant starfish, he heads off to confront Starro, with the annoying Snapper in tow. (Snapper received his nickname for his incessant habit of snapping his fingers in appreciation of anything he likes. Charming.)

The re-assembled Justice League attacks Starro, who's much more formidable than his invertebrate underlings, having mentally received all the knowledge and experience from their individual battles with the League. Starro reads Green Lantern's mind and discovers his weakness against yellow, then changes his skin color to render GL's ring useless. To find out why Snapper is immune to Starro's mind control, the Flash performs a quick chemical analy-

sis and detects traces of lime on Snapper's clothes. (Who knew sprinkling lime on the lawn was a necessary chore of the 1960s?) They gather several barrels of lime, and Green Lantern encases Starro in a hardened shell of lime, helpfully applied by J'onn J'onzz in a rare use of his Martian breath.

Once Starro is defeated, the Justice League rewards Snapper Carr for essentially standing around and doing nothing, declaring him an honorary member of the League and giving him a JLA signal device. Little do they know that their kind gesture of pity to a clearly troubled young man will result in this punk's practically living in the Justice League's Secret Sanctuary for the next five years.

Not surprisingly, the first three-issue Justice League run in *The Brave and the Bold* was a big success, leading to the first issue of its own series, *Justice League of America*, two months later in November 1960.

### A LEAGUE OF THEIR OWN

Unlike Marvel's *Avengers* series, which boasted a fluid, rotating membership as one of its strengths, for decades, the hallmark of *Justice League of America* was stability. Members weren't added easily or haphazardly, and by and large, once a hero joined up, he generally stayed, with very few exceptions. As a result, membership in the Justice League seemed far more exclusive and impressive

This was the top echelon of the DC Universe, the absolute best the company had to offer. Over at Marvel, sometimes it seemed

## CARR D'ANGELO, owner, Earth-2 Comics

### THE FIRST ISSUE OF *JLA* I EVER READ

The first issue of *Justice League of America* I ever read was #108 (December 1973) by Len Wein and Dick Dillin. It was the second part of that year's JLA-JSA crossover reintroducing the Freedom Fighters. It was great fun but horribly confusing. I don't think it ever says that Superman has gray hair because he's the 1940s Superman from Earth-Two! Needless to say, I came to love the multiverse from that moment on.

### THE BEST CREATIVE TIME ON THE TITLE

Steve Englehart came on to *Justice League of America* in 1977 after a spectacular run on *The Avengers* at Marvel. He infused the book with cool ideas like the Star-Tsar and the Construct, revived erstwhile mascot Snapper Carr, linked the interstellar Manhunter mythology to the Green Lantern Corps and solidified the Martian Manhunter's role as an essential team member with a super-cool new origin. A lot of these concepts last to this day and even made it into the new cartoon series.

### THE BEST COVER

*Justice League of America* #190 (May 1981)—they don't call him Starro the Conqueror for nothing. The heroes' faces are covered by this mind-controlling purple starfish. A creepy, haunting image by Brian Bolland. Definitely an issue where the cover is so much better than the story inside.

### THE BEST STORYLINE/ISSUE

The story that blew me away as a kid was reprinted in the 100-page *Justice League of America* #116 (April 1975), "Crisis on Earth-Three," where JLA and JSA go up against their evil counterparts, the Crime Syndicate of America. It was one of the rare times where both teams were outmatched. Heck, Ultraman got extra powers when exposed to Kryptonite! That's one nasty doppelgänger.

### THE GOOFIEST STORYLINE/ISSUE

Roy Thomas was always crafting epic storylines that outclassed the minor continuity glitch they were designed to explain. Case in point: *Justice League of America* #219-220 (October-November 1983), a JSA crossover in which it was revealed that a pregnant Earth-Two Black Canary went into suspended animation during a routine trip between Earths, and gave birth to a daughter who ultimately emerged fully grown on Earth-One to make time with Green Arrow. It had already been explained that the Earth-hopping gave Black Canary a supersonic cry; couldn't that pseudo-science also explain her de-aging? Or maybe Ollie just likes older chicks.

like anybody who hung around the mansion long enough could become an Avenger, but if a character was inducted into the JLA, it meant that the character wasn't going anywhere, and that readers would most likely be seeing them steadily for years to come. Let's take a look at the full roster of the original Justice League of America. Following the original Big Seven, DC's battling bowman the Green Arrow was the League's first recruit, followed at fairly regular intervals over the next twenty years by the size-changing hero the Atom, the winged wonder Hawkman, the blonde bombshell known as the Black Canary, the stretchable sleuth the Elongated Man, the android with a heart called the Red Tornado, Hawkman's wife and crimefighting partner Hawkgirl, the sorceress Zatanna the Magician, and the atomic powerhouse called Firestorm the Nuclear Man.

And there you have it—the Justice League of America. For our money the single best roster for a superhero team in comics. Maybe the Avengers had more fun and different combinations, and the X-Men may have been better written at times, and the Legion may have had

them beat by sheer numbers, but this is the team to which all others are compared. It's got everything. Sheer muscle in Superman and Wonder Woman, raw power in Green Lantern and Firestorm, specialists like the Atom, Flash, Aquaman, Zatanna, Black Canary and the Elongated Man, mere mortals who get by on sheer skill and willpower like Batman and Green Arrow, and lost souls looking for a new home like J'onn J'onzz, the Hawks and the Red Tornado. Most of all, it's got pedigree. It's got stature. It's got presence.

In the two decades since this first Justice League team disbanded, there have been numerous JLA lineups, some more popular than others. The most popular versions, it seems are the ones that emulate this original model: the most powerful, important characters in the company. Even with that in mind, nothing has come close in our minds to the symbolic might of this first pantheon. Other teams were just superheroes. Back in the day, at least through the eyes of a couple of 10-year-old kids, the Justice League of America felt like legends.

# Watchmen
## *The fantasy of realism*

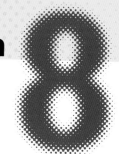

DC Comics has had a surprising tendency over the course of its existence: if a rival publisher goes out of business, DC often swoops in and buys up the rights to its characters. It happened first in the 1960s with Quality Comics, adding 1940s stars Blackhawk and Plastic Man to the roster, then in the 1980s with Fawcett, garnering the rights to the original Captain Marvel and the rest of the Marvel Family, and again in 1985, when DC purchased the "Action Heroes" from defunct publisher Charlton Comics, adding characters such as Blue Beetle, the Question and Captain Atom.

In the case of the Quality and Fawcett acquisitions, the characters were simply folded into DC's stable through its convenient "parallel Earths" theory, a DC standby. However, other plans were afoot for the Charlton characters. Alan Moore, who had just made a name for himself on *Swamp Thing*, was thinking big: a veritable deconstruction of the superhero, using the established Charlton characters as his canvas. Moore's plan was too radical for DC—it didn't want to see the properties it had just purchased altered so permanently and irrevocably their first time out of the gate. DC loved the proposal, though, and instructed Moore to continue, only with new characters of his own devising. Moore obliged, modifying Blue Beetle to Nite Owl, Captain Atom

to Doctor Manhattan and The Question to Rorschach, and the changes were all for the better. Rather than making them carry the baggage of their previous publishing histories, Moore imbued his new characters with an archetypal weight they wouldn't otherwise have: one was the gadgeteer, one was the superman, and one was the vigilante, respectively. Instead of being about the Charlton heroes, *Watchmen* would be about superheroes in total and how they'd exist in a real world, a change that gave *Watchmen* a scope and a feeling of universality.

In *Watchmen*, written by Moore and drawn by Dave Gibbons, the setting is New York City in 1985; but a very different New York City, and for a simple reason: superheroes are real, and as a result, the United States has won the Vietnam War, and Richard Nixon is still in the White House. The U.S. has retained the advantage in the Cold War against the Soviets because of its superheroes (or rather, one particular superhero, the omnipotent and near-omniscient Doctor Manhattan), and the world balances precariously on the brink of nuclear war. This is all background, of course, for the real story at hand: a murder mystery. The vigilante Rorschach discovers that his fellow superheroes, most of whom had been forced into retirement years earlier, have become targets, following the murder of the

111

Comedian, a former superhero turned government assassin. As Rorschach goes about his investigation, we're introduced to the rest of the remaining heroes in exile, and learn about their histories and intertwining relationships through flashbacks, as well as an innovative series of supplementary materials at the end of each chapter.

*Watchmen* remains both Moore's and Gibbons's strongest work, with Moore providing some of the best dialogue of his career, creating such distinct voices for his creations that the reader feels he's been reading them for years. Gibbons, meanwhile, adheres to a strict nine-panel format, only occasionally varying from the norm, and rather than feeling monotonous or confining, it acclimatizes the reader into the world of *Watchmen* without the distraction of fancy page layouts. Gibbons's designs, both for the main characters and for the slightly more futuristic yet still familiar world of 1986 New York, are inspired: his superhero costumes in particular are first-rate—you should be able to pick the characters out of a lineup having never seen them before, just by knowing their names.

The breakout star of *Watchmen* is Rorschach, Moore and Gibbons's borderline-unbalanced vigilante, hanging on to his sanity and his stark, black-and-white worldview by a tenuous thread. Some of Moore's best work in *Watchmen* is in Rorschach's first-person narration, which mixes the irrational rantings of a paranoid sociopath with moments of genuine poetry:

> *"Some of us have always lived on edge, Daniel. It is possible to survive there if you observe rules: just hang on by fingernails... and never look down."*

Moore has lamented that the popularity of *Watchmen* and Rorschach in particular helped lead comics to their "grim-and-gritty" ultra-violent and aggressive period in the 1990s. While it was never Moore's intent for Rorschach to be perceived as a hero or role model, it's hard for the reader not to empathize with such a fully rounded character.

*Watchmen* was a sensation upon its publication, first as a twelve-issue miniseries, then as a collected graphic novel. It has received numerous acclaimed awards and made *TIME* magazine's 2005 list of "100 best English language novels," the only comic book to be so honored.

Some people call it the best graphic novel ever produced. We'd be hard-pressed to disagree.

# PART IV

# MAKE MINE MARVEL

*Wherein the costumed heroes of the 1940s thaw out in the 1960s, and a predictable industry changes for the better; atomic bomb scares and irradiated spiders and fantastic foursomes abound within; team books are altered, and the early magic of the Bullpen delivers time after time.*

# Sub-Mariner

## *Under pressure*

He's a water-breathing strongman from the ocean's depths, he's the rightful king of Atlantis, and he often teams up with some of Earth's most powerful superheroes. And he's not Aquaman.

DC's Aquaman may get more publicity, but the original, accept-no-substitutes undersea hero is Marvel Comics's Prince Namor, the Sub-Mariner, who appeared a full two years before Aquaman, way back in 1939. But not only did Namor come first, he's also a far more interesting character than Aquaman, mostly because he can be such an insufferable jerk. Truly comics' first real anti-hero.

The Sub-Mariner's initial appearance was in Timely's first comic book, *Marvel Comics* #1 (October 1939). Although the story had seen print earlier in a black-and-white movie-theater giveaway entitled *Motion Pictures Funnies Weekly* #1, *Marvel Comics* #1 was Namor's first nationwide exposure.

The debut story, entitled simply "The Sub-Mariner," was written and drawn by Bill Everett, and, compared to other crude, simplistic strips of the time, was a lavishly illustrated wonder. Everett had a fully rendered, almost cinematic style that blew away most of his contemporaries. Small details such as the indication of visual distortion with light, gray-toned lines or the ever-shifting hairstyle of Namor

served as a constant reminder that the scenes were underwater.

The story opens with the curious account of a deep-sea salvage diver, who is convinced that someone or something has beaten his team to a shipwreck. Divers are sent underwater to investigate and they encounter a man swimming at crushing depths without pressure suit or oxygen helmet. The swimmer mistakes the heavy-suited divers for some sort of mechanicals and cuts their oxygen lines to the surface.

The swimmer retrieves the bodies of the murdered divers and takes them to an undersea grotto. He enters a royal chamber to show off his prize, the pressure-suited corpses, and boasts of his destruction of a surface-dweller's ship. Only after removing the helmets does he realize that the divers are in fact real men. We meet the swimmer's mother, Fen, who explains to her son, Namor, how he came to be.

Decades earlier, Fen, the Atlantean princess, had been sent to the surface as a spy to investigate the inadvertent bombing of Atlantis by a scientific vessel, the *Oracle*, captained by Commander Leonard McKenzie. Fen stowed away aboard the ship, and soon she and McKenzie fell in love and were married; all the while Fen continued to report back to the Atlanteans in secret. Despite her warnings, the Atlanteans marshaled for a counter-attack, but were all but destroyed by another bombardment from above, leaving only a few remaining. A pregnant Fen returned to Atlantis, and with the birth of Namor came the Atlanteans' last chance for revenge, since his human-Atlantean heritage means he is the only one who can live both on the land and in the water, as well as fly through the air, thanks to wings sprouting from his ankles, an accident of birth (making the Sub-Mariner Marvel's first mutant by about twenty-five years). His history now revealed, Namor takes off for the surface, set on avenging the injustices done to his people.

This was a series ahead of its time, both in the subtleties of the storyline and the slickness of the illustrations; it doesn't feel like it was created in 1939. Here we have a situation where the protagonist is clearly in the right, yet his sworn enemy is America. This kind of duality in sympathy was uncommon in popular art of the time. Everett's moody style also feels far more adult and realistic than many other strips of the day, though he was not afraid to venture into the cartoony with fishlike appearances of the male Atlanteans. As for Princess Fen, she's just human enough to remain attractive, while retaining the distinctive upswept eyebrows, large fish eyes and blue skin characteristic of male Atlanteans.

The series was renamed *Marvel Mystery Comics* as of issue #2, and the next few issues feature Namor going on a tour of destruction above in the surface world, focusing on New York City. He even betrays a bit of affection for a human woman, New York policewoman Betty Dean. The peak of Namor's uncontested rampage comes in *Marvel Mystery Comics #7* (May 1970), in which Namor plans to destroy the entire North American continent, using New York as his base of operations. Namor begins his campaign at the Statue of Liberty, not only attacking a guard upon his arrival, but also flying up to the torch and throwing tourists out the window.

It wouldn't be long before World War II would put an end to the antagonism between Sub-Mariner and the city of New York. After all, if there's one thing Namor hates more than surface-dwellers, it's Nazi surface-dwellers. Soon Namor was all over Timely's covers fighting Nazi

Namor chucks tourists out of the Statue of Liberty during his rampage across North America. Apparently, no one ever told Captain America about the incident.

troops alongside other Timely stars, Captain America and the Human Torch.

The end of the war took quite a toll on the popularity of Timely's heroes, much more than their DC rivals. Unlike Superman and Batman, who just kind of dabbled in Nazi-hunting, Timely's heroes were so identified with the war effort that their adventures in peacetime seemed somewhat pointless. By 1949, Sub-Mariner and the Torch had vanished from the pages of *Marvel Mystery*, which had changed focus and become *Marvel Tales*, a horror anthology.

With the return of superheroes to Marvel in 1961, Marvel editor Stan Lee found himself with an unexpected success on his hands in the burgeoning hit series *Fantastic Four*. Lee delved full-force into nostalgia with issue #4 (May 1962), reviving Namor as an antagonist for his new super-team, as well as the romantic rival of Reed Richards for Sue Storm's affections. After being awakened from a decades-long bout of amnesia by Sue's brother, Johnny Storm, Namor is immediately smitten with Sue and offers to spare the human race if she'll become his bride. Say what you will about Namor, at least he's not afraid of commitment.

Lee knew immediately that he had a good thing with Namor, as well as a rare storytelling commodity: a sympathetic antagonist. Instead of pushing to get him his own book, Namor was apparently given the position of "unofficial instigator of the Marvel Universe." Lee would simply move Namor from series to series in misguided altercations with various Marvel heroes.

Sub-Mariner has had several attempts at solo series over the years since his Silver Age revival, usually with limited success. A 1968 series lasted a respectable seventy-two issues, during which Namor's well-known and rather unfashionable body suit was introduced, complete with big ol' disco-style underarm wings.

Namor spent much of the 1970s as a member of the Defenders, Marvel's second-string "non-team" that united misfit and less popular characters in a loose affiliation, usually to face mystic or otherdimensional foes. In the mid-1980s, Namor even joined the Avengers, the gold standard for superhero teams in the Marvel Universe. These days, Namor has returned to his traditional role as monarch of Atlantis and wildcard in any sort of superhero struggle. It can be hard to tell whose side he's on, though the answer is obvious: the same he's always been on—his own.

By 1941, public opinion on whether or not the U.S. should get involved in the fighting in Europe was extremely mixed. One place that wasn't quite so conflicted was the comic books, particularly those published by Timely. Having already had a taste of success with Carl Burgos's Human Torch feature and Bill Everett's Sub-Mariner character, Timely opted to go for broke with its newest creation. Capitalizing on the nationalistic mood of a country on the brink of war, the company's publisher, Martin Goodman, enlisted the creative team of Joe Simon and Jack Kirby to create a patriotic hero, one that the company, and ideally readers everywhere, could rally around.

Simon and Kirby more than came through when they delivered Captain America. Goodman must have been impressed, because Captain America was the first Timely character to make his debut in his very own magazine, *Captain America Comics* (March 1940).

## SUPER SOLDIER

The tale opens with the destruction of an American munitions factory by Nazi agents working undercover in the United States. This and other acts of sabotage have prompted President Franklin Delano Roosevelt to order a new project to halt this wave of destruction, and he sends several military leaders to oversee the culmination of the plan.

Entering the lab is a frail, skinny young man, who "volunteered for army service, and was refused because of his unfit condition." A scientist, Professor Reinstein, injects him with a mysterious seething liquid and within moments the young volunteer, Steve Rogers, is transformed into a perfect specimen of humanity, and as Professor Reinstein boasts: "The first of a corps of super-agents whose mental and physical ability will make them a terror to spies and saboteurs."

Professor Reinstein's triumph is short-lived, however. Just as the scientist dubs Rogers "Captain America" ("because, like you – America shall gain the strength and the will to safeguard our shores!"), one of the military observers reveals himself as a traitor and pulls out a pistol, murdering Professor Reinstein and destroying the only remaining supply of the Super-Soldier Serum. The furious Rogers leaps in and mops the floor with the Nazi agent, who in an effort to escape stumbles into some high-voltage equipment and is electrocuted. Unfortunately, the Nazi's mission is a success—the serum and its creator are both destroyed. Despite the hopes of Professor Reinstein, there would only be one Captain America.

In this iconic World War II comic book cover, Captain America makes his debut in rare form, socking Der Führer in the jaw.

## RED, WHITE AND BLUE

Given a red, white and blue uniform and shield by the government (and, one hopes, some training), Rogers is soon making headlines foiling spies and saboteurs in the U.S. as Captain America. Stationed at Camp Lehigh as Private Steve Rogers, Cap befriends the camp's young mascot, Bucky Barnes, who excitedly follows Cap's exploits. One night, as Bucky visits Steve in his quarters, he stumbles upon Rogers changing out of his Captain America uniform. Rogers decides to train Bucky as his partner, complete with his own mask and uniform.

Whether it was intentional or not, the Captain America costume, designed by Joe Simon, made the perfect statement about America's role in the upcoming war, or at least how most Americans preferred to think it. Aside from the obvious notion of a man wrapped in the flag, note that Captain America has no offensive weapons: no gun nor sword. Instead, Captain America has a shield, which is purely a defensive weapon. The shield is unbreakable, representing the strength of America's intentions to protect the people of Europe from fascism. Even when Cap throws the shield offensively, the analogy holds: Cap is extending the strength and protection of the United States to defend the weak and helpless.

Simon and Kirby only produced the first ten issues of *Captain America Comics*, in which Cap and Bucky face all manner of spies, saboteurs and Nazi monsters. In fact, Cap's No. 1 nemesis, the Red Skull, also makes his debut in the first issue. Though the original 1940s villain is unmasked in his first appearance, the character has much more of an impact on Cap's revival in the 1960s.

Cap's original 1940s adventures were action-packed if not particularly exciting. By 1949, with post-World War II patriotism ebbing, Cap's sales began to drop, leading to the comic's cancellation. Cap and Bucky saw a brief revival in 1953 fighting Communists, but the return was short-lived.

## A MAN OUT OF TIME

By 1964, the Marvel Age of Comics was kicking into gear, and Marvel editor Stan Lee was looking for a way to punch up his newest superhero team book, *The Avengers*. Having already revived Timely's other Golden Age success, the Sub-Mariner, in the pages of *Fantastic Four*, it was time for lightning to strike twice, which it did, in *The Avengers* #4, "Captain America Joins... the Avengers!"

The story opens with a bitter, disgruntled Sub-Mariner nursing his wounds from the previous issue's battle with the Hulk and the Avengers (namely Iron Man, Thor, Giant-Man and the Wasp). The Sub-Mariner encounters a band of Eskimos worshipping a mysterious figure frozen in a block of ice. The belligerent Sub-Mariner busts up the party, rousting the Eskimos and hurling the chunk of ice far out to sea. The floating chunk hits the gulf stream, where the warmer waters begin to melt away the ice, revealing a human figure. The figure is spotted by the undersea craft and Giant-Man reaches his oversized mitt through the hatch to pull the now-defrosted figure inside. The Avengers recognize his costume beneath the tattered shreds of his army fatigues as none other than Captain America.

After a brief skirmish with the Avengers to establish his bona fides (always a good idea inside a cramped submarine), Cap tells the tragic story of what became of his final mission. While operating in Europe during World War II, Cap and Bucky were assigned to guard a new explosive-filled drone aircraft. The pilotless plane took off, and Cap and Bucky leapt after it in pursuit, but Cap couldn't hang on, and before Bucky could reach the fuse, the plane exploded, and a horrified Cap dropped into the frigid ocean below. Frozen in an ice flow, Cap has remained in suspended animation for decades until his discovery by the Avengers. (It is later revealed that the Super-Soldier Serum kept his blood from crystallizing in his veins, allowing him to survive being frozen.)

The rest of Cap's issue is fairly routine, but along with it comes the basis for Cap's characterization for the next forty years, which still holds up today. Captain America is a man out of time, lost in a new world. We see a bewildered Cap wandering around modern New York marveling at the technology and the fashions (hopefully someone was good enough to tell him that we won the war), and wondering how he could find a place to belong.

His membership in the Avengers fills that void, and while Cap eventually adjusts to the modern world, the best Captain America writ-

ers manage to keep Cap from coming across like a fossil while still reinforcing his 1940s origins and values.

There have been several exceptionally good runs of Captain America since his return in 1964. First off, naturally, are the Stan Lee/Jack Kirby stories in *Tales of Suspense*. Initially, the series focuses on Cap and Bucky's exploits in World War II, featuring frequent appearances by the Red Skull (including, finally, a look at his origin: he was originally Hitler's bellboy). Later, the series shifts to the present day, and injects Cap's adventures with a good dose of science fiction and high-octane espionage, enlisting Cap as a freelance agent in the spy agency the S.H.I.E.L.D. and introducing the high-tech terrorists known as A.I.M. (Advanced Idea Mechanics). Not only is A.I.M. responsible for the creation of the Cosmic Cube, which can convert thoughts into reality, but it also revives the Red Skull, who had fallen into suspended animation due to exposure to mysterious chemical gases.

Writer Roger Stern and artist John Byrne delivered a very solid nine-issue run in 1980, in *Captain America* #247–255. Stern's characterization of Steve Rogers is consistent and historically accurate, while Byrne's art and storytelling are clear and appealing.

The Stern/Byrne run also introduces future Cap love interest Bernadette Rosenthal and places more emphasis on Steve Rogers's attempting to build a personal life, which includes a new career as a commercial artist.

In 1985, Marvel editor and writer Mark Gruenwald took over the scripting on *Captain America* and remained for more than ten years and 136 issues. The highlight of Gruenwald's run came with issue #332 (August 1987), entitled "The Choice." Captain America is summoned by a secret presidential commission and informed that since the federal government created the uniform and identity of Captain America, they therefore own the concept of Captain America. If he wants to continue in the role of Captain America, he must put an end to his operations with the Avengers and S.H.I.E.L.D., as well as his solo operations, and report directly to them. After much deliberation, Steve Rogers refuses, citing his loyalty to the American dream and not one particular administration, and turns in his uniform and shield, giving up his life's work as Captain America. The commission attempts to replace Captain America, with disastrous results, while Steve Rogers searches for a way to adjust to his loss and find a new way of serving the American dream. While the "replace-the-superhero-with-a-crazy-dark-version" storyline was a popular one at Marvel and DC in the late 1980s and early 1990s, Gruenwald did it first and did the best job of it, as well.

When Gruenwald left the series, writer Mark Waid and artist Ron Garney took over with *Captain America* # 444 (October 1995) and kick-started the series out of its creative doldrums. Waid and Garney approached the series like a Tom Clancy thriller, and suddenly Cap did a lot less speechmaking and a lot more ass-kicking. When Cap did speak, however, his voice was dead-on.

More recently, writer Ed Brubaker and artist Steve Epting have embarked upon a critically acclaimed run on the *Cap* series, in which they pulled off the impossible: bringing Bucky Barnes back from the dead in a clever, convincing and acceptable way. Bucky is revealed as the brainwashed and cryogenically frozen Winter Soldier, an unwitting tool of the Soviet Union for decades. Only recently has Bucky regained his memories and free will.

Brubaker and Epting were behind the newsmaking "death of Captain America" storyline in *Captain America* Vol. 5 #25 (March 2007). Steve Rogers is assassinated while turning himself in for violation of the federal government's Superhuman Registration Act. Brubaker and Epting continue to tell compelling Captain America stories even without Steve Rogers, starring Bucky Barnes as the new Cap. While Steve Rogers will undoubtedly return, in the meantime the series remains in excellent hands.

Baron Zemo feels the grip of a free man, courtesy of the Star-Spangled Avenger.

# The Fantastic Four

## *The way it began*

Let us set the Wayback Machine for 1961, in which a successful comics publisher called Timely (or Atlas, depending on what month it is and who you ask) was eking out a living by treading water and following the trends. If Westerns were in vogue, it cranked out Westerns by the bushel. If romance seemed to be moving well, then it was love stories all around. At the time, the trend was monster comics, so Timely turned out Godzilla knockoffs like you wouldn't believe. Timely's managing editor and art director was Stanley Martin Lieber, although you might be more familiar with his sobriquet: Stan Lee. Lee had been working at the publisher since he was seventeen years old, and had risen from the ranks of office boy. Although his monster comics were doing OK, Stan was bored, bored, bored and about ready to leave comics for good.

Meanwhile, Timely's publisher, Martin Goodman, was having a legendary golf game with National Comics publisher Jack Liebowitz, during which he told Goodman what a big success he was having with the new *Justice League of America* comic. When Goodman left the links, he called Lee and told him to get to work on a superhero-team comic book, and fast.

As Lee tells it in *Origins of Marvel Comics*, he was also set on the right track by his wife Joan. She reminded him that since he was ready to quit anyway, why not do whatever he wanted with this new book instead of following the same comic-book clichés he'd been repeating for years?

Inspired, Lee began to flesh out his new concept for the book. First to go were secret identities. As Lee reasoned, if he himself had superpowers, he'd never be able to keep them secret, so why should they? Next, out was the classic superhero love triangle in which Our Hero's girlfriend would really fall for him if only she knew who he really was. Instead, not only would the girl know who the hero really was, they'd both be on the team, and treat each other as equals. Also, no costumes. Again, Lee couldn't see himself wearing tights and a cape, so neither would his new characters. (Of course, this rule didn't last long—about two issues. Still, they kept to the spirit of the concept by wearing more utilitarian uniforms rather than gaudy costumes.) Finally, this new team wouldn't always get along; they'd bicker, they'd squabble. Sometimes it would seem that certain members outright hated each other.

Having decided the direction he wanted this new series to take, Lee typed up a synopsis for the premiere issue and handed it off to his ace in the hole: artist Jack Kirby. Kirby had just returned from a stint at National Comics, and was currently keeping Timely/Atlas afloat with his work on the monster comics. Over the next nine years, the Lee/Kirby partnership would flourish, and generate not only 102 consecutive issues of *Fantastic Four* (an amazing body of work), but also a sizable portion of what would become the Marvel Universe. Though their partnership would later wither, at the time, neither man had any idea that the comic book they'd created would launch a publishing and merchandising empire.

## RUNNING THE SPACE RACE

In *The Fantastic Four* #1 (November 1961), readers are introduced to genius scientist Reed Richards, his fiancée Susan Storm, Sue's kid brother Johnny, and test pilot Ben Grimm, Reed's friend and college roommate. In a bid to beat those dastardly Commies to outer space, Reed and company hijack the rocket that he's designed, with plans to take it into orbit pronto, despite Ben's concerns about the rocket's insufficient shielding from cosmic radiation. You'd think Reed "Super-Genius" Richards might have listened to what seems a perfectly rational request for increased safety from a close friend and professional test pilot, right? Nope. After Sue questions Ben's manhood, he's totally on board—in retrospect, not one of Mr. Grimm's best decisions.

The foursome sneak on board the rocket and launch, and are soon in Earth orbit. Almost immediately the ship is hammered by cosmic radiation, with adverse effects on the crew, especially Ben, who manages to pilot

*Fantastic Four* #1, the start of the Marvel Universe as we know it.

## GENE SIMMONS, KISS bassist, god of thunder and Simmons Comics Group founder

### THE BEST CREATIVE TIME ON THE TITLE

*World's Finest* never really did it for me. It was simply my entree. Once I discovered Lee and Kirby's *Fantastic Four*, it wasn't long until I studied every panel and every inker (Dick Ayers, Vince Colletta and the rest). Even letterer Sam Rosen was studied by my twelve-year-old eyes. The FF's finest hour? Every issue, baby. Every issue.

### THE BEST COVER

*Spider-Man* #1's cover had the biggest impact on me. Spidey climbing up a wall, with the FF in pursuit. I loved 'em then. I love 'em now.

### THE BEST STORYLINE ON THE TITLE

Silver Surfer stories always intrigued me. Here is an alien whose world has been destroyed and his family killed and yet he is the herald for the world-eater, Galactus? When Surfer meets human beings and has second thoughts about their humanity, there is an almost Shakespearean level of literature that creeps in. "What fools these mortals be," indeed.

### THE GOOFIEST STORYLINE

The Impossible Man. And yet, no matter how goofy or impossible, I loved it.

the ship to a soft landing despite an almost unbearable heaviness in his limbs.

Back on Earth, as the quartet begins to bicker over the failed flight, the effects of the radiation become clear. First Sue fades away, then mysteriously reappears. Then Ben begins to grow and mutate, becoming an orange rock-like creature. Enraged, Ben lashes out at Reed, who, in attempting to defend himself, begins to stretch and distort, his limbs and torso freakishly elongating. Finally, emotionally upset at the conflict, Johnny suddenly bursts into flame, and then erupts into flight, soaring over the wreckage. The four resolve to serve mankind with their new abilities (some more begrudgingly than others) and dub themselves the Fantastic Four: Mr. Fantastic, the Invisible Girl, the Human Torch and the Thing.

So, was the book as revolutionary as Stan envisioned? Well, there was nothing else out there like it, that's for sure. Central to the book's uniqueness early on was the very palpable antagonism between Reed and the Thing. Unlike the others, whose powers don't preclude them from leading relatively normal lives, Ben Grimm is cursed by his powers, forced to live in hiding. He often takes out his frustrations on his own teammates, especially Reed, whom he (quite rightly) blames for his misfortune. To make matters worse, Ben, from time to time, reverts back to his human form, but never for any significant length of time. Just long enough to get his hopes up for a normal life, before being dashed once more.

## IT'S CLOBBERIN' TIME

The series' unprecedented emphasis on characterization and personal conflict struck a chord with readers, rocketing *The Fantastic Four* up the sales charts. In addition, the fan mail began to arrive in record numbers, giving Lee a pipeline to his readers he never had before, and helping to build a brand loyalty and "character first" formula that would serve him on success after success at Marvel.

The Fantastic Four's adventures were unique, as well. Rather than falling into the standard "answering a call for help" storylines, the Fantastic Four were more of explorers and adventurers rather than crimefighters, often finding themselves in peril as a result of one of Reed's experiments. There was also a sense of realism about the series. The characters grow over time; Reed and Sue eventually marry and have children. The FF lives in Manhattan, not an imaginary Gotham City or Metropolis, and they have real problems, be it angry neighbors or empty coffers. For example, when supposed genius Reed Richards puts all of the organization's money in the stock market, which then goes belly-up, the repo men show up to start taking the team's equipment. Stuff like that never happens to Batman.

But best of all are the villains. Lee and Kirby hit a period of sustained creativity, with one outstanding concept following the next. They started strong in the premiere issue with the Mole Man, an unwanted soul who rules a subterranean kingdom miles below the sur-

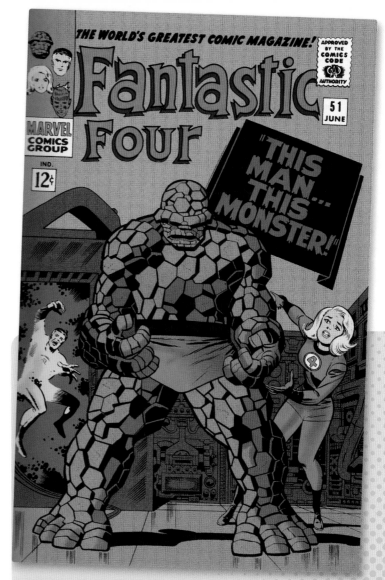

"This Man … This Monster" focuses on Ben Grimm's tortured existence as the Thing and is widely considered the best single issue of *Fantastic Four* by the Lee/Kirby team.

## MARV WOLFMAN, writer, *Fantastic Four*

### THE FIRST ISSUE OF *FANTASTIC FOUR* I EVER READ

*Fantastic Four* #4 (May 1962). I started pretty early on and quickly got the back issues. It was so different from anything I had read until then—I actually didn't know what to make of it. Within a few issues, however, I understood and loved it.

### THE BEST CREATIVE TIME ON THE TITLE

There was only one: Stan and Jack. Nobody else came close. Everyone since has only tried to continue what they did, but nobody has come close to constantly surprising us with incredible ideas and characters.

### THE BEST COVER

*Fantastic Four* #8 (November 1961), with the Puppet Master, followed by *FF* #39 (June 1965) and *FF* #48 (March 1966). This is the book that completely changed all superhero comics to come. It was the most creative, original and constantly inventive superhero comic ever done. Nobody, right up to today, has ever approached this title in sheer inventiveness.

### THE BEST STORYLINE

The Galactus saga (*FF* #48-50). Like, duh. Best and most creative superhero story ever done to its time.

face. This allowed Kirby to bring some of his trademark monsters to the forefront.

Also facing off against the FF are the alien shapechangers the Skrulls, who impersonate and frame the team; and the Puppet Master, a twisted sculptor who uses his radioactive clay to craft miniature duplicates that allow him to control the minds of others, and whose blind stepdaughter Alicia becomes the sole joy in Ben Grimm's life.

## THE DOCTOR IS IN

None of Lee and Kirby's FF creations measure up to what is arguably the single best comic-book villain ever created: Doctor Doom. Unlike previous comic-book villains, who were just evil for evil's sake, Doctor Doom is as much a fully realized character as any of the heroes, with motivations you can sympathize with and faults you can identify with.

Although Doom first appears in *Fantastic Four* #5 (which features a hilarious adventure of Reed, Johnny and Ben posing as pirates in the seventeenth century), the character's true defining moment comes in *Fantastic Four Annual* #2 (1964), in which we learn "The Fantastic Origin of Doctor Doom!"

Victor Von Doom is born the child of gypsies in the eastern European country of Latveria. His father, a gypsy healer who is marked for death by a local baron, dies trying to save Victor from the baron's wrath. After his father's death, Victor discovers that his late mother had been a sorceress, so he embraces the black arts, combining them with his own scientific genius to fleece riches from the upperclass aristocrats, then give the money to the poor. Eventually, word of the unstoppable young gypsy genius spreads to the West, and Von Doom accepts a scientific scholarship to an American university in order to have access to the latest equipment and resources. At college, he meets fellow scholarship student Reed Richards and rebuffs Reed's friendly offer to room together.

Obsessed with his work, Von Doom builds a massive device designed to breach the netherworld and allow him to contact the spirit of his mother. Wandering past Von Doom's room, Reed eyeballs his plans for the device and notices that some of his calculations are off by a few decimals. Reed tries to warn him, but Von Doom will have none of it, and haughtily shows Reed the door. When Von Doom throws the switch, the device explodes, disfiguring his face. Expelled, Von Doom leaves the university and wanders Tibet, seeking "forbidden secrets of black magic and sorcery." There, Von Doom is taken in by a mysterious order of monks, who teach him "ancient secrets and lore" and help him create his infamous armored suit and mask, behind which he hides his disfigured face from the world. From there, Doctor Doom sets off to conquer, first seizing control of his home nation of Latveria, and then making plans for the rest of the world.

Doom has real motivations and foibles. He wants to rule the world, but his reign over Latveria is shown as a benevolent dictatorship.

His subjects are devoted to his rule, and in turn, Doom is devoted to their care. He wants to retrieve his mother's soul from torment, and he's bitterly jealous of Reed's genius, exemplified in the single moment when Reed is right and Doom is wrong, his scarred face now a perpetual reminder.

## A FAMILY AFFAIR

Other than the Lee/Kirby classics, most *FF* fans consider writer/artist John Byrne's lengthy run on *Fantastic Four* (issues #232–292, 1980–1986) the next-best thing to Stan and Jack. Byrne went back to the basics, placing heavy emphasis on the Fantastic Four as a family first and a superhero team second. Byrne also reinforced Reed's status as a near-unparallelled scientific genius, stepping away from the "Mr. Fantastic" identity. Sue was also made a much stronger and more powerful character under Byrne's tenure. One noteworthy and heartbreaking Byrne story involves a desperate Reed Richards trying to convince Spider-Man villain Doctor Octopus to assist in the delivery of their second child, which is complicated by radiation poisoning.

The art doesn't disappoint, either. Byrne's clean, detailed style fit the *Fantastic Four* like a glove, and this period is some of his best work.

### SCOTT SAYS

I was lucky enough to meet Jack Kirby before he passed away, and got the chance to listen to him talk about some of his characters at length. His conception of Doom was that the explosion at the university had only left Doom with a single, tiny scar across his left cheek, but that this single imperfection of his handsome face was intolerable, and Doom would rather hide his features behind the stifling iron mask than show his imperfection to the world. A brilliant take on Doom's character, and one I'd never before considered.

# The Incredible Hulk

## *Driven by rage*

Maybe the best known of Marvel's characters after Spider-Man, the green-skinned Goliath the Incredible Hulk has found success in animation, live-action television and the silver screen, but it all started on the four-color pages of the comics.

Stan Lee was looking to follow up the success of his first big hit, *Fantastic Four*. He considered another team book, but didn't want to repeat himself. He thought about doing a Superman-style strong man, but rejected the notion as too routine. Then inspiration struck: What about a comic where the good guy is also the bad guy? A longtime fan of Mary Shelley's *Frankenstein*, as well as the classic Universal horror movies, Stan had always empathized with the misunderstood creature. Why not transfer the misunderstood monster to comics? Stan also borrowed from Robert Louis Stevenson's *Dr. Jekyll and Mr. Hyde*, giving his monster hero the ability to change back and forth from man to beast. As Stan recalls in *Origins of Marvel Comics*, "Now all that remained was to find a name... I knew I needed a perfect name for a monstrous, potentially murderous hulking brute who – and then I stopped. It was the word 'hulking' that did it. It conjured up the perfect mental image. I knew I had found his name. He had to be: The Hulk."

And with that, Stan sent his synopsis to Marvel's artistic ace, Jack Kirby, who illustrated the Hulk's first issue and designed all the major characters. Stan and Jack's creation hit newsstands in May 1962, with the premiere issue of *The Incredible Hulk*.

### SEVEN FEET OF UNFETTERED FURY

The story introduces Dr. Bruce Banner (later amended to Robert Bruce Banner, after Stan had a bit of a brain freeze and started referring to the character as "Bob Banner"), nuclear scientist and creator of the gamma bomb, a potentially devastating new atomic weapon about to be tested by the U.S. military. Banner is cautious of safety regulations, but General Thaddeus "Thunderbolt" Ross demands that the bomb be detonated immediately. Bruce is defended by the General's daughter Betty, who has eyes for the shy scientist.

Finally, Banner is ready to test the device, and the countdown commences. Surveying the detonation site, Banner notices a teenager cruising his car through the heart of ground zero. Banner yells at his assistant Igor to halt the countdown, then runs out to get the boy to safety. Unfortunately, Banner has no idea that his assistant is actually a dirty Communist spy, sent by his Soviet masters to obtain the secrets of the gamma bomb. (You'd think the name

"Igor" might have been something of a clue.) Igor decides to eliminate Banner and does not halt the countdown.

Banner reaches the test site just soon enough to throw the teenager, Rick Jones, into a protective trench, but Banner is too late to save himself, and he catches the full blast of gamma radiation released by the explosion. Banner regains consciousness later that night. He's been locked in an observation room, along with Jones, who survived without a scratch. Banner, however, is not so lucky. As night falls, Banner begins to mutate before Jones's eyes, growing much taller and more muscular, bursting through the seams of his clothes, with his skin turning a deathly gray color.

But isn't the Hulk supposed to be green? In the first issue of *The Incredible Hulk*, the Hulk is gray, as Stan intended. However, when Stan saw the final magazine, he decided that the gray color wasn't printing consistently enough. He changed the Hulk's color to green, and green it remained until the gray Hulk was re-introduced in 1986.

At first, the Hulk emerges only at night. For a short while, Banner himself triggers the transformations in an attempt to control the Hulk. (Banner knows of the Hulk's existence, but has no memory of his actions when transformed, while the childlike Hulk often forgets that he's Banner.)

## HULK SMASH!

In time, a new catalyst develops, one that cements the success of the series. When Bruce Banner becomes upset, angry or otherwise placed under stress, he loses control and transforms into the Hulk. As the Hulk grows more and more angry, his strength increases exponentially, with seemingly no limit. Or, in the words of Hulk, "The madder Hulk gets, the stronger Hulk gets!"

The Hulk's magazine only lasted six issues. After that, Stan employed Hulk as a kind of pinch-hitting guest star, touring him around the various Marvel series, before landing him in a secure spot as co-star of *Tales to Astonish*, along with perennial also-ran Ant-Man. It was in the *Tales* run, with art by Spider-Man creator Steve Ditko and later a return from Kirby, that Stan really hit his stride with the Hulk series, establishing the "Hulk-get-mad, Hulk-get-strong" motif, and building a strong supporting cast of friends and foes. Rick Jones and Betty remain Banner's closest friends, although only Jones (who later repeats his sidekick role for Captain America, Captain Marvel and even Rom the Spaceknight) knows the secret of Banner's curse. General "Thunderbolt" Ross also stays in the forefront as the Hulk's chief antagonist and major thorn in the side of Bruce Banner. Even worse, Ross now has a co-conspirator in the weaselly Major Glenn Talbot, who is not only convinced that Banner secretly works for the Soviets, but also has designs on Betty. (Some years later, believing Banner dead, Betty actually marries the pencil-mustachioed twerp on the rebound, but drops him like yesterday's papers when Bruce resurfaces.)

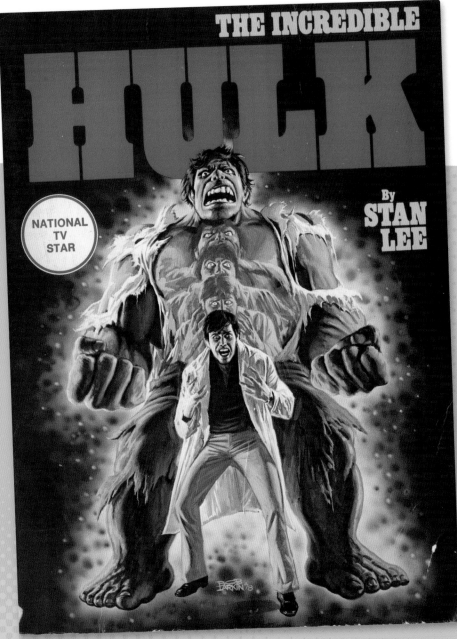

Can you believe a guy who looked like this was once a national TV star?

## BRAINS AND BRAWN

The two strongest contributions from the *Tales to Astonish* are Hulk's popular adversaries the Leader and the Abomination. The Leader first shows his long face in *Tales to Astonish* #62 (December 1964), by Lee and Ditko. An average laborer working clean-up in a chemical research plant is accidentally caught in the blast of an experimental gamma ray cylinder. Inexplicably, the man survives, but after his recovery discovers he has a voracious desire for knowledge, retaining exact recall of everything he reads. The gamma radiation has a delayed physical effect, and some weeks after the blast, his skull and brain grow to oversized proportions and his skin turns green. He abandons his former identity, and, dubbing himself the Leader, turns his unmatched intellect to matters of world conquest. The Leader often tries to use the Hulk as his unwitting pawn in his schemes, but with little success.

Where as the Leader is more than a match for the Hulk in gamma-induced intelligence, the Abomination proves to be an equal threat in gamma-induced strength. Debuting in *Tales to Astonish* #90 (April 1967), Emil Blonsky is yet another Commie spy sent to infiltrate and sabotage General Ross's Air Force base. (Maybe if Ross and Talbot weren't so busy chasing Banner around and yelling, "Traitor!" all the time, they might have noticed all these guys with Russian-sounding names suddenly getting work at the military base.) Blonsky finds Banner's latest gamma weapon that, unbeknownst to Blonsky, is designed to bombard Banner's own body with enough gamma radiation to kill himself and end the threat of the Hulk forever. When security guards bust in and haul off Banner (no doubt to face the latest trumped-up treason charge from Ross and Talbot), Blonsky uses the machine on himself and is bombarded with a far more intense blast of gamma rays than the one that transformed Banner into the Hulk. Luckily for Blonsky, he happens to possess a rare genetic factor, just as Banner and the Leader had, that prevents him from being killed by the massive dose of radiation. The gamma rays give Blonsky strength much greater than that of the Hulk, but, unlike Banner, he retains his intelligence as well.

The downside? The gamma rays mutate him dramatically, transforming him into a hideous creature that Betty Ross names the Abomination. Although Banner later invents a device to drain some of the excess gamma radiation out of the Abomination, taking away some of his strength, the Abomination maintains a baseline strength level greater than that of a relatively calm Hulk. When Hulk gets steamed, though, all bets are off.

The *Incredible Hulk* comic continues in a happy rut throughout most of the 1970s and '80s, with things finally shaking up in 1985 with the arrival of writer/artist John Byrne,

### SCOTT SAYS

What accounts for the Hulk's perennial popularity? If you ask me, it's a simple factor: rage. Everyone can identify with the helplessness of feeling pushed to the very edge, and seeing Bruce Banner get so mad that he's able to swing a Sherman tank like a Louisville Slugger. Well, it's cathartic to say the least.

who, among other things, physically separates Bruce Banner from the Hulk and finally sees that Bruce and Betty marry, despite Thunderbolt's showing up and blowing a .32-caliber hole through best man Rick Jones.

Not long after that, Banner and Hulk are reintegrated, and writer Peter David began his landmark twelve-year run on the series, playing off of a story by writer Bill Mantlo that discusses Bruce's childhood torment at the hands of his abusive father, as well as writer Al Milgrom's re-introduc-

NICE OF YOU TO WAIT AROUND.

The Hulk not only gets a new job during Peter David's tenure, but stylin' new threads, as well.

tion of the gray Hulk. Under David's pen, the fragmented consciousness of Bruce Banner is fully explored. The character is diagnosed as having multiple personality disorder—the Bruce Banner personality represents his intellect, the green Hulk his repressed rage (triggered by childhood abuse, which is why the green Hulk retains a childlike intellect and emotional state), and the gray Hulk his darker, repressed instincts, such as lust and greed.

One of the many highlights of Peter David's run is in *Incredible Hulk* #347 (September 1988), in which the gray Hulk, who retains normal intelligence and a very bad attitude, takes on a new identity as Mr. Fixit, an enforcer for a casino owner in Las Vegas. Seeing the nattily dressed Hulk pound on mobsters, then cruise back to his penthouse with a fabulous babe on his arm is surreal, to say the least; just one example of the anything-can-happen approach that Peter David brought to the title.

Between the Saturday-morning cartoons, the TV shows, the mountains of merchandise and his recent blockbuster motion picture trilogy, even people who've never seen a comic book in their lives must by now know a little something about Marvel's trademark character, and probably the single most popular superhero ever, the Amazing Spider-Man. Since he's been published for more than forty years, there's quite a lot to cover when it comes to Spidey, but we'll try to cover some of the high points. Let's open the floor to questions. Yes, you in the back?

### WHERE DID SPIDER-MAN FIRST APPEAR?

Spidey's first appearance is in *Amazing Fantasy* #15 (August 1963), in a tale called, appropriately enough, "Spider-Man!" As the legend goes, Marvel editor/writer Stan Lee, flush from the successful launches of *Fantastic Four* and *Hulk*, wanted to try an even more experimental superhero strip, one in which the hero himself would be a teenager, as opposed to the usual teen sidekick role, and which would feature a more "hard-luck hero" approach. Taking inspiration from the 1930s pulp hero the Spider, Stan dubbed his new creation Spider-Man, and premiered his new character in the final issue of *Amazing Fantasy*. Since the book was

already going to get the axe, as Stan explained to then-Marvel publisher Martin Goodman, what's the harm in trying something new?

Something new indeed. Thanks to Steve Ditko's brilliant costume design and spare, streamlined art style, along with the most inspired origin story of Stan Lee's career,

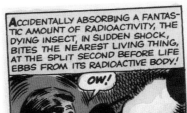

Peter Parker receives that fateful spider bite that changes his life.

Spider-Man caught the attention of comics readers in a big way. The first issue of *The Amazing Spider-Man* appeared a few months later.

## HOW CLOSE IS THE MOVIE TO THE COMICS?

Very. Sam Raimi's *Spider-Man* may not follow every bit of the Spider-Man lore chapter and verse, but man, does it come close. The only real departures are the armored Green Goblin and the fact that Spidey's webs are organic.

## ORGANIC? MEANING WHAT?

If you'll recall, in the film, after Peter Parker has been bitten by the genetically mutated spider, he soon discovers that the bite has affected him, granting him increased strength and speed, the ability to cling to walls, a mysterious "spider-sense" to warn him of danger and the ability to expel webbing from his wrists. Well, in the comics, he gets all of that except the webbing. Instead, Peter, a genius-level scientific prodigy, devises mechanical webshooter devices to wear on his wrists, which fire an adhesive "web-fluid" of his own design. By adjusting the nozzle, Spidey can fire a thick, sticky glue, a fine spray to act as a net, or long, sturdy strands that allow him to swing from building to building. (The web-fluid would dissolve after two hours, preventing someone else from gathering up the evidence and copying the formula.)

The filmmakers decided to jettison the mechanical webshooters, thinking it too far-fetched that a teenager could invent so complicated a device. Also, director Sam Raimi has stated that he felt the organic webshooters further served as a symbol of Parker's alienation and sense of being an outcast. This makes sense, and the minor detail certainly doesn't have any large effect on the film.

Still, the original version is preferable. Peter Parker's scientific genius helps set him apart from most superhero-type characters, and brings his character of "mild-mannered bookworm" into sharper focus. Also, the fact that he creates his webs somewhat validates Spidey as a hero. Random chance may have given Peter Parker his powers, but his will and intelligence make him a hero.

## WHAT ABOUT THE ORIGIN STORY? IS IT LIKE THE MOVIE?

Yes, indeed. Peter Parker, in a moment of arrogance and self-involvement, stands by and lets a criminal escape, and that same criminal later kills his beloved uncle. Some of the details change in the film: Spidey lets the criminal go at the wrestling match instead of the TV station, and Uncle Ben is killed in a carjacking rather than a home robbery, but the important stuff's all there.

Spider-Man's is the most powerful of all superhero origins because it can be boiled down to a single motivation. Why is Clark Kent Superman? Because he was raised by decent people who taught him to always do the right thing. Why is Bruce Wayne Batman? Because his parents were killed by a mugger before his eyes when he was a child, and he wants to prevent that from happening to others. Both of these are good stories, but they require a basic sense of altruism that might be hard for a reader to identify with. Why is Peter Parker Spider-Man? Guilt. Guilt over the murder of his uncle, a murder he could have stopped if he'd done the right thing. Parker is compelled to do good as Spider-Man, because the absence of his uncle is a constant reminder of his failure to be responsible. It's right there in black and white in *Amazing Fantasy* #15, and we all heard Cliff Robertson's Uncle Ben say it in the movie: "With great power comes great responsibility." There are worse things to learn from a comic book.

## WAS MARY JANE ALWAYS PETER'S GIRL?

Nope. Initially, Peter's love interest is Betty Brant, J. Jonah Jameson's secretary at the *Daily Bugle*. Also competing for Peter's attention is classmate Liz Allen, who occasionally dates Pete's jock nemesis Flash Thompson. Mary Jane doesn't enter the picture until more than three years later, after Peter has graduated high school, and after a hilarious running gag in which Aunt May continually tries to set up Peter with Mary Jane, the niece of a friend, but the reader never gets to see her face. MJ's head is obscured by houseplants, trees, lampshades, you name it. When the gorgeous Mary Jane is finally revealed in *The Amazing Spider-Man* #42 (November 1966), as drawn by the fabulous John Romita, it is a moment Spidey fans will long remember.

Mary Jane remains a presence in the series, but it is Gwen Stacy who becomes the major love interest of Peter Parker for the next five years or so. Gwen is a classmate of Peter's at Empire State University, and the daughter of police captain George Stacy, one of the few authority figures who don't automatically assume the worst about Spider-Man. Gwen is the first significant love interest for Peter in the series, at least until it all goes bad.

## UH-OH. BAD? HOW BAD?

Very bad. Moviegoers will remember the climax of Sam Raimi's *Spider-Man*, in which the Green Goblin dangles Mary Jane from the George Washington Bridge. Well, if you saw the film with any Spider-Man fans, you may have noticed a stunned, open-mouthed gape on their faces at that point. That's because this sequence is taken directly from *The Amazing Spider-Man* #121 (June 1973), except instead of Mary Jane in peril, it is Gwen. Just like in the movie, the Goblin drops her. And just like in the movie, Spidey catches her.

Unlike the movie, however, it is not enough.

### YOU MEAN SHE'S DEAD?

Yes. Spidey manages to catch her with his webbing, but it's all for naught. To further twist the blade, in the panel that shows Spidey's webbing catching her, the small sound effect "SNAP!" appears by Gwen's neck. Was she already dead from the shock of the fall, or did the abrupt stop of the rescue attempt seal her fate? Neither Spider-Man nor the reader ever gets a concrete answer. What's Spider-Man's motivation again? Guilt.

### SO WHAT HAPPENS TO THE GOBLIN?

Once again, the movie follows the events of the comic very closely. After seeing to Gwen's body and saying his goodbyes, Spider-Man furiously pursues the Goblin, dead-set on revenge. After a heated battle in which the headpiece of the Goblin's glider is damaged, forming a now-lethal point, Spider-Man pummels the Goblin mercilessly, almost killing him—but he stops himself, not wanting to become a murderer like the Goblin. Spidey coolly informs the Goblin that he's heading to prison for the murder of Gwen, knowing all too well that it will effectively ruin his life; the Goblin will undoubtedly expose Spider-Man's identity to the world if captured. The Goblin, meanwhile, has been surreptitiously controlling his glider remotely, and it is now hurtling toward Spidey's back, about to impale him. Spider-Man's spider-sense kicks in and Spidey leaps away at the last moment. No such luck

The Goblin pays the price for his sins.

AMAZING SPIDER-MAN #122: © 1973 MARVEL ENTERTAINMENT, INC. USED WITH PERMISSION. ART BY GIL KANE, JOHN ROMITA AND TONY MORTELLARO. COLOR BY ANDY YANCHUS.

## JOE HILL, novelist, writer, *Locke & Key*

**THE FIRST ISSUE OF *SPIDER-MAN* I EVER READ**

When my family went on vacation somewhere—like to Disney World—my dad would make up these multi-part Spider-Man stories for us, in which Peter Parker would just coincidentally be going on vacation in the exact same place as us. He'd tell a chapter every night at bedtime. These were really foul stories, too. Peter inevitably wound up with a case of diarrhea as the result of eating some bad road food, and would wind up fighting the Lizard and the Green Goblin, while trying not to fill his spider suit with crap. These stories would put me in an agony of suspense. As if it wasn't bad enough that Peter might be killed, there was also the possibility he'd suffer humiliation first. So those are the first Spider-Man stories I remember caring about, although it doesn't exactly answer your question.

**THE BEST CREATIVE TIME ON THE TITLE**

At the risk of providing a bland, uninteresting answer, I have to go with the first thirty-eight stories, the Ditko/Lee originals, beginning with *Amazing Fantasy* #15. Steve Ditko and Stan Lee built the sandbox that all the other Spidey writers and artists have spent the last forty years playing in.

**THE BEST COVER**

*Amazing Spider-Man* #90 (November 1970), baby. Beautifully composed, it instantly created sus-pense...and a feeling of tragedy. Oh, yeah, and one other great thing about the cover. Where it says 15 cents? Them were the days.

**THE BEST STORYLINE/ISSUE**

It was bad enough when her dad got killed (felled by falling bricks—and Spidey took the blame!) but nothing matches up to Gwen Stacy's death in *The Amazing Spider-Man* #121. For me, as a young reader, it was a big emotional shock. She wasn't just murdered by one of the bad guys, remember. Her neck was snapped when Spider-Man tried to save her, and stopped her fall too abruptly with one of his web strands. It was my first introduc-tion to the idea that no matter how clever you are, no matter how smart or heroic or kind, you can still catastrophically mess things up.

**THE GOOFIEST STORYLINE/ISSUE**

Oh, probably this sorry rubbish they just pulled with Mephisto unwriting history, and undoing the last ten years of Peter Parker's life ("One More Day"). That's a cowardly, corporate decision, not a valid storytelling choice. The moment you become afraid to let a character grow and change, that character dies on the page. This is true even of four-panel funnies in the newspaper. After a while, *Garfield* isn't funny anymore because he never changes.

# SPIDER-MAN'S ROGUES' GALLERY

**GREEN GOBLIN** The most dangerous of all Spidey's foes, because only he knows who's under Spider-Man's mask.

**DOCTOR OCTOPUS** With four powerful robotic arms bonded to his spine, Otto Octavius's genius is only matched by his insanity.

**SANDMAN** After a radioactive day at the beach, bank robber Flint Marko can turn to solid granite or a fine powder.

**ELECTRO** Lineman Max Dillon becomes a living battery, and sends thousands of villainous volts Spider-Man's way.

**SCORPION** The first of J. Jonah Jameson's attempts to defeat Spidey, private eye Mac Gargan is given superstrength and a high-tech tail.

**VULTURE** Senior citizen Adrian Toomes swoops through the canyons of New York on artificial wings, snatching up cash and jewels along the way.

**VENOM** An alien symbiote and a jealous photojournalist rival combine to create one of Spider-Man's most dangerous and popular foes.

**KRAVEN THE HUNTER** A world-famous big-game hunter who sets his sights on the most elusive target of all: Spider-Man.

for the Goblin, who is speared in the chest by his glider, killing him.

As writer Gerry Conway put it, "So do the proud men die. Crucified not on a cross of gold, but a stake of humble tin." Pretty heady stuff for a superhero comic, especially in 1973.

## I FEEL LIKE READING SOME SPIDEY. WHAT DO YOU RECOMMEND?

When in doubt, go to the source. It can't get any better than the original tales of Spider-Man by Stan Lee, Steve Ditko and John Romita. Luckily, you can own the first eighty-nine issues of *The Amazing Spider-Man* in *The Essential Spider-Man*, Vol. 1–4. Check out the first appearances of Spider-Man and all his friends and foes, in chronological order: Doctor Octopus, the Green Goblin, Electro, the Lizard, the Sandman, the Chameleon, Kraven the Hunter, Mysterio, the Vulture, the Rhino—the list goes on and on. While it's a shame they're only in black and white, it's hard to be too upset over the volume of pages you get for the price.

As for the epic Green Goblin/Gwen Stacy tragedy previously detailed, check out *Spider-Man: The Death of Gwen Stacy*, written by Gerry Conway with art by Gil Kane. It's much, much better and more affecting than our meager prose can convey.

*The Best of Marvel Comics, Volume 1* is tough to find, but should you stumble across it at a used bookstore or convention, hip-check whoever's next to you out of the way and pay the man what he wants for it. A lot of books

## BRIAN LYNCH, screenwriter/writer, *Spider-Man Unlimited*

### THE FIRST ISSUE OF *SPIDER-MAN* I EVER READ

My first exposure to Spider-Man was either his quick vignettes on *The Electric Company* television show or the cartoon *Spider-Man and His Amazing Friends*. As for the first comic, I was at a yard sale, and there was a comic featuring Spider-Man fighting Man-Wolf that came with a tape featuring actors reading the script, some music and sound effects. I bought it, and was at first disappointed that Iceman and Firestar weren't in it, but soon got caught up in Spider-Man's world.

### THE BEST CREATIVE TIME ON THE TITLE

When the whole "Who is the Hobgoblin?" story arc was going on in the mid-1980s, I couldn't get issues quick enough. Keep in mind there was no Internet back then, so I didn't even know when new Spidey books were coming out. I would go with my mom to the supermarket every week on the off-chance there was a new issue.

### THE BEST COVER

The cover I think of when I think of Spider-Man is Peter Parker walking away from the suit, which has been jammed into a trashcan (*The Amazing Spider-Man* #50). That said, Todd McFarlane always had covers that wowed me. His cover to *Spider-Man* #1 was great, and at the time, the fact that they had two versions of it (one with metallic webs!) blew my little mind. And the next printing had gold webs! Yes, I bought all of them.

### THE BEST STORYLINE/ISSUE

"Kraven's Last Hunt" by J.M. DeMatteis and Mike Zeck was amazing, but more a Kraven story than a Spidey tale. I love the entire Sin-Eater storyline by Peter David and Rich Buckler, and the Hobgoblin arc was great. Venom's intro and the return to the red-and-blue costume (*The Amazing Spider-Man* #300) stands out, too. And while I'm not a fan of the original Clone Saga, the *Ultimate Spider-Man* version of it was a lot of fun.

### THE GOOFIEST STORYLINE/ISSUE

Saying the Clone Saga or "One More Day" is too easy. I think Slyde's first appearance (*The Amazing Spider-Man* #272, January 1986) is pretty goofy (non-stick coating on a super-villain suit? Sure!), but for all-time goofy, I'd go with "The Other." Spider-Man gets into a cocoon, dies, sheds his skin, eats a dude's head, kinda gets new powers. Wait, now I just remembered the Gwen Stacy/Norman Osborn love child arc. I need more time on this . . .

boast something similar in the title, but this one has the goods to back it up. A handsome red leather-bound edition published in 1987, not only does the collection feature Lee/Kirby *Fantastic Four* and *Thor* stories, Roger Stern/John Byrne collaborations on *Hulk* and *Captain America*, a gorgeous Stern/Paul Smith *Doctor Strange* story and a great *X-Men* tale by Chris Claremont and John Romita, Jr., it also contains two of the best Spider-Man stories ever published.

The first is a three-part Master Planner storyline from *The Amazing Spider-Man* #31–33 (December 1965–February 1966), a tense action story pitting Spider-Man against the aforementioned Doctor Octopus, while a gravely ill Aunt May's life hangs in the balance. The second is "The Kid Who Collects Spider-Man," from *Amazing Spider-Man* #248 (January 1984), by Roger Stern and Ron Frenz. In the story, Spider-Man pays a visit to nine-year-old Timothy Harrison, the world's biggest Spider-Man fan. It's easily the most poignant and touching Spider-Man story ever published. If you can't find this collection, go ahead and track down the back issue. It'll be worth the effort.

## CHRIS SAYS

If you delve into Spider-Man's world at all, you're sure to come across references to "the Clone Saga," arguably one of the worst Spider-Man stories of all time, and it committed the compound sin of being a bad idea that dragged on far too long. In it, Spider-Man is replaced by a clone of himself, a plotline flawed from the start and too convoluted to delve into here (we'd prefer that you actually *want* to read comics after you finish this book). The story was Marvel's early-'90s attempt to reinvigorate Spidey's line of comics, and things went seriously awry by implying that the past decade of Spider-Man stories were merely the adventures of a clone. The ham-fisted way they tried to rectify the problem was nearly as bad.

But as with all ongoing comics, if you wait them out long enough, they'll eventually self-correct. Writer Brian Michael Bendis revisited the idea of the clone saga in the Spider-Man reboot series, *Ultimate Spider-Man*, to much greater effect, even though the stink of the previous storyline still hasn't fully faded.

# The Mighty Thor
## *Journey into mystery*

The year was 1962, and Marvel editor Stan Lee was feeling the pressure. Stan had come out of the gate strong: his new comics had been met with unexpected success at the newsstands. *Fantastic Four* and *The Amazing Spider-Man* were not only selling better than anything the company had put out in years, but Stan was achieving critical success unlike anything he'd ever experienced. The fan mail was pouring in (in excess of a thousand letters a week), and Stan and Marvel were suddenly the darling of the press, with Stan and Marvel doing all kinds of print and radio interviews about the new generation of comic-book heroes.

The problem was, now what?

As Stan recounts in *Origins of Marvel Comics*, "But what was left to invent? Who could be stronger than the Hulk? Who could be smarter than Mr. Fantastic? We already had a kid who could fly, one who could walk on walls and ceilings, and a female who could fade away whenever danger threatened – or whenever the artist ran out of ink. As you can see, we were hooked on superlatives at that time, always trying to come up with characters who were bigger, better, stronger. However, we had painted ourselves into a corner. The only one who could top the heroes we already had would be Super-God, but I didn't think the world was quite ready for that concept just yet. So, it was back to the ol' drawing board."

Stan was racking his brain for new heroes, but he kept coming back to the notion of "Super-God." He knew there was no way to feature God in a comic without offending, well, practically everybody. In the midst of all this, Stan remembered a radio interview he had done in which the host had referred to the new Marvel stories as "twentieth-century mythology," comparing them to Greek and Norse mythology. With that, Stan had his solution. Sure, there was no way they could publish a comic book featuring God as a superhero, but a comic book featuring a god as a superhero? No problem. Soon enough, Stan had settled on a mythological deity to receive the Marvel treatment, and the Mighty Thor was on his way.

Feeling that he was handling too much of the company's writing himself, Stan turned over the Thor concept to his brother Larry Lieber, who had been working on the company's line of monster comics. For the art, Stan once again turned to Jack Kirby to bring his rough concept to life. Lee, Lieber and Kirby's vision of the Norse god of thunder made its debut in *Journey Into Mystery* #83 (August 1962) in "The Stone Men From Saturn!"

Dr. Don Blake discovers that the hammer makes the man in Thor's Marvel comic debut.

## IF HE BE WORTHY...

In the premiere story, we're introduced to Dr. Donald Blake, a crippled physician vacationing on the coast of Norway. Coincidentally, also visiting the lovely Norwegian coast are the Stone Men from Saturn. However, they're not there for the scenery. A scouting force for a planned invasion of Earth, the stone chaps amuse themselves by uprooting and disintegrating trees. (A little-known fact: Saturnian Stone Men apparently hate trees.) The Stone Men are spotted by a local fisherman, whose warnings fall on mostly deaf ears, except for our good Dr. Blake, who decides to go investigate for himself.

Blake stumbles upon the aliens, but is quickly spotted, and the Stone Men are soon in hot pursuit. Running for his life, Blake stumbles and drops his cane, which slows him down even more. Seeking refuge in a cave, Blake finds the only way out blocked by an enormous boulder. Leaning against the cave wall, he accidentally activates a hidden trigger, revealing a secret chamber. Inside is only a "gnarled wooden stick – like an ancient cane." When the stick turns out to be of little use in moving the boulder, Blake strikes the stick against the boulder in frustration, and with a flash of lightning, both Blake and the stick are transformed. To his disbelief, Blake is now the Mighty Thor, Norse god of thunder. Looking down at the wooden stick, he sees that it too has changed, becoming a war hammer, bearing a peculiar inscription: "Whosoever holds the hammer, if he be worthy, shall possess the power of Thor."

The boulder that had seemed immovable mere moments before is now lifted with ease, and Thor begins to experiment with his new weapon and physical form. Thor discovers that he must continuously hold the hammer to remain Thor (after sixty seconds without contact, Thor will change back into Blake, although the hammer will remain), and that by striking the hammer against the ground, both he and the hammer return to their original shapes. Thor also discovers the hammer's ability to control the weather, and that it always returns to his hand after it's thrown. Best of all, Thor learns that by throwing the hammer, and then immediately catching the leather thong at the end of the handle, he's able to hurtle through the air like a missile.

Thor's lesson in hammer-handling comes none too soon, because before long the full Saturnian invasion force has arrived in Norway. Thor quickly dispatches the Stone Men's ground troops, and handily dismantles the invaders' "mechano-monster," as well. The Stone Men are freaked, and split for Saturn pronto, not knowing how many more like Thor may be on Earth.

## ENTER THE ASGARDIANS

After the first fourteen issues, the book was placed in the hands of Stan and Jack. Once Stan took over the scripting, a distinct difference was seen in the dialogue: Thor (and later his fellow Asgardians, as well) began to speak in a sort of archaic pseudo-Shakespearean old English, which doesn't make a whole lot of sense considering he was Norwegian, but succeeded in giving the character a sort of regal nobility that served the character well in setting him apart from the rest of Marvel's costume-types.

Early on, Thor focused more on Earth-bound villains and threats, but the series really kicked into gear when Stan and Jack began to center the series around Thor's Asgardian heritage. It is later revealed that Don Blake has never truly existed, that Thor's human identity has all been a lesson in humility from Thor's father, Odin, mightiest of the Norse gods and ruler of Asgard. Despite this, Thor continues to live a double life as both Thor and Blake, partly because of the strong bond he has forged with Midgard (that's Earth for you non-Asgardian types) while in temporary exile from Asgard, and partly because of his love for Blake's nurse, Jane Foster. Thor also finds new allies in Balder the Brave, Thor's loyal right-hand man, and in the beautiful but deadly warrior Sif, Thor's intended bride since childhood.

The central conflict of the series involves Thor and his half-brother Loki, the god of mischief. Bitterly jealous of Thor and longing for Odin's throne, Loki unleashes evil scheme after evil scheme in

### CHRIS SAYS

There's an inscription on the face of Thor's hammer that reads "Whosoever Holds This Hammer, If He Be Worthy, Shall Possess the Power of Thor." Surprisingly, others beyond Thor have proven worthy of hoisting Mjölnir over the years: a horse-faced alien named Beta Ray Bill, Captain America and even Superman (in the *JLA/Avengers* crossover).

efforts to either destroy Thor or discredit him in the eyes of Odin the All-Father. Some of Loki's plots even result in the creation of new foes for Thor to deal with, bruisers such as the Absorbing Man and the Wrecker, who reappear many times over the years.

Besides the Lee/Kirby issues, the most acclaimed run on *Thor* was created by writer/artist Walt Simonson during the mid-1980s. Lasting for thirty issues (#337–367), Simonson brought a new vitality to the series that it hadn't seen in years, and his classic, illustrative art style returned *Thor* to a scope and grandeur that had been missing since the days of Jack Kirby. As for the writing, Simonson brought two sorely needed aspects to the series: a return to the strong emphasis on Norse mythology and a genuine sense that anything could happen—from aliens stealing Thor's hammer to Thor being transformed into a six-foot-tall frog. There have been several notable *Thor* runs since Simonson's, but none that measures up to his ambitious, epic storytelling. Highly recommended.

# Iron Man

## *Isn't it iron-ic*

The best superhero origins are timeless. You can pick them up at any time, and the story and concepts are as fresh as they were the day they were created.

"A shy teenager is bitten by a radioactive spider, and learns a tragic lesson about responsibility."

"Rocketed to Earth from a dying world, a newborn child is raised by Midwestern farmers and grows up to be humanity's greatest champion."

Then there's Iron Man.

Although the basic origin itself can be tinkered with to fit a more current time frame, the original story is, shall we say, problematic, involving as it does the Vietnam War. However, if you look past the dated trappings, there's a concept at its core that still works quite well, and is as relevant today as ever.

Back in 1963, Stan had an idea for a superhero who was also a successful businessman, a jet-setting Howard Hughes type. But Stan's rich protagonist needed a reason to go out in a costume and risk his life fighting bad guys. Once more, Lee put it all together. As he recounts in *Son of Origins of Marvel Comics*, "What if our hero had an injured heart – a heart that required him to wear some sort of metal device to keep it beating? The metal device could be the basic element in an entire suit of armor which could both power him and conceal his identity. I loved it. It had the right ring to it. I knew it would work."

Dubbing his new creation Iron Man, Stan turned over the plot to his brother Larry Lieber, who the previous year had conceptualized Stan's Thor notion, to provide the script. As for the art, Don Heck provided the pencils, as he would for many of the succeeding *Iron Man* adventures. Jack Kirby, meanwhile, contributed the design of the original Iron Man armor, as well as the cover for the debut appearance. Compared to the power of Jack Kirby's work,

Tony Stark's first armor tended to favor function over fashion.

or the sleek dynamism of Steve Ditko's style, some have called Don Heck's work boring or staid, a position with which we heartily disagree. Heck provided a sophistication to the series that fit the high-society feel of the Tony Stark character. Likewise, the streamlined look of Iron Man's armor, as opposed to Marvel's overly muscled superheroes, exemplified Heck's strengths as a draftsman. Lee, Lieber and Heck presented their new creation to the world in *Tales of Suspense* #39 (March 1963), in "Iron Man Is Born!"

Here we meet Tony Stark, a millionaire industrialist who is demonstrating the power of his newfangled "transistors" to the U.S. Army. While in Vietnam to ground-test his new "transistor-powered" mortar cannons, Stark accidentally triggers an explosive booby-trap and is mortally wounded and captured by Wong-Chu, "the red guerrilla tyrant" of South Vietnam. When Wong-Chu's Commie doctors get a hold of Stark, who conveniently has papers identifying himself as "famous Yankee weapons inventor," they determine that shrapnel from the explosion is traveling ever closer to his heart and will kill him within a week. Wong-Chu lies to the injured prisoner, telling Stark that if he builds a new weapon for them, surgeons will save his life. Stark sees through Wong-Chu's ruse, and sets to work creating a chestplate that will keep his damaged heart beating, while also powering a suit of armor that will liberate him from prison.

Stark is assisted by Professor Yinsen, another of Wong-Chu's prisoners, who turns out to be, in the words of Stark himself, "once the greatest physicist of them all." How absolutely convenient. With Yinsen's assistance, Stark completes the armored suit just before the shrapnel reaches his heart. Unfortunately, Wong-Chu and his men approach the cell while the armor is charging and Stark lies helpless. To prevent them from capturing Stark, Yinsen charges into the hallway, distracting the guards at the cost of his own life.

Now fully charged and operational, and with the chestplate keeping him alive, Stark quickly learns to function within his gray iron shell. With the help of the many attachments he and Yinsen built into the armor, Stark eludes his captors in the prison, then goes on to face Wong-Chu. Stark lays a capitalist smackdown on the Commie warlord, and then puts away Wong-Chu for good, blowing up the guerrilla's ammo dump just as he runs toward it.

More than any of the other Marvel comics of the era, *Iron Man* was caught up in the fervor of Cold War America—Iron Man represented the power of American technology and scientific know-how that would quash those backwards Commies. Iron Man's Silver Age rogues' gallery tells the tale, boasting such baddies as the Soviet armored doppelgänger the Crimson Dynamo, the Red Chinese warlord the Mandarin (sporting ten super-powered rings, one for each finger), the Soviet spy known as the Black Widow (who would later defect to the U.S. and become Iron Man's teammate), and another Russian armored-type, Titanium Man.

## CLOTHES MAKE THE MAN

Along the way, Iron Man's armor evolves as well, starting in the second issue. Stark returns to the United States and his playboy lifestyle, and shows off the first of many upgrades, changing color from gray to gold. The most significant upgrade happens in *Tales of Suspense* #48 (December 1963), courtesy of artist Steve Ditko. He put together the sleek, streamlined red and gold ensemble, the most influential in the series' run.  To this day, most new interpretations fall back on Ditko's as a template. For more than twenty years, the only significant alteration to the Ditko suit was in the helmet, which would occasionally feature a forked faceplate, visible rivets and, very briefly, a nose, thanks to artist George Tuska.

The armor's abilities have stayed fairly consistent throughout the series: increased strength and resistance to harm, boot-jets for flight, "repulsor" beams of concussive force from the gloves and a "unibeam" laser from the chest. Occasionally special attachments or add-ons are utilized, from jet boosters for increased speed to roller skates for, well, increased funkitude. Specialized armor is also created for specific situations, such as outer space, underwater depths or stealth missions.

In the 1970s, the Cold War angle is downplayed, and more emphasis is placed on Stark's business interests, and matters of corporate intrigue and sabotage. The issue of Stark's bad heart is finally settled; he receives a synthetic heart in an experimental operation. This takes away a fair amount of the series' central concept, however, namely "the millionaire playboy with the fatal flaw."

## A CHINK IN THE ARMOR

Writer David Michelinie and artist Bob Layton solved this problem with their landmark run in *Iron Man* #120–128 (March–November 1979), "Demon in a Bottle," in which Tony Stark faces up to his alcoholism. In Michelinie's tense thriller, Stark's company is ever so slowly wrested from his grasp, while competing industrialist Justin Hammer frames Iron Man for the murder of a foreign ambassador on live television. Under constant pressure— he loses his company, and Iron Man's reputation is in ruins— Stark increasingly turns to alcohol. He eventually hits rock bottom, then finds the strength to turn away from the bottle. The subject is maturely handled, and Layton's art is clean and appealing. It was first collected in trade back in 1984, and is currently available in hardcover—highly recommended.

His alcoholism is brought back in *Iron Man* #169 (April 1983), in a lengthy storyline by writer Denny O'Neil in which Stark completely loses control of his company (which he had regained after his last bout with alcoholism) and personal fortune to competing businessman Obadiah Stane. Stark suffers a major relapse, and even gives up his Iron Man identity entirely, passing the armor on to his longtime pilot James Rhodes.

Rhodes remains as Iron Man for more than three and a half years, even after Stark sobers up and moves to California. Eventually, in *Iron*

*Man* #200 (November 1985), Stark returns to the armor (albeit one of the ugliest armored suits Iron Man ever wore), and returns to his corporate glories at the helm of Stark Industries. Rhodes is eventually given his own armor and sporadically operates as War Machine.

Tony Stark first confronts his battle with the bottle in an *Iron Man* run by David Michelinie and Bob Layton.

# The Avengers
## *Earth's mightiest heroes*

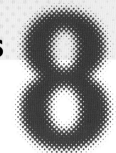

DC Comics may have invented the concept of the "superhero team" with the Justice Society and later the Justice League, but it was never much on refining it. In the DC Universe, superheroes formed super-teams because, well, that's just what superheroes did. Sure, there are rare exceptions such as the Doom Patrol, but they were short-lived. DC had the JLA and its junior version, the Teen Titans, and that is pretty much it.

Marvel, on the other hand, developed distinct identities and purposes for each of its superhero teams. The Fantastic Four are a family, first and foremost. The X-Men are outcasts, banded together by human society's hatred and mistrust. The Defenders, a successful 1970s team book, are a "non-team" consisting of misfits who find themselves hanging together out of a need to belong to something. And the Avengers? The Avengers are the varsity team, the first line of defense, the big guns of the Marvel Universe. Anybody could be a Defender, and no one wanted to be an X-Man, but if you were a superhero and were invited to join the Avengers, you'd made it to the big leagues.

It's this air of prestige and responsibility about the Avengers that helps make them so consistently popular. While the Fantastic Four explore the cosmos and the X-Men look after

their own, the Avengers are in the trenches, saving the world, year in and year out. Combine that with one of the best core memberships in comics and a frequently changing roster, and you get one of the best superhero team series ever published.

Unlike most of Marvel's other Silver Age launches, the Avengers were created as a direct result of fan requests. By 1962, Stan Lee was besieged by requests for more Marvel team-ups, particularly a new collaboration of Marvel's solo stars. Never one to let a good idea pass him by, Stan put his head together with Marvel's master storyteller Jack Kirby, and the two put together their newest team. Here's how Stan tells it in *Son of Origins of Marvel Comics*: "After kicking it around for awhile, we came up with what seemed like a perfect combo. We'd start with the Hulk, just to make it difficult. Then, we'd include Thor, 'cause there's always room for a god of thunder. Iron Man would be able to supply them all with weapons and bread whenever they needed it, and we'd toss in Ant-Man and the Wasp just for the sheer lunacy of it."

Now that a team had been chosen, all that was needed was an origin. After all, said Lee, "it wouldn't make a terribly interesting story merely to have someone send the others a note inviting them to join a group of superheroes." (This, by the way, was the origin of the 1940s Justice Society of America, until a more satisfying origin adventure was retroactively created for the team in the 1970s.) Since a suitably big menace was necessary to bring this powerful a group together, Lee and Kirby opted to use one of their biggest: Loki, the god of evil (or mischief depending on the day) from the *Thor* series.

In *The Avengers* #1 (September 1963), "The Coming of the Avengers," Loki frames the Hulk in an attack on a passenger train, with the hopes of provoking his hated half brother Thor to pursue him. When the Hulk's young sidekick Rick Jones contacts the Fantastic Four via ham radio for assistance in locating the Hulk, Loki jams the signal, diverting it to a frequency he knows Thor's alter ego, Don Blake, to be listening to. However, Loki doesn't realize that others could be listening to the frequency and might answer Rick Jones's call for help, namely Iron Man, Ant-Man and the Wasp.

Soon, Thor, Iron Man, Ant-Man and the Wasp meet up at the southwestern clubhouse of the Teen Brigade, Rick Jones's club of ham radio enthusiasts (don't ask), ready to help track down the Hulk. When Thor is lured away by an illusionary image of the Hulk, he deduces that Loki is involved, and heads to Asgard to track down his half brother. Iron Man, Ant-Man and the Wasp brawl with the Hulk all across the Southwest, until Thor shows up with a captive Loki and reveals that they've all been manipulated.

Before the heroes can go their separate ways, Ant-Man suggests that they continue to work together in the future. Iron Man and Thor agree, as does the Hulk, who remarks, "I'm sick of bein' hunted and hounded! I'd rather be with you than against you!" At the suggestion of the Wasp, the newly formed team dubs itself the Avengers, and there you have it.

The Hulk's naturally suspicious and belligerent nature would eventually win out, and by issue #3, the Hulk is gone from the Avengers for good. With the next issue comes the arrival of the final "founding member:" Captain America. Even though he was not around when the team originated, Captain America has become nearly synonymous with the Avengers over time. In fact, in recognition of this important factor, *Avengers* writer Kurt Busiek later notes that the team has given Cap "founding member" status, granting him a permanent say in all Avengers decisions and policy.

When Captain America joins the Avengers in *The Avengers* #4 (March 1964), his arrival really solidifies the team. The book finds a renewed focus that it had lacked before, both in Captain America's relationship with honorary member Rick Jones, who elicits Cap's memories of his wartime partner Bucky Barnes, and in the team's struggle with Cap's World War II adversary Baron Zemo, who emerges from hiding in South America to seek out revenge on Captain America for the permanent damage to his face.

As any reader of the '70s can tell you, Marvel used to place a caption at the top of the first page of every Marvel comic, giving the new reader a quick explanation of the series' premise. It was quick, elegant and unobtrusive. So rather than try to explain to you the Avengers' "mission statement," as it were, we'll let you learn it the same way we did:

> *"And there came a day, a day unlike any other, when Earth's mightiest heroes and heroines found themselves united against a common threat. On that day, the Avengers were born – to fight the foes no single super-hero could withstand! Through the years, their roster has prospered, changing many times, but their glory has never been denied! Heed the call, then – for now the Avengers Assemble!"*

Everything you need, right there at the top of the page.

The debut issue of *The Avengers*, by Stan Lee and Jack Kirby.

Captain America makes his triumphant, if a little damp, return, after decades on ice.

## THE EARLY DAYS

Over the years, different writers would take the "foes no single super-hero could withstand" in a few different directions. Let's take a look at a few influential *Avengers* writers and some of the important villains and concepts they brought to the table.

First and foremost, of course, we have Avengers creators Stan Lee and Jack Kirby. Kirby's influence past the origin was minimal—only drawing the first eight issues of the entire series—however, those issues were some of Kirby's best action storytelling of the era, and *The Avengers* #3 (January 1964) set a surprising precedent for team books of the time: membership was not fixed. Anybody could leave the team at any time, as evidenced by the Hulk's turning on the Avengers after only three issues. The Avengers' unpredictable nature was reinforced in the very next issue, when the long-absent Captain America joined the team, reuniting Kirby with his most famous Golden Age creation.

Lee and Kirby's *Avengers* #6 introduced another extremely long-running Avengers opponent, the Masters of Evil, made up of enemies of the individual members from their solo series, in this case Iron Man's foe the Melter, Thor's opponent Radioactive Man, and Giant-Man (the first of many name and costume changes for Ant-Man) and the Wasp's sparring partner the Black Knight, led by Cap's old foe Baron Zemo.

After Kirby left, the *Avengers* art duties were taken over by Don Heck, a much maligned penciller who, in our opinion, never gets the respect he's due. Though his action sequences could be a little stiffer than Kirby's, Heck brought a leaner, less musclebound look to the characters, and rendered some of the most consistently gorgeous women in comics. Kirby returned to the series for layouts for one issue only, and what an issue. In *Avengers* #16 (May 1965), Stan set the tone for the Avengers for decades to come with just one story: "The Old Order Changeth!" All the members but Captain America quit the team, leaving Cap with a

The best thing about Roy Thomas's introduction of the killer robot Ultron and the Vision is the way it eventually ties up the Avengers into a sick little dysfunctional family. Follow along:

- Hank "Ant-Man" Pym creates Ultron, who, upon achieving sentience, immediately attacks his creator and subjects him to treatments that remove all memory of the incident.

- Ultron uses the defunct android body of the original 1940s-era Human Torch to create the Vision, and uses the brain patterns of the fallen Avengers ally Wonder Man (which are for some reason recorded by Hank Pym upon Wonder Man's death, in another example of Pym's somewhat cavalier approach to science) to create the Vision's personality and consciousness.

- Vision eventually falls in love with and marries his fellow Avenger the Scarlet Witch.

- When Ultron desires a mate, he kidnaps Hank Pym's wife Janet (the Wasp) in a plan to transplant her persona into an android body (no Oedipal issues here or anything), and although the plan is foiled, the resulting female android, Jocasta, briefly joins the Avengers.

- When Wonder Man returns from the dead, he and the Vision eventually declare themselves "twin brothers," because of the whole "shared brain patterns" deal. However, things get complicated when Wonder Man finds himself attracted to the Scarlet Witch (which makes sense, since the Vision's brain is based on Wonder Man's).

- Ultron allies himself with another Avengers foe, the Grim Reaper, who is the brother of Simon Williams (Wonder Man). The Reaper hates the Vision for bearing his brother's brain patterns, and never accepts the resurrected Wonder Man as his real brother.

trio of reformed supervillains as Avengers, as well as some heavy expectations to fulfill.

## "THE OLD ORDER CHANGETH"

Stan's complete overhaul of the team set up a new dynamic for the series: not only could anyone leave the Avengers, but absolutely anybody could wind up a member. This fluidity of concept allowed the series to adapt to the changes in the industry and the culture far more easily than other team books, and no doubt guaranteed its longevity. In addition, the new team—Captain America, Hawkeye, Quicksilver and the Scarlet Witch—had a "regular guy" persona (Cap, Hawkeye and Quicksilver weren't particularly musclebound) that perfectly meshed with Don Heck's leaner, slimmer figures and linework, and his art flourished.

Roy Thomas took over as writer after Stan left the book and began bringing in new members almost immediately. The most significant of Thomas's additions was the Vision. Though the red-skinned synthezoid (Thomas's term for a synthetic human) was inspired by a Golden Age Timely character in name, the Vision adds a Mr. Spock-like dose of pathos to the team as the cold, emotionless android who secretly yearns for humanity. The Vision's powers are innovative, as well. He can control his body's density, allowing him to float in the air like a wraith and pass through solid objects, or reach maximum density and become as hard as a diamond. Thomas also introduced the Vision's creator, the murderous robot Ultron, who has been in turn created by founding Avenger Hank "Ant-Man" Pym.

A variety of writers helmed *The Avengers* throughout the 1970s and early 1980s, including Steve Englehart, Gerry Conway, David Michelinie, Bill Mantlo and Marvel's then-editor-in-chief Jim Shooter. Working with the last four, if sporadically, was artist George Pérez. His *Avengers* work helped him make a name for himself with his insane attention to detail and ability to deftly handle the rendering of a large cast.

In the late 1980s, writer Roger Stern put out some of the best *Avengers* stories seen in years. Following up the lengthy storyline in which founder Hank Pym is framed and leaves the team, Stern shifted focus to the Wasp, giving her the chairmanship of the team for a lengthy tenure. This move, along with the strong female emphasis from members like the new Captain Marvel, She-Hulk and the Scarlet Witch, took the team in some excellent new directions.

One of the high points of Stern's run was the "Avengers Under Siege" storyline in *The Avengers* # 270–277 (August 1986–March 1987). The son of the original Baron Zemo puts together a massive team of supervillains sixteen or so strong (including such powerhouses as the Wrecking Crew, Mr. Hyde, Goliath and the Absorbing Man), creating the most powerful and dangerous version of the Masters of Evil ever assembled. In a well-planned and coordinated attack, Zemo's new Masters seize Avengers Mansion, beat an inebriated Hercules so badly as to put the immortal demigod into a coma and torture the Avengers' majordomo, Edwin Jarvis, before the eyes of a helpless and enraged Captain America. Only through a daring rescue attempt by the Wasp, the second Ant-Man, Thor and the mentalist Doctor Druid is the Mansion regained and the Masters of Evil captured.

## THE HOME FRONT

A word about Jarvis: part of the reason the notion of a rotating lineup of Avengers works so well is the presence of certain constants in the Avengers' life, whoever they may be, namely, Avengers Mansion and its master, Edwin Jarvis. Rather than using a nameless stereotype as a butler, Avengers writers through the years (particularly Roger Stern and Kurt Busiek) invested Jarvis with a genuine sense of loyalty and duty to the team. Jarvis's presence provides a very human element. Not only is his unflagging loyalty a credit to the Avengers, but his willingness to chastise and encourage them provides a much-needed human element in a roomful of androids, legends, gods and monarchs.

As for the Mansion, it serves a similar purpose. There's a reason the Avengers live in the Mansion and not a shiny chrome HQ—the homey atmosphere grounds the team, allowing the reader to identify with them more easily. Over the years, various writers have tried setting up the Avengers in different compounds, headquarters, embassies and

155

Avengers Mansion: one of the more comfortable super-headquarters.

hydrobases, but they inevitably wind up home at the Mansion.

## THE LINEUP

The core Avengers lineup is so perfect an archetype for the superhero team that parts of it have been lifted over the years and applied to DC's Justice League formula. DC revised Green Arrow as a loudmouth reactionary (mirroring Marvel's hotheaded Hawkeye), added an emotionless android like Marvel's Vision in the Red Tornado, and incorporated the armored scientist Steel in the Iron Man role.

At the center of the core team is Captain America, the human, all-too-mortal touchstone for the team, and the group's natural leader, even when he's not officially serving as chairman (a rotating position that's decided by election).

In the "heavy hitter" roles are Thor and Iron Man, who both add significant muscle to the team. While Thor's status as an Asgardian god lends the team a cachet of mythology and godhood, Iron Man provides the team's solid technological base.

Hank Pym, whether he's Ant-Man, Giant-Man or Yellowjacket, provides the team's hard science and analysis. On the other hand, his fragile mental state, troubled past and diminutive stature give the Avengers a touch of all-too-human vulnerability.

The Wasp adds a lighthearted femininity to the team, and has grown over the years into one of the most capable and dependable members.

The Vision's struggles toward humanity act as a reminder of just what the Avengers are fighting for, and his courtship and eventual marriage to the Scarlet Witch (who balances out the team's scientific emphasis with her sorcerous nature) gives the series some much-needed romance and a sense of family.

Hawkeye's inclusion reinforces the fact that the Avengers aren't just a collection of gods and near-gods, but that a mere mortal with unerring skill and undeniable willpower can contribute to and even lead the team.

Finally, the addition of the wisecracking Beast provides a steady dose of humor to a book that is sometimes too serious for its own good.

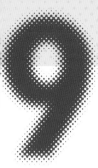

# The X-Men

## Protecting a world that hates and fears them

A runaway hit in comics shops in the 1980s and '90s and movie theaters in 2000, 2003 and 2006, the X-Men have been heavy hitters in Marvel's lineup for decades. However, it's easy to forget that for much of the series' existence, the X-Men were distant third-stringers in the Marvel Universe, with their comic book often relegated to reprints and even a lengthy stretch in cancellation. Much like one of its members, the X-Men would eventually rise from the ashes to become one of the company's most popular and profitable books, leading Marvel's expansion into toys, animation and the silver screen.

The X-Men first appeared in *The X-Men* #1 (September 1963), yet another creation of Marvel's Silver Age team supreme, writer/editor Stan Lee and artist/storyteller Jack Kirby. *The X-Men* starts off with a deceptively simple premise, and one that still holds much significance to this day. Professor Charles Xavier, the most powerful mutant telepath on the planet, founds Xavier's School for Gifted Youngsters, a haven for children born just a little different—as mutants.

Later defined as *Homo superior*, mutants are those born with extra powers or abilities that normal humans lack. At Xavier's School, these children can learn to use their powers safely, without fear of persecution from a world that is growing more and more fearful of mutants. After sufficiently mastering their powers, Professor Xavier's students often continue to serve their mentor as members of the X-Men, protecting the world against the machinations of other mutants who do not share Xavier's enlightened philosophy. Rather than co-existing peacefully with normal humans, these "evil" mutants seek conquest.

Lee's premise is ingenious on a number of levels. The central theme of the series, young people ostracized for being different, is a perfect metaphor for the isolation and sense of removal most teens feel going through adolescence. Further, the series' continuing message of tolerance translates to readers of all races, faiths and orientations.

In his book *Son of Origins of Marvel Comics*, Stan relates how, when he was dreaming up this new team book, he was having trouble coming up with fresh and exciting ways for his heroes to gain their superpowers. Utilizing the idea of mutation seemed a great, easy way to get a series going without devoting a lot of time to an origin. As Lee put it, "Whatever power we conceived of could be justified on the basis of its being a mutated trait." In fact, Stan wanted to title his new book *The Mutants*, but Marvel's then-publisher, Martin Goodman, ixnayed the idea, feeling that little kids wouldn't understand the title. Sent back to the drawing board, Lee reasoned that since mutants are people with something "extra," these "extra-people" could be dubbed the X-Men.

The original team is close to what moviegoers have seen: Professor Xavier, of course, Scott Summers as Cyclops, and Jean Grey, then referred to as Marvel Girl. Other members include Bobby Drake, whose ability to generate and control snow and ice earns him the nickname Iceman; Henry McCoy, referred to as the Beast for his apelike build and oversized hands and feet; and trust-fund rich boy Warren Worthington III, better known as the Angel because of his enormous feathered wings. Joining the team later are Cyclops's brother Alex, who generates concussive bolts of energy as Havok, and his girlfriend Lorna Dane (also known as Polaris), who is able to control the forces of magnetism.

The series wasn't a big hit like Spider-Man and the Fantastic Four. The book suffered through some lackluster art by Werner Roth after Kirby left the book, and although writer Roy Thomas and artist Neal Adams did some outstanding work starting in 1969, it wasn't enough to save the series. *The X-Men* was canceled after issue #66 in 1970, with reprints published for another twenty-five issues.

## ALL-NEW, ALL-DIFFERENT

In 1974, a suggestion was made by then-Marvel President Al Landau to introduce an international team of superheroes that could then be sold in various countries. Marvel's editor-in-chief at the time, Roy Thomas, felt this request could serve as an excellent means of reviving the X-Men, and assigned writer Len Wein and artist Dave Cockrum to create the "all-new, all-different" international X-Men. Of course, by the time the book was published, the "international publishing" directive had been abandoned, and many of the characters came from countries that would never have been a viable publishing market for Marvel. But who cared? The X-Men were back and creatively stronger than ever. In *Giant-Size X-Men* #1 (May 1975), Len Wein and Dave Cockrum introduced comics fans to seven new X-Men. Aside from the returning Professor Xavier and Cyclops, there were the Russian Colossus, the Canadian Wolverine, the German Nightcrawler, the Japanese Sunfire, the Irish Banshee, the African Storm and the Native-American Thunderbird.

The series resumed publication where it left off, with issue #94 (August 1975). After just two issues, Wein was promoted to editor-in-chief. He left the series and turned over the scripting to newcomer Chris Claremont, who went on to write the series for sixteen years. It was in Claremont's hands that the series really coalesced into what most people think of when you say "X-Men." Claremont developed subplotting that carried storylines through years of advancement, and created an ever-shifting and evolving cast of characters. He also had a willingness to tell big stories and break many of the conventions of Marvel's comics up to that point (such as killing off main characters or portraying heroes that weren't always entirely heroic). Most important, though, he placed an emphasis on character. Sure, what the X-Men did made them interesting to read about, but it was *who they were* that kept readers coming back.

## CLAREMONT AND BYRNE

If Chris Claremont gave the X-Men heart, then without a doubt it was the team of Claremont and artist John Byrne that gave the series what it had lacked: star quality. By 1979, *The Uncanny X-Men* was really starting to pick up steam as one of Marvel's most popular series. *The Uncanny X-Men* combined tense, action-packed drama with Claremont's keen characterization, illustrated with heart and flair by Byrne, who was providing some of the best art of his career. The Claremont-Byrne team hit its zenith with issues #129–138 (1980), known nowadays as "The Dark Phoenix Saga." There's a lot going on in these issues. New characters are introduced, particularly Kitty Pryde, the new "kid sister" for the team. Wolverine is brought even more to the forefront as the X-Men's lethal loose cannon. And most significantly, the team is changed forever as Jean Grey finds herself unable to control her ever-growing power as the Phoenix, and elects to commit suicide before the horrified eyes of her lover, Scott Summers.

This was heavy stuff, and a breakthrough story in a lot of ways for Marvel. Aside from its mature handling of such issues as Scott and Jean's romance and Wolverine's lethal tenden-

cies, there hadn't been a series that killed off one of its main characters permanently (at least it was expected to be permanent, and was treated as such for a decade or so), and this monumental, now-classic turn of events almost didn't happen. As the story goes, the creators' original intention was not to kill Jean off, but instead to psychically neuter her, rendering her completely powerless. However, when penciller Byrne drew the sequence of Phoenix consuming a sun in a far-off galaxy, he included scenes of the planet of the "asparagus people," as he later called them, being destroyed in the process. When then-editor-in-chief Jim Shooter saw this, he insisted that the Phoenix be killed off as a consequence of her actions, refusing to publish a series featuring a genocidal mass-murderer as a hero. Under heavy editorial pressure from above, Claremont and Byrne reluctantly altered the finale of their story: in the new ending, a remorseful Jean commits suicide to save the planet from herself.

The Scott Summers–Jean Grey romance hit a climax here that is never quite reached again, even after Jean is resurrected and the characters marry in the mid-1990s. Claremont does a remarkable job at bringing Scott's emotions to the forefront (primarily through his concern for Jean's welfare), and the few moments of peace and happiness Scott and Jean manage to claim for themselves are all the sweeter because of Scott's near-constant worry over Jean's rapidly developing powers. It's a tough thing to sell a romance as believable in the comic-book pages, but between Claremont's words and Byrne's renderings, they manage to pull it off, making Scott's grief all the more palpable.

## AGE OF MUTANTS

There's a lot here to admire besides the Jean Grey storyline. The introduction of Kitty Pryde helps to fill the void created by the loss of Jean, reconnecting the book with its original school-based concept by injecting a much-needed dose of youth and vitality into a school that by now is populated almost entirely by adults. Thanks to Claremont's charming characterization and Byrne's appeal-

ing design, Miss Pryde becomes one of the series' most popular characters and remains a mainstay of the book for the next fifteen years or so.

While not yet remotely the breakout star of the book he would eventually become, Wolverine comes into the forefront for the first time during the "Dark Phoenix Saga," exhibiting more and more of the lethal ferocity that would eventually make the character famous. The introduction of the Hellfire Club also adds a steady stream of new stories and adversaries, while the suggestive S&M-influenced attire of

A prominent scene from the landmark Claremont/Byrne "Dark Phoenix Saga." Jean Grey makes the ultimate sacrifice to save her lover, her friends and the whole planet.

Emma Frost and the Black Queen adds a hint of sexiness to the series without crossing the line for an all-ages book.

Wolverine's transition into more of a starring role in *The Uncanny X-Men* begins in "The Dark Phoenix Saga" as well, but no one could have predicted just how much the homicidal little Canuck would really catch on with fans. In the years that followed, Wolverine's mysterious backstory was ever-so-slowly fleshed out, revealing both a noble side, as recounted in his adventures in Japan in the pages of Chris Claremont and Frank Miller's extremely popular *Wolverine* miniseries, and a tortured origin, as revealed in Barry Windsor-Smith's "Weapon X," which explains the excruciating process behind the implantation of Wolverine's adamantine skeleton. While his popularity remains strong, at times eclipsing Spider-Man as the company's most popular character, the continual morass of revised origins, false memories and newly revealed secrets have taken away much of Wolverine's cool "man-of-mystery" sheen.

Though Byrne left only a few months after the end of the Phoenix story, Claremont would stay on the series for another decade and contribute many excellent stories and characters to the ever-growing X-Universe. Still, the "Dark Phoenix Saga" remains the crown jewel in the X-Men library.

## CHRIS SAYS

Chris Claremont's tenure on the book was marked by collaborations with remarkable artists, many of whom had their first Marvel work published within the pages of *X-Men*. In his time, Chris produced his very best work with rising star John Byrne, who catapulted to superstardom on the book even as Claremont did. There was also Dave Cockrum, who launched the new version of the X-Men before Byrne and got even more attention for his return to the title after Byrne left; and newcomer Paul Smith, who followed Cockrum and became an immediate smash. Other fledgling talents such as John Romita Jr., Marc Silvestri and Jim Lee also went on to become superstars following their work on the title. This good fortune followed Claremont to other X-titles, too, where he worked with future fan-favorites Bill Sienkiewicz, Michael Golden, Butch Guice, Kyle Baker and Art Adams.

Part V

# AROUND THE FOUR-COLOR WORLD

*Wherein the publishers of the past and the present come together; history is made, books are recommended, awards are detailed, and publishing titans of yesteryear and present day get their due.*

# Disney Comics

## *The mouse's house*

Back in the 1930s, Walt Disney was quick to move his characters into the then wildly popular medium of newspaper strips, with Mickey Mouse receiving his own strip in 1930 and Donald Duck following suit in 1938. As comic books began gaining popularity in the late 1930s, Disney, never one to miss out on a promotional opportunity, licensed the comic-book rights to his characters to Western Publishing, who first reprinted the newspaper material in Dell Comics's *Four Color* in 1940. When the Disney features in *Four Color* met with overwhelmingly positive response, Western debuted in October of that same year *Walt Disney's Comics and Sto-*ries, soon followed by solo magazines *Mickey Mouse* and *Donald Duck*.

When talking about Disney comic books, there's only one name you really need to know, and that's the man for years known to Disney comics fans only as "The Good Duck Artist" (since all the work in the Disney comics was uncredited): Carl Barks.

Beginning in the 1930s, Barks labored for years in anonymity working on Dell's line of Walt Disney comics, not only writing and drawing dozens of pages per month for decades but also creating the familiar characters Uncle Scrooge, the Beagle Boys, Gladstone Gander, Gyro Gearloose and many more.

Barks first found success on the *Donald Duck* series, where he introduced Scrooge McDuck—Donald's hyper-fantasticatillionaire uncle—an industrialist tycoon who is constantly dragging Donald and his nephews on globe-trotting adventures to either protect his fortune or expand it. The scripts and art in these comics are first-rate and marvelous. Barks excelled at both physical comedy and high adventure, and gave Donald much more of a personality here than he ever had in the cartoons.

Aside from gorgeous backgrounds and authentic, painstakingly researched details, Barks's true gift as a comic-book artist was his

Carl Barks's Scrooge had his priorities firmly in place.

ability to so convincingly wring emotions from his ducks, creating characterizations deeper and more keenly felt than anything found in more "grown-up" comics of the time.

It was only after Barks's retirement in the 1970s that he finally received recognition for his work, as determined fans, now grown, learned his identity and tracked him down. By producing oil paintings of his duck characters that became big hits in galleries nationwide, he earned the well-deserved financial success that had eluded him for most of his life. Barks passed away in 2000 at the age of ninety-nine. Thankfully, his work is once again available to an American audience with Gemstone Publishing's new *Donald Duck* and *Uncle Scrooge* comics, which each month offer a steady diet of Barks reprints.

The modern inheritor of Barks's throne is writer and artist Don Rosa. A lifelong fan of Barks's *Uncle Scrooge* comics, he painstakingly crafts masterful sequels to many of Barks's classic Scrooge tales, as well as fills in the gaps from Barks's stories of Scrooge's younger days in his critically acclaimed twelve-part series *The Life and Times of Scrooge McDuck*. Rosa's work is sharply written and beautifully drawn with a sparkling wit and a charming tendency to sprinkle the panels with cute little animals peeking out of nooks and crannies.

Although Rosa is acclaimed throughout Europe as a top talent and masterful storyteller, he remains somewhat unknown here in his home country. For many years, Disney comics were unavailable because of Disney's difficulties with earlier licensees and its own failed attempt to start its own comics imprint. Thankfully, Disney's current comics licensee Gemstone gives Rosa's work the respect it deserves, publishing collected versions of *Scrooge McDuck*, as well as a series of smaller graphic novels containing a Carl Barks classic and its Don Rosa sequel.

Disney's duck comics are popular in other parts of the world. In Finland, it's tradition to purchase a subscription to *Donald Duck* for children when they are born.

# Image Comics

## Image central casting

When Image Comics first formed in 1992, it was comprised of six studios run by Image's partners (a seventh creator involved in the company's start-up, Whilce Portacio, never became a full partner or owned his own studio):

1. Extreme Studios, run by Rob Liefeld

2. Highbrow Entertainment, run by Erik Larsen

3. ShadowLine, run by Jim Valentino

4. Todd McFarlane Productions, run by Todd McFarlane

5. Top Cow Productions, run by Marc Silvestri

6. Wildstorm Productions, run by Jim Lee

Rob Liefeld's *Youngblood,* Erik Larsen's *The Savage Dragon,* Todd McFarlane's *Spawn* and Jim Lee's *WildC.A.T.s* enjoyed record-breaking sales and multimedia attention upon their launches, and toys and animated series spun out of the comics to varying degrees of success. In *Spawn*'s case, the toys were such a huge success that they became a major component of Todd McFarlane Productions. McFarlane's toy line, known for its attention to detail and authentic likenesses, has expanded to include many movie characters, sports figures and musicians, among others. In addition, *Spawn* inspired an HBO animated series and became a major motion picture.

*Youngblood, WildC.A.T.s* and *The Savage Dragon* had short-lived animated series, as well. Of these titles launched in 1992, only *Spawn* and *The Savage Dragon* are still published regularly, and only *Dragon* is still written and illustrated by its creator, Erik Larsen.

In the intervening years, Image has published hundreds of new comics from other high-profile creators and expanded far beyond its origins. Sam Kieth's *The Maxx* was an early favorite. Kieth's distinctive, moody art style first caught fans' attention in Neil Gaiman's *Sandman* series for DC. With *The Maxx*, Kieth also tackled writing chores, co-writing with William Messner-Loebs at the start. The series eventually inspired a thirteen-episode animated series that aired on MTV.

Kurt Busiek, Brent Anderson and Alex Ross's *Astro City* was a hugely popular Image series. *Astro City*, a superhero title set in its titular city, has one distinct difference between it and many other superhero titles: it focuses as much on the regular people in the city and their perceptions of the heroics going on around them as it does on the caped and costumed figures.

As the different studios expanded their respective lines, there was talk of integrating the different universes into one, which would allow all the different titles and characters to cross over into one another. But by then, the sort of fare Image was offering was so diverse and widespread that doing so didn't make sense.

Image books have been created by many superstar writers and artists, but none has been bigger than *Watchmen* writer Alan Moore. Moore released the retro-leaning series *1963* before taking over writing chores on several Image titles, including Rob Liefeld's *Youngblood* spin-off, *Supreme*. His work on *Supreme* used many ideas Moore originally developed for DC's *Superman*, and functioned as a running commentary on superhero comics even as it celebrated their clichés. Though *Supreme* was at times dogged by lackluster artwork as other artists aped Liefeld's style to lesser effect, it remains one of the most unique comic-book runs ever released.

Along the way, the company established smaller imprints under its partner studios, too. Jim Valentino brought on many new creator-owned titles, offering new creators full ownership of their characters in exchange for an upfront administrative fee. Some of the founding partners have moved on, and today Image Comics consists of three partner studios: Image Central, Todd McFarlane Productions and Top Cow Productions.

While sales of Image titles don't approach the staggering levels of its heyday, newer titles such as *Invincible, The Walking Dead, Casanova, Fell, NYC Mech* and the Frazetta comics line, along with transplanted titles such as *True Story, Swear to God*, keep the company's offerings as diverse and interesting as ever.

---

## RECOMMENDED READING 101
### IMAGE COMICS

*Astro City: Life In the Big City* by Kurt Busiek, Brent Anderson and Alex Ross

*Gen¹³: Who They Are and How They Came to Be* by Jim Lee, Brandon Choi and J. Scott Campbell

*Invincible: Family Matters* by Robert Kirkman and Cory Walker

*Liberty Meadows: Eden* by Frank Cho

*Mage: The Hero Defined* by Matt Wagner

*Rising Stars: Born in Fire* by J. Michael Straczynski

*The Savage Dragon Archives*, Vol. 1 by Erik Larsen

*ShadowHawk: Out of the Shadows* by Jim Valentino

*Spawn: Beginnings* by Todd McFarlane

*Supreme: The Story of the Year* by Alan Moore

*The Walking Dead* by Robert Kirkman

*WildC.A.T.s: Covert Action Teams* by Jim Lee and Brandon Choi

*Youngblood* #1 by Rob Liefeld

## 3

# Dark Horse Comics

## *Presenting Dark Horse*

Portland, Oregon-based Dark Horse Comics was the brainchild of Mike Richardson, a local comic retailer. Richardson owned and operated a number of stores in the Oregon area before deciding to jump into the publishing game. As a retailer, Richardson recognized the dearth of quality non-superhero titles, and in 1986, he pooled funds from his stores to launch the publishing division with two titles, *Dark Horse Presents* and *Boris the Bear*. The first of the two, *Dark Horse Presents*, was an anthology series that gave birth to such acclaimed series as Paul Chadwick's *Concrete* and Frank Miller's *Sin City*.

*Concrete* tells the tale of a congressional speechwriter who finds himself transformed into a bulky stone giant. Rather than turning into the standard superhero action smash-'em-up, *Concrete* develops into a thoughtful, wistful examination of the human condition, as the title character looks for ways to give his life meaning while longing for his lost humanity. As for *Sin City*, after breaking from DC, artist Frank Miller was finally free to tell the kind of hard-boiled crime stories he'd been longing to create. Both *Sin City* the comic and the movie co-directed by Miller became smash hits.

Following Dark Horse's success with creator-owned titles, the company began publishing licensed comics based on successful science-fiction movies, starting with *Aliens* in 1988, followed by *Predator* in 1989. It soon signed on as the comic publisher for *Star Wars*, a license Dark Horse has held for close to two decades, publishing hundreds of comics

Dark Horse founder Mike Richardson's creation *The Mask* was next worn by Jim Carrey in the 1994 film.

based on the property and expanding George Lucas's universe into exciting new areas.

The classic comic-book staple—the crossover—was used to great effect by Dark Horse. The company paired up two of its film licenses in one title, leading to the successful *Aliens vs. Predator* comic in 1989. The comic book was so well-received that it kick-started a fan push for a movie of the same name, which culminated in two big-screen efforts. *The Mask*, a title created by Richardson in 1982, became a Jim Carrey vehicle in 1994. Meanwhile, Dark Horse carried on with other new titles, licensed comics such as Joss Whedon's *Buffy the Vampire Slayer* and Robert E. Howard's *Conan*, and creator-owned titles such as Stan Sakai's long-running *Usagi Yojimbo*.

The company helped strike a blow for creators' rights in the early 1990s, offering enough creative freedom and ownership to high-profile creators that some of the industry's top talent left Marvel and DC to create all-new titles for Dark Horse, including Frank Miller and Dave Gibbons's *Give Me Liberty*, John Byrne's *Next Men* and Mike Mignola's *Hellboy*. *Hellboy* has proven

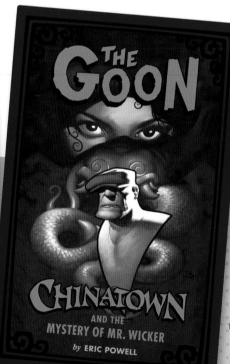

Does this look like an image that could launch a big-screen film franchise? Thankfully, yes.

Eric Powell's *The Goon* tops many recommended reading lists, and ours is no different.

especially successful, leading to numerous spin-offs and two major motion picture adaptations. Similarly, two properties Frank Miller created for the company, *Sin City* and *300*, have also been turned into successful and acclaimed movies.

Further adding to the company's portfolio is Dark Horse's early championing of Japanese manga in the American comic market. Manga is big business here now, but at the time the company first signed on to bring translated versions of these black-and-white comics to our shores, it was anything but a safe bet. Early editions of acclaimed, long-running series such as *Lone Wolf and Cub* have sold huge numbers in America.

Dark Horse continues to expand upon its wide array of titles through recent offerings—a line of novels based on licensed characters and their own creations, independent films, and new comics such as *Buffy* creator Joss Whedon's *Sugar Shock*, singer Gerard Way's *The Umbrella Academy* and Robert E. Howard's *Pigeons From Hell*.

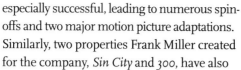

**CHRIS SAYS**

When Dark Horse took on the *Star Wars* license, it brought a new level of gravitas to the material that the Marvel Comics of the late 1970s never had. And at the same time, licensed books seemed to enter a more serious, less playful phase, too. Don't get me wrong: the comics were great—they needed to get serious for the long-term viability of the license. But while this new material was more faithful to the movies and novels, the Marvel comics, well, they featured, among other things, a giant green gun-totin' rabbit palling around with Han Solo. You just don't get that same level of whimsy and playfulness nowadays. Although maybe that's a good thing.

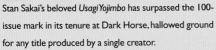

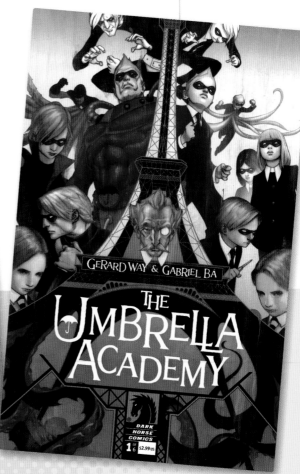

Stan Sakai's beloved *Usagi Yojimbo* has surpassed the 100-issue mark in its tenure at Dark Horse, hallowed ground for any title produced by a single creator.

With *The Umbrella Academy*, My Chemical Romance lead singer Gerard Way is one of the few rock stars to aspire to be a comic book writer.

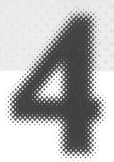

# Bone

## Tickling your phoney bone

Every now and then a book comes along and completely takes you by surprise, a perfect blend of influences that coalesce to create something entirely new, yet so distinctive, you can't imagine it being any different. In the early 1990s, that book would have been *Bone*, the series self-published by writer/artist Jeff Smith.

Smith, a self-taught cartoonist, first conceived the characters that would populate *Bone* in a daily comic strip entitled *Thorn* for the student newspaper *The Lantern* at Ohio State University. A polished version made its debut in 1991 with the release of *Bone* #1, the first issue of Smith's self-published comic book. Almost immediately, *Bone* became a cult sensation. Smith's confident cartoony style and sharp wit immediately won over readers as they got to know Smith's trio of protagonists, three rounded, cartoony creatures known as the Bone cousins—Fone Bone (the friendly, even-tempered everyman), Phoney Bone (the scheming, greedy instigator) and Smiley Bone (the dopey, happy-go-lucky doofus).

Exiled from their hometown of Boneville thanks to one of Phoney's get-rich-quick

A rat creature sneaks up on our hero Fone Bone in Jeff Smith's *Bone*.

schemes gone awry, the Bone cousins find themselves in a mysterious forested valley populated by foul rat creatures, talking bugs and humans. One human in particular, the beautiful blonde Thorn, immediately becomes the unrequited love of Fone Bone's life.

Equal parts Carl Barks's *Uncle Scrooge*, Walt Kelly's *Pogo* and J.R.R. Tolkien's *The Lord of the Rings*, *Bone* manages to achieve a precarious mix of farce, sweet romance, slapstick and high adventure, as the Bone cousins adjust to life in the valley among the humans, and eventually become drawn into a battle against evil most foul—all while avoiding stupid, stupid rat creatures and occasionally enjoying some breakfast cakes. The influence of Walt Kelly's *Pogo* is particularly apparent with Smith's three main characters, Fone Bone, Phoney Bone and Smiley Bone, who bear more than a slight resemblance in personality and appearance to Kelly's Pogo Possum, Porky Pine and Albert Alligator.

Early on, the series is primarily played to comedic effect, with the storylines often revolving around Phoney's attempt to take financial advantage of their new human neighbors—in one, he attempts to "fix" the village's annual Great Cow Race. Later on, the storylines get much darker and more serious, with the introduction of some creepy villains like Kingdok, the leader of the rat creatures, and the Hooded One, servant of the Lord of the Locusts. The shift in tone from comedy to dark fantasy is a little unexpected, but Smith handles the transition so adroitly, the reader never misses a beat.

Smith had long envisioned *Bone* as a finite story, and brought the series to an end with issue #55 (2004). The series continues to be popular in collections, available in black-and-white graphic novels, a truly mammoth "One Volume" single collection, and its current re-release in colorized collections from Scholastic Books. *Bone* has also found its way to action figures, video games and several attempts at a feature film, none of which has quite found its way to fruition. But with a story so fun and characters so lovable, it's only a matter of time.

---

## RECOMMENDED READING 101

### BONE

Bone One Volume Edition
Bone Volume 1: Out From Boneville
Bone Volume 2: The Great Cow Race
Bone Volume 3: Eyes of the Storm
Bone Volume 4: The Dragonslayer
Bone Volume 5: Rock Jaw
Bone Volume 6: Old Man's Cave
Bone Volume 7: Ghost Circles
Bone Volume 8: Treasure Hunters

---

### SCOTT SAYS

One of the most immediately addictive facets of *Bone* is Jeff Smith's exquisite comedic timing, often employed through the pacing of panels and dialogue. In a favorite sequence from an early issue, Fone Bone, who is running from the monstrous rat creatures, finds refuge at the end of a long branch, hanging off the side of a cliff. Relieved, Fone Bone remarks to himself, "Those rat creatures would have to be pretty stupid to follow me on to this frail, little branch." Cut to the next panel, with the two rat creatures now hanging on the end of the branch, which is about to snap away, as Fone Bone yells "Stupid, stupid rat creatures!!" I was hooked.

# Top Shelf Productions

## Top of the pops

Independent comic companies need two things to really stand out in a world so dominated by the two biggest companies' superhero lines: intelligent, innovative titles and proper promotion to help expose the books to fans. Top Shelf Productions, a Marietta, Georgia-based publisher, has both.

Top Shelf's owners, Brett Warnock and Chris Staros, had these two needs in mind from the start of the company in 1995. Staros, an agent representing international artists and author of *The Staros Report*, an annual

*Too Cool to Be Forgotten* is the latest project from Alex Robinson, creator of one of Chris's all-time favorites, *Box Office Poison*.

exploration of the best comics released in a given year, hooked up with Warnock, who that year had self-published a book called *Top Shelf*, an anthology featuring creations from talented newcomers.

The company launched its first title in 1997, Pete Sickman-Garner's *Hey, Mister*, but it was the publication of writer/artist Craig Thompson's *Good-Bye, Chunky Rice* that really established the company as a champion of comics as a literary art form. *Rice* is a poignant story of friendship and loneliness about a turtle who leaves behind his best friend, a skittish mouse, as he goes off to follow his dreams. The story's sensitive writing and whimsical artwork captivated its readers and won the company a Harvey Award.

Top Shelf gained further acclaim when it agreed to distribute *From Hell*, the acclaimed graphic novel by creators Alan Moore and Eddie Campbell. This incredibly detailed, beautifully illustrated (and very long—572 pages) look at the possible secret behind Jack the Ripper won numerous awards.

A sign of fandom's appreciation for Top Shelf occurred in 2002 when one of the company's primary bookstore distributors went under, causing severe problems for Top Shelf. In desperate need of quick support, the company went public with this news, and

TOO COOL TO BE FORGOTTEN: © 2008 BY ALEX ROBINSON. PUBLISHED BY TOP SHELF PRODUCTIONS.

fandom responded in a big way. In less than twelve hours, the company's fan support was great enough to pull Top Shelf through this financial difficulty.

Top Shelf continues to take creative risks that proves successful and creatively inspiring at the same time. Its line of books has expanded to include projects such as Craig Thompson's sensitive coming-of-age *Blankets*, James Kochalka's *American Elf*, as well as Jeffrey Brown's *Clumsy*, Alex Robinson's *Box Office Poison* and Andy Runton's *Owly*. Rather than relying on only bookstore distribution, Top Shelf does considerable business every year through comic conventions.

In 2006, the company took its biggest risk and produced its biggest success yet: the publication of Alan Moore and Melinda Gebbie's *Lost Girls*. *Lost Girls* is celebrated creator Alan Moore's erotic graphic novel series that details the sexual awakening of three literary characters: Dorothy Gale from *The Wonderful Wizard of Oz*, Wendy Darling from *Peter Pan* and Alice from *Alice's Adventures in Wonderland*. The book might seem like a safe bet now, since any new project from Moore is met with headlines, positive press and immense fan support. But at the time, it was a big gamble for Top Shelf, since just the printing costs for the three oversized, slipcased hardcover volumes were astronomical.

Though the success of the book was anything but assured—the controversial content has caused concerns about child pornography, incest and other themes (Moore himself even

Jeff Lemire's second of three *Essex County* books experiences middle-chapter syndrome.

## THE COMIC BOOK LEGAL DEFENSE FUND

Another way in which Top Shelf co-founder Chris Staros supports the comic-book industry is through his work with the Comic Book Legal Defense Fund. Staros serves as president for the non-profit organization dedicated to the preservation of First Amendment rights for members of the comics community. The CBLDF has been in existence since 1986 and has diligently fought against censorship, raising funds for court battles and holding benefits for creators, retailers and fans. The organization offers membership for just twenty-five dollars a year, and the donations are of vital importance to the organization and to the industry in general. The fund's website, www.cbldf.org, offers full information on its many efforts to ensure comics' long-term viability and freedom.

referred to the book as "pornography"), and it has a high retail cost ($75)—the first two printings of the book both sold out on the day of release. The book has gone on to be a steady seller and creative success. While the furor over the book's release has faded, the entire experience served to typify Top Shelf's approach to business—the company is willing to take great chances as it continues on with its mission to advance comic books as an art form. Happily, the market supports this approach and Top Shelf continues on unabated.

### RECOMMENDED READING 101

#### TOP SHELF

*American Elf* by James Kochalka

*Blankets* by Craig Thompson

*Box Office Poison* by Alex Robinson

*Clumsy* by Jeffrey Brown

*Essex County* Trilogy by Jeff Lemire

*From Hell* by Alan Moore and Eddie Campbell

*Incredible Change-Bots* by Jeffrey Brown

*Lost Girls* by Alan Moore and Melinda Gebbie

*Owly* by Andy Runton

*Super Spy* by Matt Kindt

*The Surrogates* by Robert Venditti and Brett Weldele

*Too Cool to Be Forgotten* by Alex Robinson

## THE AWARDS

Top Shelf is also a perennial contender for comic-book awards. There are many such awards that are handed out to comic books and graphic novels, everything from the *Wizard* magazine Fan Awards to the Lulu Awards (given out to female creators) and even the very occasional Pulitzer Prize. These are the primary awards handed out to comic creators and cartoonists.

**THE REUBEN AWARDS** The Reuben Award is given to the Outstanding Cartoonist of the Year by the National Cartoonists Society, the world's largest and most prestigious organization of professional cartoonists. Named after Reuben "Rube" Goldberg, the award has been in existence since 1954, longer than any other comic-book award. Division awards also are given in dozens of categories, including excellence in the fields of newspaper strips, illustration, greeting cards, feature animation and comic books. All members of the society vote on Cartoonist of the Year, but division awards are chosen by both general society and separate juries overseen by the regional chapters.

**THE EISNER AWARDS—** formally called the Will Eisner Comic Industry Awards, but referred to informally as "the comic-book Oscars"— replaced the Kirby Awards in 1987. Will Eisner presided over the awards until his passing in 2005. The categories are nominated by a rotating five-person panel and then voted on by comic-book industry professionals. The winners are awarded at a ceremony at Comic-Con International: San Diego every summer.

**THE HARVEY AWARDS**, named after writer/artist Harvey Kurtzman, was the second awards show to be created out of the disbanding of the Kirby Awards in 1987. The Harveys also award achievement in comic books, although, unlike the Eisners, the nominees are chosen by any comic-book professionals, who then also vote on the winners. The winners are traditionally awarded at a ceremony at a comic convention. The location of the award ceremony has changed over the years, but has taken place at the Baltimore Comic-Con since 2006.

**THE IGNATZ AWARDS** are named for creator George Herriman's influential *Krazy Kat* newspaper strip (one of the lead characters in the strip was a mouse, Ignatz) and recognize outstanding achievement from small-press or indie comic creators. The nominees are named by a five-panel jury, and the winners are voted on by attendees at the annual Small Press Expo (SPX).

**THE EAGLE AWARDS** are the primary U.K. comic-book awards. They have been in existence since 1976 and are named after a popular 1950s U.K. comic magazine of the same name. These awards are open to fandom, both for nominations and voting on the winners. The awards are given out during the annual Comic Expo held every spring in Bristol.

# 6 IDW Publishing

## *Designing an idea that works*

Sometimes, the best-laid plans of a start-up company can take an unexpected turn and lead to even better things. Such was the case for IDW Publishing, a company that began with no plans to publish comic books.

A decade ago, four people—Ted Adams, Robbie Robbins, Kris Oprisko and Alex Garner, all of whom had years of experience in the comic-book industry—formed Idea and Design Works (IDW) as a full-service graphic design company. In 1999, they experimented with publishing, releasing the art book *Uno Fanta*, created by artist Ashley Wood, though they had no real intentions of publishing comic books on a regular basis.

Plans changed in 2001. Writer Steve Niles and artist Ben Templesmith, two friends of the partners, approached them about taking on a comic that had been rejected by nearly every other comic publisher: *30 Days of Night*. Although the book has become the company's flagship title and a solid success story, its beginnings were more humble.

The first issue featured a cover by Ashley Wood and debuted to little fanfare. But the serious nature of the vampire story, the intriguing, painterly artwork by Templesmith and some press attention from *Wizard* magazine focused more eyes on it. Its 3,000-copy print run sold out, and it became the focus of a Hollywood bidding war and eventually optioned by Sony Pictures. The comic and the company jumped to the forefront of a new era of horror comics. The company re-considered its stance and delved deeper into comics publishing.

IDW's next innovative move was licensing the comic rights to the top-rated television series *CSI: Crime Scene Investigation*. The show had millions of viewers, but it was not considered workable as a comic because it did not feature costumes, colorful characters or super-

October 2007: when vampires ruled the box office.

natural settings. Though there was no reason to think that a crime-procedural comic would resonate with fans, the first *CSI* miniseries debuted to huge sales and widespread acclaim. And thanks to mail order, it attracted a sizable number of buyers who normally don't set foot in comic-book shops.

In its developing years, the company followed two paths: producing additional horror comics and producing high-quality licensed titles. IDW comics such as *30 Days of Night*, *Bigfoot* (by Steve Niles and comic legend Richard Corben) and *Wake the Dead* (an update of the Frankenstein mythos) further cemented IDW's reputation at the forefront of the horror-comics revival.

In 2004, around the time that the company began to diversify its line even more, IDW hired *Comic Books 101* co-author Chris Ryall as its publisher and editor-in-chief. While the company's horror titles expanded to include some author-driven projects (adaptations of Richard Matheson's *Hell House*, Clive Barker's *The Thief of Always* and *The Great and Secret Show*, author F. Paul Wilson's retelling of his own novel *The Keep* and novelist Joe Hill's all-new comic-book creation, *Locke & Key*), it expanded into new arenas, too.

The signing of the *Transformers* comic license in 2005 was foremost among the company's expansion plans. The title, based on the 1980s toy brand, had fallen into disrepair after its previous publisher closed its doors under bankruptcy. IDW returned the title to its former glory, producing numerous series based on the existing brand as well as the big-budget movie release in 2007. The publisher further cemented its relationship with *Transformers* toy-makers Hasbro when it signed on to produce *G.I. Joe* comics in 2008.

IDW has re-released and relaunched cancelled titles from the past, too. Popular independent comics from the 1980s such as First Comics's *Grimjack, Jon Sable Freelance* and *Badger* have all relaunched new series and reprint volumes under IDW. In 2005, writer Peter David brought his acclaimed-but-canceled DC title *Fallen Angel* into IDW's fold, and writer Alan Martin

Novelist Joe Hill's debut topped critics' lists and was snatched up by Dimension Films.

LOCKE & KEY #1 © 2007 BY JOE HILL AND IDEA AND DESIGN WORKS, LLC. ART BY GABRIEL RODRIGUEZ.

# CLIVE BARKER, author/filmmaker/painter

**THE BEST COMIC-BOOK SERIES I'VE EVER READ**

Alan Moore's *Promethea*, without question.

**THE BEST CREATIVE TIME ON A TITLE**

I have to go with the conventional here, Kirby/Lee's *Fantastic Four*.

**THE BEST COVER**

The white cover of *Promethea* (#23 by J.H. Williams III). The simple gold lines against the white background are stunning. A very close second favorite is *Fantastic Four* #49, with Galactus pursuing the FF. He's waving his hands with his fingers pointed earthward, and the ground is erupting all around them.

**THE BEST STORYLINE/ISSUE**

There's an embarrassment of riches ... do I go to *Doctor Strange* by Steve Ditko? I think I must. This was my first introduction to the idea of comic books as art. This intro into the world of Ditko's *Doctor Strange* redefined the way we see comics. Ditko truly embraced the lessons of the surrealists. His style was the dominant thing that drew you to that book; his flavor was all over it. His art was best served by Doctor Strange's world—in his hands, magic became a plausible reality. No one drew with the delirious specificity of Ditko.

**GOOFIEST COVER**

Anything by Jim Starlin. Starlin, while talented, is guilty of over-mythologizing everything he worked on. Every story had to be bigger and more cosmic than the last.

**BEST GAY STORYLINE**

*Enigma* by Peter Milligan. An amazing story of the layers a gay man uncovers on his way to discovery. Also, Grant Morrison's *Marvel Boy*, the most homoerotically illustrated comic ever done.

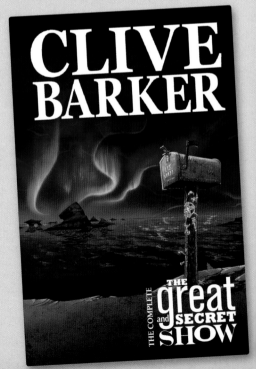

Chris and *Comic Books 101* cover artist Gabriel Rodriguez adapted Barker's epic novel into an epic graphic novel.

created new comics based on his popular Tank Girl character.

Among the many licensed comics that IDW has published, perhaps its biggest success has been Joss Whedon's *Angel* series. The comics, based on the popular television series, captured a small but passionate audience when first debuted. This early success exploded when creator Whedon returned to the story, continuing it where the TV show left off. Whedon and writer Brian Lynch's efforts on 2007's *Angel: After the Fall* led to the largest sales the company had ever seen for a monthly comic and helped propel the company to its position as the fourth-largest publisher in 2008.

IDW is also home to high-profile license *Star Trek*, a property that's been in the hands of four previous publishers (Gold Key, Marvel, DC, and Wildstorm). *Comic Books 101* co-author Scott Tipton has written numerous *Star Trek* titles for the company, including a *Klingons* comic published entirely in the Klingon language.

In 2007, interest in *30 Days of Night* hit a peak when the big-screen adaptation of the comic debuted at number one in its opening weekend. The movie, a faithful retelling of the original miniseries, was directed by David Slade and starred Josh Hartnett in the lead role. The movie took great care to maintain the look and feel of the comics, and delivered one of the more faithful comic-book adaptations.

The company has expanded its line with the creation of new imprints. Under the Library of American Comics imprint, IDW produces deluxe hardcover collections of acclaimed newspaper strips such as Chester Gould's *Dick Tracy,* Milton Caniff's *Terry and the Pirates* and Harold Gray's *Little Orphan Annie.*

IDW's Worthwhile Books imprint was launched in 2008, focusing on children's picture books. The line's debut title, *Michael Recycle,* launched on Earth Day and was embraced by many elementary schools' reading programs.

IDW has long been determined to leave the creation of superhero universes to the publishers who've mastered such a thing over the last half-century, but it continues to have success in a variety of other areas in the vast comic-book arena.

In 2007, the Eisner-nominated pairing of Chris and acclaimed painter Ashley Wood teamed up to present the ultimate team-up book.

ZOMBIES VS. ROBOTS © 2007 IDEA AND DESIGN WORKS, LLC. PUBLISHED BY IDW PUBLISHING. ART BY ASHLEY WOOD.

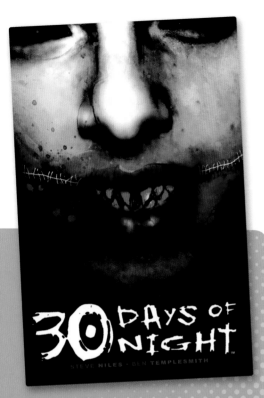

The *30 Days of Night* graphic novel.

## RECOMMENDED READING 101

### IDW PUBLISHING

*30 Days of Night* by Steve Niles and Ben Templesmith

*Angel: After the Fall*, Vol. 1 by Joss Whedon, Brian Lynch and Franco Urru

*Angel: Auld Lang Syne* by Scott Tipton and David Messina**

*Clive Barker's The Great and Secret Show* by Chris Ryall and Gabriel Rodriguez*

*Clive Barker's The Thief of Always* by Kris Oprisko and Gabriel Hernandez

*The Complete Chester Gould's Dick Tracy*, Vol. 1 by Chester Gould

*The Complete Terry and the Pirates*, Vol. 1 by Milton Caniff

*Completely Doomed* by Robert Bloch, Richard Matheson, David J. Schow, F. Paul Wilson and others

*Cory Doctorow's Futuristic Tales of the Here and Now* by Cory Doctorow

*Fallen Angel: To Serve in Heaven* by Peter David and J.K. Woodward

*Locke & Key* by Joe Hill and Gabriel Rodriguez

*Star Trek: Klingons: Blood Will Tell* by Scott Tipton, David Tipton and David Messina**

*Supermarket* by Brian Wood and Kristian Donaldson

*Tank Girl: The Gifting* by Alan C. Martin, Rufus Dayglo and Ashley Wood

*The Transformers: Infiltration* by Simon Furman and E.J. Su

*Wormwood: Gentleman Corpse* by Ben Templesmith

*Zombies vs. Robots* by Chris Ryall and Ashley Wood

*Yes, I'm admittedly a bit biased about these. —Chris

**What he said. —Scott

# PART VI

# THE CREATORS:
## THE MEN BEHIND THE SUPERMEN

*Wherein dues are paid to those who paid their dues; ink-stained fingers are celebrated; and the captains of this industry are hailed. The opportunity to learn about the names behind the creations, as well as the greatest hits they've recorded on paper, is afforded the reader within this chapter.*

# Jerry Siegel & Joe Shuster

Sometimes fate can be cruel.

In retrospect, there's no way these two teenagers from Cleveland could have possibly conceived of the ironies in store for them. Even if you could've warned them somehow, they'd have never believed it.

"Jerry, Joe, listen up. The two of you are going to create a character so universally beloved, it will revolutionize an industry. Your creation will be known worldwide for decades, with no end in sight. It'll spawn radio shows, television shows, stage plays, movies and countless spin-offs. Just the money from merchandising alone would make you rich beyond the dreams of avarice.

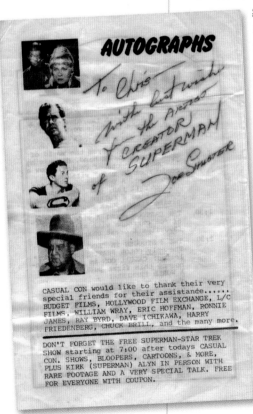

The first autograph of Chris's life, from 1975 when he was too young to appreciate the greatness in front of him. He appreciates it now.

"And you won't see any of it.

"Oh, you'll be well-compensated for a while, but after it's clear that you're no longer necessary, you'll be edged out of the operation, and lose control of your creation. Over the ensuing decades, you'll eke out a modest living, and wind up in near-poverty in your golden years, until a combination of corporate guilt and fear of bad publicity will restore you proper credit to your creation, and you'll be given a reasonable (if nowhere near appropriate) pension. Your example will stand as a shameful lesson of everything that's wrong with the comics industry.

"But your creation will live on forever as an example of everything that's right."

Would they still think it was worth it?

These days, anyone with even a remote interest in comics knows the story: how writer Jerry Siegel and artist Joe Shuster shopped their proposal for a newspaper strip called *Superman* around to every syndicate and comic-book publisher in town with no luck; how editor Vin Sullivan finally took a chance on the project no one believed in and purchased it for use in *Action Comics*; how Siegel and Shuster quickly cut apart their newspaper strips and converted them into a comic-book format; and most infamously, how National Comics purchased the character of Superman outright for $130 as a condition of publication, in a move that would make the company untold millions in profits, and relegate Siegel and Shuster to mere hired hands on their own creation.

It's an ugly story, and one that could discourage any positive discussion of Superman, just from the sheer stinking injustice of it. Here's why we should discuss, and enjoy, Superman in spite of the indignities visited upon his fathers: despite their shabby treatment, Siegel and Shuster remained proud of their creation and its impact on the world, and certainly were proud of all their work on the character. In addition, over the following six decades, a small army of writers and artists have toiled on the character, each adding to and shaping the Superman legend. One can sympathize with Siegel and Shuster's plight, and condemn those whose actions led to it, yet still admire and enjoy the work.

Siegel and Shuster had a ten-year contract to write and draw Superman comics, and with that agreement near its end in 1947, the two sued National, for which they received a modest cash settlement and rights to the character Superboy, which they then sold to National as well. Siegel returned to National in 1959 to again write Superman comics, a relationship that continued until 1967, when he once again sued over the Superman rights, with little success. Shuster, meanwhile, continued to eke out a living as a cartoonist, a situation made problematic by his failing eyesight.

It wasn't until 1975 that Jerry Siegel and Joe Shuster finally received some recognition for their creation. With *Superman: The Movie* looming on the horizon, Siegel began a public-relations campaign about the way he and his partner Shuster had been treated, a move aided and abetted by comic-book artist Neal Adams. Fearing bad publicity just before their multi-million-dollar blockbuster was about to hit movie screens, Warner Communications (then DC Comics's parent company) came to an agreement with Siegel and Shuster: the two men would receive a modest pension for the rest of their lives, and the credit line "Superman created by Jerry Siegel and Joe Shuster" would appear wherever Superman did, be it comic books, movies, television shows, you name it. Was it enough? No, not nearly enough. But at least it was something.

In recent years, Siegel's heirs have continued to fight for ownership of their father's creation, with some success. In 2008, the Federal District Court ruled that Siegel's estate was entitled to share in the United States copyright to Superman. To what extent remains to be seen, but at least for now, it looks like there may be something to this "truth and justice" business after all.

---

**RECOMMENDED READING 101**

### SIEGEL & SHUSTER

*Superman Archives*, Vol. 1–7

*Superman: The Action Comics Archives*, Vol. 1–5

# 2 Bob Kane

As much as one has to empathize with the plight of folks like Superman's creators Jerry Siegel and Joe Shuster, it is important to remember that there were also creators in the Golden Age of comics who, through a combination of hard work, creative inspiration and canny business instincts, managed to do pretty well for themselves. To quote Carl Barks's Uncle Scrooge, these guys were "tougher than the toughies and smarter than the smarties." Guys like the creator of Batman, Bob Kane.

Kane got his start as a cartoonist early, selling humor stories first to Jerry Iger's publishing concern in 1936, then to Eisner & Iger in 1937, before moving on to adventure strips such as "Rusty and His Pals" for National Comics. When Superman took the comics world by storm in 1938, Kane responded, working with writer Finger to create an all-new mystery man Kane conceived as the Bat-Man. Beginning with Leonardo da Vinci's famous drawings of the ornithopter, a machine that da Vinci hoped would allow man to fly with giant, scalloped wings, Kane began to develop his Batman, a strictly mortal vigilante to contrast against the decidedly superhuman Superman. While Bill Finger was an integral part of Batman's creation, Bob Kane held the contract with National Comics and was officially considered the creator of Batman, a situation

that has rankled comics historians for decades, and one which Kane himself, in his later years, admitted was probably a mistake. He conceded how much Finger brought to the character and how important he was to Batman's conception and development.

Kane secured for himself a much more favorable deal than Siegel and Shuster had, operating under a longer-term agreement that guaranteed him much better financial compensation for his work, as well as the retention of his "Created by" credit on the *Batman* comics—a situation made all the more ironic by Kane's gradually decreasing involvement in the actual production of the comic, as Kane would rely more and more over the years on ghost artists Dick Sprang and Sheldon Moldoff, artists whose conceptions of the Caped Crusader would become just as well-known as Kane's, if not more so.

Not that Kane was without influence on the character. A fan of Orson Welles's *Citizen Kane* and the Warner Bros. gangster films, Kane worked to bring that kind of cinematic approach to the early Batman strips, which exhibited a darker, moody feel and exaggerated, almost outlandish approach. In the series' early days, Kane worked closely with Finger and assistant Jerry Robinson, and together the three created nearly all of the trademark Batman elements still known and loved today, from the Batcave, Batmobile and utility belt to Batman's bizarre array of villains like the Joker, the Penguin and Catwoman. While precisely who created what has long been a source of debate, it's clear that there was a congruency of thought that made for the creation of some very entertaining comics.

An even more influential creation of Kane and company was Robin the Boy Wonder. In fact, the addition of Robin turned out to be such a hit with the comics readership that the idea spread like wildfire, and soon no tights-wearing mystery man would be seen without a similarly dressed youngster at his side.

As the years went by, Kane became less involved with the creation of the comic books. In 1943, he tackled the daily *Batman* newspaper strip, and after the strip ended in 1946, Kane relied on his personal ghost artists for the comic books, such as Moldoff, who labored for years on the Bat-books in anonym-ity. Kane found some success in animation in the 1960s with television programs like *Courageous Cat* and *Cool McCool*, and spent his elder years painting, showing his work in galleries nationwide, and generally basking in the spotlight of being the creator of Batman, especially after the character enjoyed new-found mass-media popularity in 1989 with Tim Burton's film. Bob Kane died November 3, 1998, and remains one of the rare examples of Golden Age greats who received the rewards and recognition they deserved.

---

### RECOMMENDED READING 101

#### BOB KANE

*Batman Archives*, Vol. 1–7

*Batman: The Dark Knight Archives*, Vol. 1–5

---

# Will Eisner

Actively writing, drawing and publishing comics from 1936 until his death in 2005, Will Eisner is the closest thing there is to the patron saint of comics. One of the founding fathers of the Golden Age, Eisner created and worked on characters and series from a variety of publishers. In 1940, Eisner created his trademark character, the Spirit, which was tremendously popular and saw an exposure unprecedented in today's comics market, and which served as a venue for Eisner to develop and hone his craft, taking the standard adventure strip in countless new directions. When Eisner ended *The Spirit* in 1952, he turned to new ventures, creating the modern graphic novel with his landmark work *A Contract With God*, thus beginning a series of intensely personal works that focused on the simplest of humanity's pleasures and sins. But let's not get ahead of ourselves...

Chris shared panel space with Will Eisner upon joining IDW in 2004, which has made all subsequent panels suffer by comparison.

### THE EARLY DAYS

A nineteen-year-old Eisner cut his teeth in the comics biz in 1936 just as things were starting out. One of his first jobs was at the now-forgotten Fox Comics, creating the thinly disguised Superman knockoff Wonder Man at the behest of Fox's publisher, an assignment that soon found the young artist testifying at the lawsuit brought by National, alleging copyright infringement. When National prevailed, Eisner's days at Fox were over.

### EISNER'S BIG BREAK

Eisner partnered with Jerry Iger to create the Eisner & Iger Studios, a production house that provided comics material to a number of publishers, most notably Quality Comics, producing such features as Uncle Sam, Doll Man and Blackhawk. Some of the all-time greats in comics art got their start at E & I, including Lou Fine, Jack Cole and Jack Kirby. Business was booming, but in 1939, Eisner got an offer he found hard to refuse.

Eisner was approached by Quality publisher Busy Arnold and Henry Martin, the sales manager for the Register & Tribune Newspaper Syndicate. The men had a radical idea. Concerned about the growing competition they faced from comic books for young readers, the men proposed that Eisner produce for them a weekly sixteen-page comic book, which would be syndicated nationwide, appearing in Sunday papers across the country. Wise beyond his years, Eisner saw the artistic and financial potential of this new venture and negotiated a partnership agreement granting him complete ownership of the characters and material, a move unheard of in comics publishing of the time. Eisner thought that it was his artistic ability that gave him the extra leverage to gain this kind of agreement, but as he later discovered, they were less concerned with quality than with reliability: after all, this would be appearing week after week, and Eisner was one of the few producers they thought able to pull it off.

Eisner sold his half of E & I to Iger, and threw himself into the new project. The sixteen-page section would be split into three features: four pages for Chuck Mazoujian's *Lady Luck*, five pages for Bob Powell's *Mr. Mystic* and seven pages for the feature Eisner himself would produce. Eisner had long thought that the comic-book medium was capable of work much more sophisticated than was commercially viable in the monthly magazines. With a syndicated weekly newspaper release, Eisner now had access to an older, more adult reader, and far more flexibility than was possible with a daily newspaper strip. He had gained the best of both worlds: the length and format of comic books and the much larger and more mature audience of comic strips.

For the lead feature, Eisner wanted a detective strip with a very vulnerable, human protagonist, something miles away from the Supermen that were ruling over comics at the time. Eisner's hero, Denny Colt, wore no costume. Instead he sported a blue suit, gloves, a fedora and a domino mask. The flashy alias the Spirit was added at the insistence of the syndicate, who wanted something a little closer to the mystery men of the day.

In his premiere appearance, criminologist Denny Colt pays a visit to Central City Police Commissioner Dolan, letting him know that he's on the trail of criminal scientist Dr. Cobra. Colt tracks down Dr. Cobra, and in attempting to apprehend him is drenched in a mysterious chemical, seemingly killing him. Dolan and the police arrive on the scene, and, assuming Colt is dead, haul him away to a waiting grave in Wildwood Cemetery. However, it turns out that the chemical only put Colt in a death-like state of suspended animation—a real bummer when he wakes up the next night six feet under. Presumed dead by the world, Colt assumes the identity of the Spirit, to go after criminals beyond the reach of the police, taking up residence in a hidden HQ beneath Denny Colt's crypt in Wildwood Cemetery. Only Police Commissioner Dolan and his daughter Ellen know who the Spirit is and where he can be found.

Commercially, the strip was an immediate success, with some newspapers citing a 10 percent gain in circulation as a result of the Sunday insert. The strip was entertaining, and head and shoulders above anything else in crime comics, but nowhere near the heights it would later reach. In 1942, Eisner was drafted, but *The Spirit*, whose subscribing newspapers had tripled, continued right on schedule, with art by Lou Fine and scripts from Manly Wade Wellman, Dick French and Jack Cole.

## AFTER THE WAR

It wasn't until Eisner came back to *The Spirit* after World War II in 1946 that the strip really began to hit its stride. Eisner was revitalized in returning to the work, and began to alter his approach to the already innovative strip by varying his storytelling and not always utilizing the Spirit as the center of the story. In addtion, Eisner couldn't afford the luxury of a traditional cover with only eight pages to work with each week. Instead, Eisner began to use his opening splash page to immediately set the mood and draw the reader into the story, incorporating the Spirit logo somewhere in the background, often as part of the landscape.

In the postwar years, Eisner began to treat the Spirit as an antihero, becoming less and less the straight-shooting good guy he is at the series' inception. Often the Spirit is only peripherally involved in his own adventures. Eisner focused on telling a wide variety of stories, from comedy to tragedy, parable to suspense, with only a brief appearance by the Spirit to keep the reader connected to the strip as a whole. Just as Eisner was experimenting with story, so was he experimenting with art, as well. The storytelling became wildly different from week to week, mixing traditional panel-to-panel storytelling with prose sections, utilizing layout in brand-new ways to convey sensations or sounds, at times breaking format entirely when the story called for it.

Eisner also created a number of femmes fatales for the Spirit to contend. There was Sand Saref, a girl from Denny Colt's youth turned smuggler and black marketer, whom the Spirit can never bring himself to apprehend. There's also Lorelei Rox, a modern-day siren with a voice that can kill. But no femme fatale can compete with P'Gell, the gorgeous international black widow who moves from husband to husband, from scheme to scheme, sometimes pausing in her plans to either tempt the Spirit away from the righteous path, or occasionally to warn him of some dire threat about to befall him. Eisner's women were usually dangerous, sometimes tragic and always damned sexy.

Probably the most famous of the Spirit sections is "The Story of Gerhard Shnobble" (September 5, 1948). Another of Eisner's luckless schlubs, Gerhard Shnobble is a thirty-five-year veteran bank guard who is fired when he's unable to stop a robbery. Desperate to prove his value, Gerhard suddenly remembers that as a child, he discovered he could fly, until his parents forbade it, insisting he be normal. Determined to show the world, Gerhard heads to the top of a nearby building, where the Spirit is coincidentally headed to stop the same bank robbers. Gerhard leaps off the building and indeed can fly . . . at least for a moment. Eisner uses full-page spreads to express the feeling of height when Gerhard is in flight, and as he does in many of his later stories, utilizes the narrator's voice to provide a bit of poetic irony. "The Story of Gerhard Shnobble" is everything that made *The Spirit* great: funny, whimsical and tragic, with a spare but elegiac tone in narration and breakthrough storytelling unlike any seen before.

By 1952, skyrocketing paper and printing costs made *The Spirit* section no longer profitable, and the syndicate pulled the plug. They asked Eisner to keep the character alive in a daily strip, but he refused. He continued to work for the U.S. Army, writing and illustrating *P.S. Magazine*, a series of comic-style instruction manuals for enlisted men. Eisner spent the next two decades applying the comics form to "education, instruction and other pragmatic directions," as he himself put it. In 1978, Eisner was ready to return to storytelling, and did so in grand form with what most comics historians consider the first graphic novel, *A Contract With God*.

## A NOVEL IDEA

*A Contract With God* was the first of Eisner's autobiographical graphic novels, telling stories of life in the tenements of the Bronx in the 1930s. *Contract* is made up of four stories, tales of lost faith, lost hope, despair and coming of age, illustrated by a cartoonist at the height of his form, and with rough dialogue that rings true; the voices of immigrants not heard for fifty years speak out again through Eisner's pen.

In 1986, Eisner published another autobiographical work, *The Dreamer*, about his early days trying to find work and success in the then-burgeoning comic-book industry. Eisner recants his own only slightly fictionalized telling of the founding of the E & I studio, the Wonder Man lawsuit and his decision to jump to the syndicate. He also provides character studies of Jack Kirby, Lou Fine, Jack Cole and other Golden Age greats.

In *The Building* (1987), Eisner tells the stories of four different residents of a New York building, how their lives intermingle without ever knowing it and how, after death, their spirits remain a part of the structure, even after it's been demolished. Often overlooked by readers, *The Building* may be Eisner's best single work, combining the authenticity and heart of his autobiographies with the unmatched plotting and storytelling skills he demonstrated in *The Spirit*. Highly recommended.

Though advancing in years, Eisner's productivity continued unabated. In *To The Heart of the Storm* (1991), Eisner returned to autobiography with a much more ambitious work, devoting attention to his father's youth in Vienna and his own struggles growing up as a Jewish kid in a predominantly Italian and Irish neighborhood.

After signing a long-term contract with DC Comics to keep all of his works in print, including the entire run of *The Spirit*, Eisner produced three major works, putting to shame contemporaries one-third his age. Eisner's *Last Day in Vietnam* (2000) tells the small stories of military life in wartime, gleaned from Eisner's own military experience, as well as field trips to Korea and Vietnam during his stint producing *P.S. Magazine*. *Minor Miracles* (2000) comprises Eisner's retellings of the tales of modern folklore passed on to him by his family growing up.

Eisner's following book, *The Name of the Game* (2002), was a generational novel about a wealthy Jewish family and their attempts to gain social advantage through marrying "the right people." *The Name of the Game* expands on some of the themes touched upon by Eisner as early as *A Contract With God*, and does so with vitality, wit and Eisner's ever-improving sense of draftsmanship and design.

In his final work, *The Plot: The Secret Story of the Protocols of the Elders of Zion* (2005), Eisner tried to raise public consciousness of anti-Semitism with his exploration of a 100-year-old hoax that falsely accused Jewish leaders of planning to take over the world. Primarily a historical piece, *The Plot* has none of the heart that made Eisner's other works so powerful, but the artwork is astonishing, the work of a man who spent a lifetime developing his craft.

Will Eisner passed away January 3, 2005, at the age of eighty-seven. He left behind a legacy unprecedented in the comic-book industry, and a body of work to be studied for decades to come by those who look to learn at the feet of the master.

---

### RECOMMENDED READING 101

#### WILL EISNER

*The Best of the Spirit*

*The Building* (Scott's personal favorite)

*Comics and Sequential Art*

*A Contract With God* (Chris's personal favorite)

*The Dreamer*

*The Name of the Game*

*To the Heart of the Storm*

# Stan Lee

## 4

If you're looking for the most influential name in American comics, how can it not be Stan Lee? The Fantastic Four. The Hulk. Spider-Man. The Mighty Thor. Doctor Strange. The X-Men. Iron Man. The Avengers. As kids, thanks to the *Origins of Marvel Comics* reprint series, our first exposure to these characters wasn't necessarily current comics, but their original appearances by Stan, Jack Kirby and Steve Ditko. Much is made of the fact that Kirby and Ditko don't get enough credit for their work at Marvel; there's no denying that. However, it was the voices of the characters that made Marvel's heroes more alive than DC's —the humor and angst of Spider-Man, the depression of Ben Grimm, the cool confidence of Captain America, the tortured soul of the Silver Surfer.

And even with the more than considerable partnership of fine artists and co-plotters like Kirby, Ditko, Gene Colan, John Romita, John Buscema and many others, it often goes unremarked that Stan was for quite a few years writing the bulk of Marvel's output himself, not only balancing dozens of characterizations, but creating all of the countless connections that are woven back and forth between all the Marvel series. Lee created the notion of the "Marvel Universe" that DC and practically every other comic-book publisher would eventually imitate.

So how to recommend the best Lee-penned stories? In looking at the hundreds of great comics in Lee's long, storied career, this makes for a difficult if not unpleasant task. As always, it's a matter of opinion. Is "The Spider-Man Unmasked" in *The Amazing Spider-Man* #39–40 (August–September 1966) the best? Or "The Galactus Saga" in *Fantastic Four* #48–50 (March–May 1966)? "The Return of Captain America" in *The Avengers* #4 (March 1964)? *The Silver Surfer* #4 (February 1969)? It's hard to say. The crowning glory of Lee's initial output at Marvel—beyond the sheer inventiveness that he brought to all of the characters he helped create—is the 102 issues of *Fantastic Four* that he and Jack Kirby produced together. While later creators have surpassed the sheer number of consecutive issues created by a single team, the creativity, originality and sheer mastery of this centennial accomplishment will never be matched. Another early and amazing feat for which Lee is renowned is his long tenure on *The Amazing Spider-Man* with Steve Ditko and

Smilin' Stan Lee

PHOTO COURTESY OF STAN LEE AND POW! ENTERTAINMENT.

## STAN LEE: MASTER THESPIAN

Of course, in addition to his distinguished career as editor, writer and publisher, Stan has yet another calling in which he's flourished in recent years—acting! Just take a look at these performances from some of the most popular movies ever made! Stan Lee: the new Robert De Niro? The evidence speaks for itself.

| | |
|---|---|
| The Trial of the Incredible Hulk (TV movie) | Guy in Jury Box |
| The Ambulance | Marvel Comics Editor |
| Mallrats | Smilin' Stan Lee |
| X-Men | Hot Dog Vendor |
| Spider-Man | Guy Looking Up |
| Daredevil | Guy at Traffic Light |
| Hulk | Security Guard |
| The Princess Diaries 2: Royal Engagement | Foreign Diplomat |
| Spider-Man 2 | Guy Dodging Debris |
| Fantastic Four | Postman Willie Lumpkin |
| X-Men: The Last Stand | Guy with Garden Hose |
| Spider-Man 3 | Guy in Times Square |
| Fantastic Four: Rise of the Silver Surfer | Uninvited Wedding Guest |
| Iron Man | Guy Who Looks Like Hugh Hefner |
| | Guy Who Drinks Gamma Soda |
| The Incredible Hulk | |

then John Romita. And the list only starts with these two titles.

Fortunately, the bulk of Lee's creative output is now readily available, both in handsome full-color hardcovers and much more affordable *Essential* black-and-white editions. The ambitious new comics reader should start with *Fantastic Four* and *The Amazing Spider-Man* and go forward from there.

## MAKE YOURS MARVEL

One feat for which Stan should be heralded is the sheer force of will he brought to bear in promoting the comics that Marvel produced. Beyond the act of creation and his scripting chores, Stan was (and is) a tireless, enthusiastic promoter of comics. Before Stan, comics were appreciated by fans for their colorful characters. Stan had the foresight to become a colorful character in his own right. He oversaw the letters pages, which allowed fans to have their say about a previous issue and receive bombastic replies from the folks creating the comics. Even his nicknames for himself and the creators in the credits boxes of Marvel's comics ("Rascally" Roy Thomas, Jack "the King" Kirby, "Sturdy" Steve Ditko, and so on) added to the sense of familiarity between creator and fan.

Stan further created "Stan Lee's Soapbox," a column in the letters pages where he talked up the comics in inimitable fashion. He talked about Marvel's comics and fans' support of them in a conspiratorial manner, making the readers feel like they were on the same team as the Marvel staff, all aligned in solidarity against the more staid "Distinguished Competition," Stan's gentle barb of a nickname for Marvel's main competitor, DC Comics. He signed off his columns with "Excelsior!" because he liked the sound of it, and it was a call to arms that would stick in readers' minds. While Stan was in charge, as far as he made fans feel, Marvel was the only place to be. Stan also talked up Marvel's comics at conventions. He made the rivalry with DC a personal, but never mean-spirited, thing. And he oversaw the creation of Marvel fan clubs such as the 1960s M.M.M.S. (Merry Marvel Marching Society) and *FOOM* (a fan club/fan magazine) in the 1970s.

---

### RECOMMENDED READING 101
#### *STAN LEE*

The Amazing Spider-Man Omnibus

Bring on the Bad Guys

The Fantastic Four Omnibus

The Incredible Hulk Omnibus

Origins of Marvel Comics

Son of Origins of Marvel Comics

The Superhero Women

---

## EXCELSIOR!

It was the development of Stan Lee as a public persona that led to his eventual positions as president, publisher and finally chairman emeritus of Marvel. In the early 1980s, Stan headed west to Southern California to function as publisher while simultaneously developing Marvel's properties for Hollywood. Stan has been very active in helping develop Marvel's characters as animated series, television shows and big-budget motion pictures. He also pursued other ventures outside of Marvel, creating new entertainment companies and developing all-new creations for print, Web and broadcast.

In 2001, Stan crossed a line that longtime fans never thought they'd see—he wrote comics for the Distinguished Competition. *Just Imagine... Stan Lee Creating the DC Universe* allowed Stan to pair up with acclaimed artists and re-cast DC's flagship characters in their own style. All of which was just one more way for Stan to do what he does best: find new and exciting ways to create comic books and promote them to eager fans.

# 5 Jack Kirby

What do you say about Jack Kirby? The man practically invented the superhero comic, or at least what most people think of when they see one. Jack Kirby was one of the top guys in the business in the 1940s, on books such as *Captain America*, *The Sandman*, *Boy Commandos* and dozens more, and he out-and-out revolutionized the industry in the 1960s, creating nearly all of Marvel Comics's trademark characters, from the Fantastic Four to the Hulk to Thor, from the Avengers to the X-Men. Kirby's dynamic sense of storytelling and larger-than-life style swept the comics world, and his timeless ability in character design can still be seen to this day.

Nearly everyone working at Marvel Comics is still in some shape or form playing with the toys Jack "the King" Kirby created, and while there's certainly no shame in that, it bears repeating from time to time.

In the time it took to take this photo of Joe Simon and Jack Kirby, the King likely could have drawn three more pages.

## FROM MARVEL TO DC

As more and more of the plotting fell on Kirby for Marvel works such as *Fantastic Four* and *Thor*, Kirby reportedly disliked that Stan Lee's scripting often did not properly reflect the direction or tone of the stories as he'd conceived them. So, during his last few years at Marvel, Jack developed a whole new army of characters and kept them to himself. Since there was no creator ownership in mainstream comics at the time, Kirby wasn't about to turn his newest, most personal concepts over to Marvel, so away they went into the drawer.

Frustrated, Jack Kirby quit working at Marvel Comics in 1970. According to a famous rumor, no one working at Marvel at the time received a formal memorandum that Jack Kirby had left the company. Instead, there was only one of Jack's trademark cigars pinned to a wall with a note attached reading "I quit!"

When then-DC Comics publisher Carmine Infantino made Jack an offer to come over to DC, Kirby accepted, and brought his new concepts with him. Infantino wanted Kirby to handle at least one existing title in addition to the new books he had in the works. Kirby had no great love for any of the DC books, and didn't want to boot another artist out of a job, so he told Infantino to give him whatever book didn't have an artist even if it was the lowest-selling title DC published. As a result, Jack Kirby made his post-Marvel DC debut on *Superman's Pal Jimmy Olsen* #133 (October 1970).

Readers who were expecting the placid, Mort Weisinger-style Jimmy Olsen stories they'd seen for years were in for a shock. Suddenly every issue was full of new concepts: the Whiz Wagon, Project Cadmus, the Hairies, a new Newsboy Legion and Guardian (revivals of previous Golden Age Kirby work for DC). And lurking in the background was a mysterious new villain that would soon become very important in the rest of Kirby's DC work: Darkseid, the uncontested dictator of the hellish world Apokolips.

The new Kirby take on Jimmy Olsen was so revolutionary that Infantino ordered the faces of established Superman characters Superman, Perry White and Jimmy Olsen to be either redrawn or heavily inked by established Superman artists Al Plastino and Murphy Anderson. Kirby fans were outraged that DC tampered with his art, and Jack himself reportedly wasn't pleased, but he was busy putting the finishing touches on the debut issues of his three new series for DC, which he would write, draw and edit. Kirby was in complete control of his work, for probably the first time in his career, and his enthusiasm showed.

## THE FOURTH WORLD

In 1971, Kirby debuted his signature work at DC, later dubbed the "Fourth World" saga: *New Gods, Mister Miracle* and *The Forever People*. Together with *Superman's Pal Jimmy Olsen,*

Kirby intended these stories to be part of an interconnected epic. This epic would run forty or fifty issues of each of the three central titles and culminate in a grand finale for the entire saga, which would then be slightly condensed and reissued as a series of hardcover collections for mass-market bookstores. It's important to remember the time frame: this is 1971 we're talking about. There were no miniseries in comics, never had been, and comics weren't designed to be finite and have endings. And the idea of reprinting the comics in a hardcover? Selling to bookstores? Ludicrous. Comics are sold at newsstands and grocery stores, and that's it. Kirby was about twenty-five years ahead of the industry, correctly

Before joining DC in 1970, Kirby created many titles alongside Joe Simon, including *Black Magic* from the late 1940s.

BLACK MAGIC #17 © 1952 CRESTWOOD PRIZE GROUP.

predicting what would eventually become the lifeblood of today's modern comics market.

Sadly, Kirby's epic was never properly finished. After less than two years (only eleven issues each of *New Gods* and *The Forever People,* and eighteen issues of *Mister Miracle*), Kirby's series were canceled, ostensibly for low sales, a claim that remains in question. Some fans and critics have accused Infantino of canceling the books because he didn't "get" them or because they looked too much like Marvel books, but he steadfastly maintains that the sales weren't there and that it was purely a business decision. Other historians claim the sales were steady if not spectacular, and certainly not the worst-selling DC titles by far. Still, it's easy to imagine that the average 1970s-era DC comics reader might have been a little taken aback by Kirby's dynamic, explosive work, not to mention Kirby's, shall we say, unique approach to dialogue, which often sounds little like any form of discourse commonly used, and could more properly be termed a kind of "free-form word jazz."

After the books were axed, Kirby created a second wave of titles for DC, including *OMAC, Kamandi: The Last Boy on Earth* and *The Demon,* then returned to Marvel for a brief stint, eventually winding up working in animation. When DC editors later realized the genius of the original Kirby "Fourth World" series, they asked him to return to the series for a grand finale. Kirby made several attempts, first in a new *New Gods* reprint series and then with the DC graphic novel *The Hunger Dogs,* but both DC and Kirby agreed that they were less than successful. Even so, Kirby's characters have remained active in the DC Universe ever since.

## KIRBY UNLEASHED

Kirby often referred to "The Pact!" in *New Gods* #7 (February 1971) as his favorite of all the stories he'd created. It's easy to see why. Before this, the story moved along at a breakneck pace, introducing concepts and characters non-stop. In "The Pact!" we get the first glimpse of backstory in the saga. Darkseid engineers the murder of the wife of his enemy Izaya, the Highfather of New Genesis, setting off the war between the idyllic paradise New Genesis and Darkseid's hellish planet Apokolips. The ferocity of war and the despondency of Izaya as he realizes war has ravaged his once-verdant world is portrayed as only Kirby could. The moment is both evocative of his best work at Marvel yet entirely new, and uniquely Kirby.

As for Darkseid himself, he's probably Jack Kirby's single greatest creation. Over the years, Darkseid has become the most dominant villain in the DC Universe. His thirst for power motivates his every action, with his schemes for conquest often taking years to come to fruition. Looking as if he is carved from solid stone, Darkseid doesn't exhibit the weakness for honor shown by other Kirby villains, such

as Doctor Doom. One of Darkseid's weaknesses is emotion, namely pride in his son Orion, who opposes him at every turn. Kirby found interesting ways to convey this visually: when Darkseid is meant to be intimidating, implacable or otherwise inscrutable, his eyes are a solid mass of red, conveying no emotion. However, when he's exhibiting fear, concern or jealousy, he's drawn with normal pupils, appearing more human and mortal.

If *New Gods* provided the grand epic in Kirby's new universe, *Mister Miracle* was meant to show off a ground-level, human struggle on top of the requisite Kirby high adventure. *Mister Miracle* recounts the adventures of Scott Free, son of Izaya, who escapes the slave pits of Apokolips and flees to Earth, where he performs as Mister Miracle, escape-artist extraordinaire. According to Kirby biographer Mark Evanier, Kirby saw the *Mister Miracle* comics as an analogue to his own life, "writing of his feelings of imprisonment in the comic-book industry and certain employment situations." *Mister Miracle* is probably the most creatively successful of Kirby's "Fourth World" books thanks to its down-to-earth setting, human appeal and extremely likable characters Scott Free, his love interest Big Barda, and Oberon.

*The Forever People* tells the story of five adolescents from New Genesis who explore the Earth on their Super-Cycle, protecting the planet from Darkseid's threats while learning about Earth's people and customs. Basically, super-hippies from outer space. Though well-intentioned, *Forever People* lacks the high-

octane drama of *New Gods* and the character appeal of *Mister Miracle*, and is the weakest of the three series.

Kirby's *New Gods* characters had some limited, but still pretty cool, media exposure in the popular *Super Friends* animated series, *Super Friends: The Legendary Super Powers Show* and *The Super Powers Team: Galactic Guardians*. Over the two seasons (1984–1986), Darkseid

Mark Evanier paid proper tribute to his old "boss" in this 2008 biographical art book.

KIRBY: KING OF COMICS © 2008 MARK EVANIER. PUBLISHED BY ABRAMS PUBLISHING.

and his gang of villains on Apokolips are featured as the primary antagonists. As a running subplot, Darkseid has a curious fixation with Wonder Woman, probably an easier sell to kids (and more important, to network executives) than Darkseid's usual murky motives.

In conjunction with the animated series, Darkseid, Desaad, Kalibak, Mantis, Orion, Mister Miracle and other Kirby characters were also featured in the popular *Super Powers* action-figure line from Kenner. Not only were the figures very well done and quite faithful (some nowadays go for big money on the collector's market), but the toys and characters for the TV show were redesigned by Jack Kirby himself, thus providing him with his first

royalties in over forty years of comics work. (DC Comics has occasionally remarked, with no undue pride, that it paid Kirby more for creating Darkseid than Marvel did for creating its entire universe.)

After leaving DC Comics in the early 1980s, Kirby was courted by a new publisher, Pacific Comics, one of a few new independent publishers to arise during the birth of the direct market. Pacific offered Kirby something he'd never had in his long, storied career—full ownership over his creations, as well as royalties on the comics he produced for them. *Captain Victory and the Galactic Rangers* and *Silver Star* sold well for Pacific but were never received with the same fanfare as Kirby's earlier works. Some other creations that Kirby had intended for Pacific ended up at another new publisher, Topps Comics, after Pacific folded in the early 1990s. Topps let the King create *Jack Kirby's Secret City Saga*, also referred to as "the Kirbyverse," again offering him ownership of his creations.

Although we're sadly unable to enjoy any new work from the King, between hardcover archives, trade collections and back issues, we're still constantly delighted by new, never-before-seen Kirby material. Long live the King.

---

## RECOMMENDED READING 101

### JACK KIRBY

*The Fantastic Four Omnibus*

*Jack Kirby's The Demon Omnibus*

*Jack Kirby's Fourth World Omnibus*, Vol. 1-4

*Jack Kirby's O.M.A.C.: One Man Army Corps*

*Kamandi Archives*, Vol. 1-2

*The Losers*

---

## LEE AND KIRBY

At this stage of the game, no one can really know for certain who invented what in the Lee/Kirby partnership. All we have to go by are their interviews and their work.

In interviews, Stan has always credited Jack Kirby and Steve Ditko (and others) as co-creators. He's been seen going out of his way to do so many a time. People who want to discredit Lee for being in the press for all these movie premieres need to realize that Kirby would be too, if he were alive. (And as for Spider-Man co-creator Ditko, it's his choice that he hasn't allowed a photograph of himself to be taken in decades, not Stan elbowing him to the side.) As far back as the 1970s, Stan was crediting Kirby and Ditko as co-creators of Marvel characters, in print, well before any lawsuits or movie deals.

As for Kirby, many of the interviews in which he claimed sole credit for works such as *Fantastic Four* and *Hulk* took place toward the end of his life, when he was embroiled in a lawsuit with Marvel over his artwork, and in our opinion anyway, may have been getting some poor advice from people who encouraged him to hit the comics press and make headlines.

It was during that period that Kirby was even claiming creator credit on *Spider-Man*, of all things. True, Kirby did an early sketch of Spider-Man, but it mostly resembled an earlier work he did called The Fly, and looked nothing at all like Ditko's Spider-Man.

So, if interviews are inconclusive to prove Kirby's claim, let's look at the work. Together, Lee and Kirby created the Fantastic Four, the Hulk, Thor, the X-Men and Nick Fury, to name just a few. Now let's remove Kirby from the equation. With Steve Ditko, Lee created Spider-Man (arguably the company's greatest success) and Dr. Strange. With Don Heck, Lee created Iron Man. With Bill Everett, Lee created Daredevil. It seems difficult to believe that the common denominator in these successes was not the editorial hand and writer's voice of Lee.

Now let's look at the reverse. Some of Kirby's solo creations include the New Gods, Mr. Miracle, the Forever People, Kamandi and the Demon. All of these are extremely strong concepts with innovative designs and knockout storytelling. However, the absence of Stan Lee's dialogue and editorial eye is noticeable. Another example of the two masters' strengths as a team is evident in their work on *Captain America* compared to the later work that Kirby did on the title when he returned to it as both writer and artist. Are we saying that "Kirby can't write," as his detractors are wont to do? *Certainly not.* What we are saying is that if Lee had as little to do with the process as Kirby alleged, then his absence should be less apparent in Kirby's post-Lee and post-Marvel work. And that's not the case.

To us, Lee and Kirby were an artistic collaboration in the best sense of the word, each suitably complementing the other's strengths.

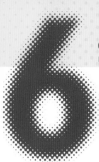

# Steve Ditko

While it's a common enough sentiment to refer to Marvel as "The House That Stan and Jack Built," there's a third column holding up the theoretical structure, one as absolutely essential as Stan Lee and Jack Kirby. His name is Steve Ditko.

Ditko had been with the company since its days operating under the name Atlas Comics, illustrating science-fiction and monster comics for the publisher since the mid-1950s. In 1963, when Lee decided to introduce a new teen hero called Spider-Man, he felt Jack Kirby's power-packed approach was a bad fit for the "everyman" kind of hero he had in mind, and instead turned to Ditko to design the character and illustrate his adventures. Ditko's lanky, outlandish style was a perfect fit for Spider-Man, and his shorter, wiry hero was the perfect counterpoint to all the other musclebound hero-types on the racks.

The design for Spider-Man's costume was also a brilliant stroke: bizarre and almost completely non-representational, with only the webbing and small emblem really getting across the spider motif. As a result, Spider-Man's costume (and often outlandish physical poses) came to signify the character more personally than most other great superhero archetypes; he doesn't look like a spider at all, but like Spider-Man. The Lee/Ditko run of *The Amazing Spider-Man* introduced almost all of Spider-Man's rogues' gallery and most of the significant supporting characters. It also established the baseline for the character, one that all successive Spidey creators would follow. If Marvel's eventual domination of the comics industry can be chalked up to Spider-Man's runaway success, then Ditko deserves as much of the credit as Lee and Kirby.

Following the success of Spider-Man came another Lee/Ditko collaboration, Doctor Strange, Marvel's master of the mystic arts. Whether the character was originally the brainchild of Lee or Ditko is unclear, but its success can most definitely be attributed to both. Lee's knack for creating insanely catchy names and phrases that easily roll off the tongue was at full bore in this strip, as evidenced in Doctor Strange's opponents, like the Dread Dormammu, his spells and mystic talismans, like the Eye of Agamotto, and his expressions: "By the Hoary Hosts of Hoggoth!" Thanks to Stan's dialogue, *Doctor Strange* sounded like nothing else out there, and thanks to Steve Ditko's psychedelic dreamscapes, it looked like nothing else, too. As for the storytelling, Ditko's conception of, for example, Strange's astral form leaving his body and entering the dreamworld was groundbreaking stuff in comics back in 1963, and his heavy use of inks and shadows gave the book an overall sense of moodiness not seen in any other books Marvel was publishing at the time.

Ditko left Marvel in 1966, and no one knows precisely his reasons. The most common belief is that Ditko disagreed with the decision by writer-editor Stan Lee to reveal Spidey's enemy the Green Goblin as Norman Osborn, the father of Spider-Man's best friend. Ditko felt crime in general to be anonymous, and to reveal the Goblin as someone Peter already knew went against Ditko's intentions, and the very point he was trying to make. Ditko has denied that this was the reason for his departure from Marvel. More likely, it was Ditko's increasing frustration with his lack of control over his work, as well as a lack of credit; Ditko was reportedly doing most of the plotting on *The Amazing Spider-Man*, while Lee still received full credit as writer. Whatever the reason, by 1966 Ditko was gone, baby, gone, and smaller publishing rival Charlton Comics was only too happy to give him a new home.

## RAISING THE QUESTION

In an earlier, pre-Marvel stint at Charlton, Ditko had (with writer Joe Gill) created the character Captain Atom. When he returned to the publisher in 1966, he returned to the character, as well. Ditko also created two more characters that would come to be what Charlton is best remembered for: the Blue Beetle and the Question.

A revamped version of a pre-existing character, Ditko's Blue Beetle was reminiscent of his work on *Spider-Man*, an acrobatic jokester with an aptitude for science. However, it was on *The Question* that readers would first see Ditko spread his wings. It was soon evident in examining Ditko's new work that his new employer was giving him the freedom to express himself more fully, a freedom he'd never enjoyed at Marvel. Suddenly some of Ditko's politics and personal beliefs began to come into play.

With the Question, Steve Ditko created an unforgettable character in both visual design and philosophical concept in just a few appearances. The Question is a hero with no face (a specially designed featureless mask obscures his identity), no compunctions about using intimidation to get answers, and such a secure moral high ground that he's willing to allow criminals to die in the course of their criminal acts. What was Ditko saying in making his hero faceless? A comment on the nature of heroism, that the individual must sacrifice himself to the greater good in order to stand against evil? Like all really intriguing ideas, there are no easy answers, and Lord knows we'll never get any out of Ditko.

Ditko took his Question concept even further in his later creation Mr. A, a similar character who wears a steel face mask with a suit and fedora, and leaves a calling card just like the Question. Unlike the Question's card—just a question mark—Mr. A's card is half black and half white, symbolic of the

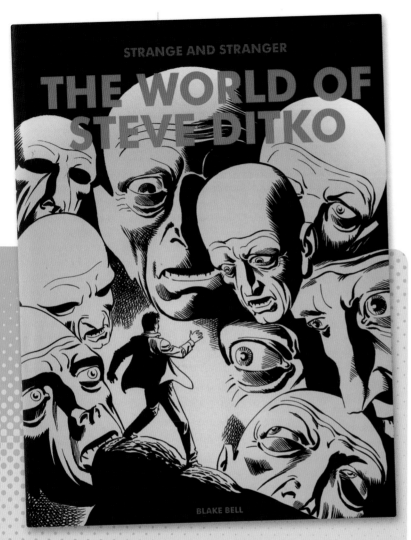

STRANGE AND STRANGER

# THE WORLD OF STEVE DITKO

BLAKE BELL

Perhaps the best—and one of the only—thorough explorations of Ditko's work was released last year.

character's belief that there is pure good and pure evil, and no moral gray areas.

After leaving Charlton, Ditko moved over to DC in the late 1960s, where he created characters like the Creeper, and Hawk and Dove. He even returned to Marvel, although never to the characters he'd made famous, Spider-Man and Doctor Strange.

Maddeningly protective of his privacy, the almost-never-photographed Steve Ditko still resides in New York, refusing to give interviews, although on rare occasions he releases statements regarding his comic-book work. While we have to respect the wishes of a man so steadfast in his convictions, we can't help but wish that he'd lower his guard just a little, to allow the countless fans who've gained so much from his work the opportunity to say "thanks." Hopefully, he at least knows we're out there.

---

### RECOMMENDED READING 101
#### STEVE DITKO

*Action Heroes Archives*, Vol. 1–2
*The Amazing Spider-Man Omnibus*
*Essential Doctor Strange*, Volume 1

---

# Chris Claremont

## 7

Think back for a minute to, say, high school or college. A pretty sizable chunk of your life, right? Now imagine spending *four times* that long writing a single group of characters.

Sixteen years. That's how long Chris Claremont was the writer on Marvel's *The Uncanny X-Men*, the series he revitalized, which in turn revitalized the American comic-book market with its breakthrough success, and supplanted Spider-Man as Marvel Comics's trademark series and primary cash cow.

Claremont got his first break at Marvel writing *Iron Fist*, about the company's kung-fu hero, before being assigned *X-Men* just as the series returned to print in 1975 after a long layoff. Although the new team and its superheroic mutant characters had been earlier created by Len Wein for their debut appearance in *Giant-Size X-Men* #1 (May 1975), their personalities and relationships were the sole creation of Claremont, who took over the series with issue #94 (August 1975), the first to follow their *Giant-Size* return.

In Claremont's hands *The Uncanny X-Men* was like nothing Marvel was publishing at the time. Claremont was plotting for the long haul, with lengthy, continued storylines that would last for months at a time, and subplots that would linger on for years. In Claremont's hands, the book was a true ensemble, with all of the team members getting a fair share of the spotlight (with the exception of Professor Xavier, who Claremont had a tendency to remove from the picture so as not to let his perhaps-too-powerful psychic abilities solve things too easily and too often). Another trademark of Claremont's run was strong female protagonists, from Jean Grey, Storm and Moira MacTaggert in the series' early years to later additions Rogue and Kitty Pryde.

From a narrative perspective, Claremont made great use of third-person narration, almost to the point of intrusion, although, Claremont managed to keep readers drawn in,

## CHRIS SAYS

In addition to being revered for his work on *X-Men* (and its spin-off book, *New Mutants*), another skill of Claremont's was to write nearly every character in its perfect "voice," whether it was one he'd handled before or not. Beyond fully developing new X-Men like Wolverine—particularly in a groundbreaking miniseries he and artist Frank Miller produced in 1982—Claremont's deft touch included memorable interpretations of Marvel icons as disparate as Spider-Man (*Marvel Team-Up*), the Avengers (*The X-Men vs. the Avengers*) and even the Micronauts (*The X-Men and the Micronauts*). For kids of the 1980s, there weren't too many superhero books better than those helmed by Claremont.

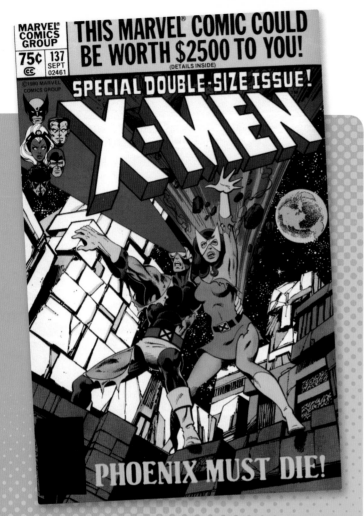

"The Fate of the Phoenix!" capped off a brilliant and creative storyline in a tragic way, as you could surmise by the issue's sub-title.

thanks to his elegant turns of phrase. In terms of theme, Claremont found the right tone to make *X-Men* constantly relevant to young readers. He keyed in on the feelings of alienation and awkwardness familiar to adolescents, allowing readers to strongly identify with the characters. At the same time, he used the anti-mutant hatred as a stand-in for very real issues such as racism and homophobia.

Claremont's best work is probably his most famous one, "The Dark Phoenix Saga" from the pages of *The Uncanny X-Men*, which traumatized a generation of young readers with the unexpected death of the series' lead heroine, Jean Grey. However, to really appreciate the scope of what Claremont accomplished, you have to look at his sixteen-year *X-Men* run as a whole. The more than 4,000-page literary work continues to influence popular culture to this day. Many of the *X-Men* comics currently created bear its influence, and hundreds of X-Men-themed television shows and movies still mine Claremont's work for material.

---

### RECOMMENDED READING 101

#### CHRIS CLAREMONT

*The Uncanny X-Men Omnibus*

*Wolverine* by Chris Claremont and Frank Miller

*X-Men: The Dark Phoenix Saga* by Chris Claremont and John Byrne

*X-Men: God Loves, Man Kills* by Chris Claremont and Brent Anderson

---

# John Byrne

**8**

Not many creators can lay claim to being a true successor to the legacy of Jack "The King" Kirby. John Byrne, through his decades of impressive output as both an artist and a writer/artist, is one of the few.

Byrne, British-born but Canadian-raised, began his artistic career humbly enough. In the mid-1970s, he worked for Charlton, drawing a back-up strip called *ROG-2000* and illustrating licensed books such as *Wheelie and the Chopper Bunch* and *Space: 1999*. His work on these titles caught the attention of Marvel Comics, which brought him on to tackle some of its floundering titles such as *Marvel Team-Up* and *Iron Fist*. Even then, his dynamic, naturalistic linework stood above many of his peers', and he began to elevate these low-selling titles to sales levels Marvel hadn't experienced before. But it was his work on another of Marvel's titles that would produce the first landmark work of Byrne's artistic career.

In the late 1970s, Byrne took over the art chores on *The Uncanny X-Men* from Dave Cockrum. Cockrum was the artist since the title's relaunch in issue #94, the first to feature the "all-new, all-different" X-Men. Byrne came aboard on issue #108 (December 1977), and his star and that of the title rose together nearly overnight. The creative team on this book, writer Chris Claremont, Byrne and inker Terry Austin, produced one of the most classic runs in all of comics, still the yardstick by which all subsequent *X-Men* comics (and movies) have been measured. During Byrne's tenure, the team defined the character of Wolverine, making him one of the most popular characters in all of Marvel; they produced "The Dark Phoenix Saga," a truly epic and shocking story that inspired the plot of the recent big-screen movies; and they introduced the Canadian super-team Alpha Flight, a team that would eventually spin off into its own title written and drawn by Byrne.

An opinionated, outspoken storyteller, Byrne was involved in much of the plotting on *X-Men*. When he disagreed with the editorial decision to kill Phoenix, he left the book soon after that storyline was complete. Nearly every title Byrne worked on at the time became a fan-favorite—his work with Roger Stern on *Captain America*, while only nine issues in length, is another such example. But he would take a huge step forward when he began his lengthy run as both the writer and artist on *Fantastic Four* in 1981.

While Lee and Kirby produced 102 consecutive issues of the title, Byrne stuck around for sixty-two issues (plus a few annuals he either wrote or drew or both). In that time, he returned the title to a prominence it hadn't seen since the Lee/Kirby team broke up (and arguably hasn't seen since Byrne left).

Byrne's work on *Fantastic Four* showcased his strength as a writer right from the start, and began his habit of introducing lasting changes on a title, a move that would both win over and alienate fans in the years to come. Here, it worked masterfully. He created characters and concepts that not only epitomized the anything-goes era of Lee and Kirby but also moved the title forward, emphasizing both the familial aspects of the team and the huge, innovative ideas that had been long missing. It took him five issues to fully make the book his own. While his first few issues were serviceable, it was the title's twentieth-anniversary issue, *Fantastic Four* #236 (November 1981), that clued people in that he had bigger things in mind for his run. The extra-length story, "Terror in a Tiny Town," spent as much time developing the family dynamic of the characters as it did introducing an interesting new threat from a perfectly characterized Doctor Doom.

Byrne took the team in directions that felt organic to what had come before while also being truly innovative. He further mutated the misshapen, tragic Thing; he turned the Human Torch's girlfriend into a herald of Galactus; he even managed to juggle lighter storylines, such as adding She-Hulk to the team alongside his most serious direction for the title, Sue Richards's sensitively handled miscarriage. Nearly the entirety of Byrne's *Fantastic Four* run has been collected in trade paperback form now, and all are well worth checking out.

When Byrne left the title under circumstances that have never been fully explained —

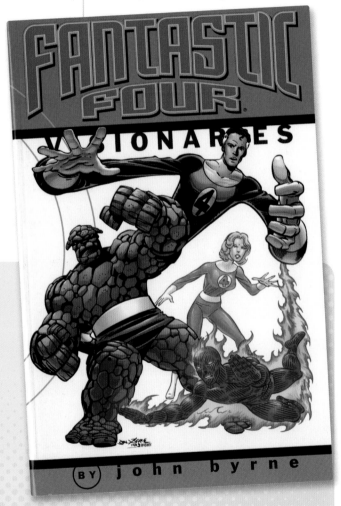

Byrne's *Fantastic Four* is second only to Lee's and Kirby's in creativity and adoration.

he left his final storyline midstream—he took his revisionist talent to DC Comics, which had just produced the *Crisis on Infinite Earths* miniseries that effectively reset its universe. Byrne was hired on to relaunch Superman in the form of a miniseries called *The Man of Steel*, and then a new *Superman* title or two to follow. His retelling of Superman's beginnings updated some aspects of the origin laid down a half-century before, but it also changed some aspects of the character that fans didn't appreciate.

In the intervening decades, Byrne would alternate between Marvel and DC, revamping titles like *The West Coast Avengers* and *The Sensational She-Hulk* for Marvel and *Wonder Woman*, *New Gods* and *Doom Patrol* for DC. He did return to the *X-Men* titles as writer, too, but his run there was rather short and unremarkable. After working on other Marvel titles, including *Namor* and *Iron Man*, Byrne left behind work-for-hire jobs and went off to create some characters of his own.

Byrne headed to Dark Horse Comics to help kick off its burgeoning Legends line. His post-superhero title for this line, *John Byrne's Next Men*, was a true return to form. It was an advancement of his previous work on superhero titles and told a more mature story than people had previously seen from him. The complete series has been collected in two volumes and is an excellent showcase of Byrne's many strengths as a creator.

In 1998, Byrne again returned to Marvel, this time in an attempt to give Spider-Man his

*John Byrne's Next Men* was a fitting addition to Dark Horse's Legends line.

own reboot and makeover. *Spider-Man: Chapter One* managed to change the 1962 origin in unnecessary places while at the same time staying too slavish to what Lee and Ditko created to actually make any substantial changes that mattered to fans. But you can't win 'em all, especially in a career that's lasted more than three decades.

Byrne has produced an amazing amount of pages in his career, working at a pace of two or three finished pages per day. He has written the majority of comics he's illustrated since originally leaving *X-Men*, and at times he's even lettered his own work. His tendency to change elements in long-running characters (he's working in an industry built on maintaining some form of character status quo, after all) as well as his outspoken, forthright personality have worked to his detriment at times, but in these days of Internet anonymity and an impassioned fanbase, that's not unexpected or even uncourted by Byrne every now and then.

A long-time *Star Trek* fan, John has in recent years turned to writing and drawing comics based on that property. He admits his pace has "slowed" to producing two pages of scripted, pencilled and inked pages per day, but that's still a King-ly pace that outmatches nearly every other artist working today.

A cover to 2008's *FX* shows that all roads eventually lead Byrne back to superhero comics.

---

### RECOMMENDED READING 101

#### *JOHN BYRNE*

*Fantastic Four Visionaries* – John Byrne, Vol. 1–8

*John Byrne's Compleat Next Men*, Vol. 1–2

*Superman: The Man of Steel*, Vol. 1–6

*X-Men: The Dark Phoenix Saga* by Chris Claremont and John Byrne

# George Pérez

## 9

When people don't know how else to compliment a piece of comic-book art, many times they fall back on the obvious: the detail. "Just look at the detail…" Nowhere is that somewhat trite piece of praise more appropriate than when discussing the work of artist George Pérez. He is certainly known for his insanely intricate linework, but to focus on that alone glosses over so much more in the artistic style of the man who has become known as comics' premier "team-book" illustrator, and who has remained a fan favorite for well over three decades.

A self-taught artist from Queens, New York, George Pérez got his start in comics at Marvel in the mid-1970s, providing art for the publisher's kung-fu feature *Sons of the Tiger*, before moving up to more high-profile assignments such as *The Avengers* and *Fantastic Four*. Young and eager to work, Pérez often found himself taking on team books that were less popular with the older, more established artists, simply because they had so many more characters to draw each month. Here, especially on *The Avengers*, is where Pérez first made a name for himself.

Soon other publishers were knocking on Pérez's door, and he made the jump to DC in the early 1980s, first on a well-received run on DC's *Justice League of America* and then on a book with writer Marv Wolfman that would become DC's biggest hit in years, *The New Teen Titans*. Suddenly the 800-pound gorillas

Pérez helped ring in the U.S. Bicentennial with this image from Marvel's 1976 calendar.

MARVEL CALENDAR: © 1976 MARVEL ENTERTAINMENT, INC. USED WITH PERMISSION. ART BY GEORGE PÉREZ AND JOE SINNOTT.

at DC (and rightfully so—*The New Teen Titans* was more exciting and vibrant than anything DC had published in years), Wolfman and Peréz, stepped right over to *Crisis on Infinite Earths* in 1985. This twelve-issue maxiseries set out to redefine DC's universe, and gave Pérez the opportunity to draw every single character in DC Comics history, or at least as close as any one man will ever come.

After a somewhat fallow period in the late 1980s and early 1990s, Pérez came back strong in 1994, providing the art for Peter David's Incredible Hulk graphic novel *Future Imperfect*. In 1998, he returned to the book that started it all for him, providing the art-work for Kurt Busiek's revival of *The Avengers*, staying on the series for a critically acclaimed three-year stint. Back at Marvel, Pérez had the chance to return to his dream project that had been aborted decades earlier, the victim of inter-company politics: *JLA/Avengers*. The long-awaited crossover of DC's and Marvel's biggest superhero teams was larger and more ambitious than anyone could have imagined, with Pérez and writer Busiek managing to include every character who had ever been a member of either team, in a globe-trotting adventure that spanned space and time. It's one of Pérez's most impressive single pieces of work.

So what makes Pérez so great besides the aforementioned intricate detail and willing-ness to include a cast of thousands? Pérez is not only a great artist, but he's just as great a storyteller, able to convey great emotion in his characters through body language and facial expression. Pérez also is extremely innovative at page layout, often employing dozens of tiny panels on a page to get across a multiplicity of action, yet keeping the storytelling clear and understandable. And there's also Pérez's gift with faces, a skill shown off best in his most recent *Avengers* run. He often depicts scenes of members Captain America, Hawkeye and Goliath with their masks off: three blonde-haired Caucasian men in their early 30s, but not a moment of confusion as to who is who.

Now back at DC Comics, Pérez works on such comics as the team-up series *The Brave & the Bold*, another *Crisis* series and *Legion of Super-Heroes,* all or which offer the requisite team-book challenges on which Pérez thrives.

---

## RECOMMENDED READING 101
### GEORGE PÉREZ

*Avengers Assemble*, Vol. 1–2 by Kurt Busiek and George Pérez

*Crisis on Infinite Earths* by Marv Wolfman and George Pérez

*The Incredible Hulk: Future Imperfect* by Peter David and George Pérez

*JLA/Avengers* by Kurt Busiek and George Pérez

*The New Teen Titans Archives*, Vol. 1–3 by Marv Wolfman and George Pérez

# Frank Miller

## 10

Frank Miller has gotten his share of the spotlight in recent years as he's transitioned into film, first as co-director with Robert Rodriguez on the movie adaptation of *Sin City*, then as the visual inspiration for Zack Snyder's bravura adaptation of Miller's book *300*, and most recently for his solo directorial debut on the adaptation of Will Eisner's *The Spirit*. It's therefore somehow pleasing to realize that it all got started because once upon a time, Frank Miller was just a guy who wanted to draw comic books.

Miller broke into comics in the late 1970s, with a two-issue stint on *Peter Parker* which led to his assignment as regular *Daredevil* artist. Not until Frank Miller took over the writing duties on the series did the tone fully shift to what Miller was looking to create: more serious, gritty drama. Miller, a big fan of the 1950s EC crime comics, applied much of that feel to *Daredevil*. By redefining characters such as the Kingpin and Bullseye to be more realistic and genuinely menacing, and introducing the femme fatale Elektra, inspired by strong female characters P'Gell and Sand Saref in Will Eisner's *The Spirit*, the ground was set for a landmark run on *Daredevil* that would influence the series for the next two decades.

Spanning roughly thirty issues of *Daredevil* (#158–190, 1979–1983), these stories are where Frank Miller truly came into his own as a writer and artist. Here can be found the introduction and loss of Elektra, and the classic clashes with Bullseye and the Kingpin. Everyone who's worked on *Daredevil* for the past twenty years has done so in the shadow of Miller's remarkable work. Looking back, it may seem a bit tame and melodramatic compared to what's out there today, but it's important to remember that no one was doing this kind of storytelling at the time, especially at Marvel.

While just about everyone considers Miller's first run on the series to be revolutionary stuff, his second stint is much more powerful. In "Born Again" (#227–233, 1986), we see what happens when the Kingpin is handed a slip of paper with that most precious of commodities: information. To be exact, Daredevil's real name. After the Kingpin succeeds in completely destroying Matt Murdock's life, Murdock slowly loses his grip on the world around him and descends into what can only be described as a full nervous breakdown. Miller takes us through hell with Matt Murdock, and sees us through to the other side. Some of the best writing of Miller's career is matched by fantastic pencils and inks from David Mazzucchelli that evoke Miller's style without merely copying it.

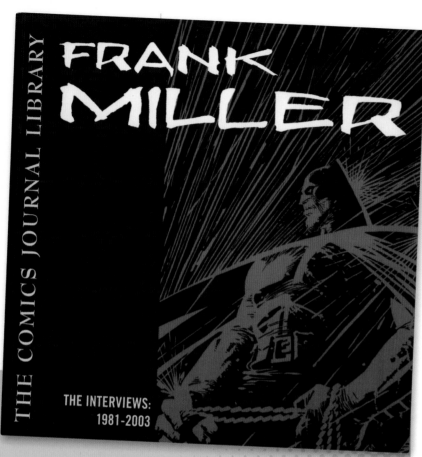

THE COMICS JOURNAL LIBRARY

FRANK MILLER

THE INTERVIEWS:
1981-2003

Miller's opinionated interviews are as captivating to read as the stories and art he produces.

One of Miller's most widely read works is his 1986 graphic novel *Batman: The Dark Knight Returns*. Miller's conception—Batman as a tersely speaking urban vigilante with a tendency to play a little rougher than longtime Bat-fans were accustomed to—had such an impact on the popular culture that it forever affected the character in whatever genre it appeared in, whether in film, animation or the comics themselves. Driving this four-issue series is a strong, compelling story, one of Miller's best, which holds up more

## RECOMMENDED READING 101

### FRANK MILLER

*Batman: The Dark Knight Returns*

*Batman: Year One* by Frank Miller and Dave Mazzucchelli

*Daredevil: Born Again* by Frank Miller and Dave Mazzucchelli

*Daredevil Visionaries–Frank Miller*, Vol. 1–3

*Elektra: Assassin* by Frank Miller and Bill Sienkiewicz

*Hard Boiled* by Frank Miller and Geof Darrow

*Ronin*

*Sin City: The Big Fat Kill*

*Sin City: The Hard Goodbye*

*Sin City: That Yellow Bastard*

*300*

than two decades later, and still has the crackle and spark of a brand-new book.

*The Dark Knight Returns* still stands as a high point in Frank Miller's artistic development. While some of his later work on *Sin City* revealed a singular, more impressionistic approach some consider more aesthetically pleasing, here Miller is still tempering that with a more traditional mainstream style, which is quite effective for this particular book. Miller also delves heavily into media influence in *Dark Knight*. Much of the storyline's background and exposition are established by the talking heads of network television news anchors and commentators, a device seen so often nowadays it is almost cliché, but which was a bold new approach in 1986. Miller keenly anticipated the overpowering presence of today's media. What then seemed like a parody of television now can pass by the reader practically unnoticed. The notion of a cranky middle-aged Batman coming out of retirement and struggling to do the things that once came so easy is a deliciously appealing one. Miller takes full advantage, both for humor and for drama's sake, as Batman's crusade seems all the more heroic now that it hurts him so much to continue, and he has to try so much harder.

After the astounding critical and commercial acclaim of *Dark Knight*, Miller was catapulted into another realm as a creator—he could now do anything he wanted and feel secure that there would be an audience for his work. With this newfound freedom, Miller

## CHRIS SAYS

Miller's *Daredevil* run was something that snuck up on me when I was twelve. My local retailer told me about this new comic that Marvel was producing, *Marvel Fanfare*. At $1.25, it was a bit pricey at the time, but "worth it," he told me, "because the back cover is by the next superstar at Marvel." It was a dark, sketchy image of Daredevil drawn by Frank Miller, an unknown to me. And it was nothing that spoke of greatness, really. But it was different. I was twelve, I was ready for different, so I gave *Daredevil* a shot. The first issue I picked up turned out to be issue #181 (April 1982), the monumental death of Elektra issue (talk about coming in at the end of a story). And soon I was spending all my paper-route income on every back issue I could find. This Frank Miller guy blew me away with his darker stories, his ninjas, his ability to turn a character I always remembered as a jokey, blind Spider-Man-type into something totally new and yet totally organic. And he got better from there, with *Ronin* and "Born Again" and *Elektra: Assassin* and so many others. Not to mention *Dark Knight Returns* and *Batman: Year One*. Even though I came to *Daredevil* a bit late, I have my retailer to thank for not allowing me to miss all the greatness to come. Listen to your retailer, kids—they really know their stuff.

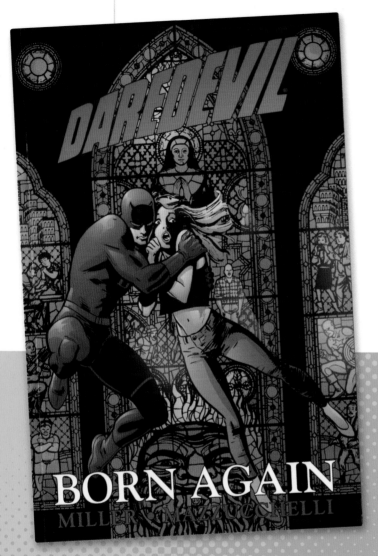

threw himself into a work that could never be published at DC or Marvel, not only because neither publisher had any interest in publishing non-superhero work, but also because Miller's new series would be unashamedly sexy and violent, oft-disturbing rampage of fists, babes and bullets, combining the best of all of Miller's influences (EC crime comics, writers Mickey Spillane, Dashiell Hammett and Raymond Chandler, artists Jack Kirby and Bernie Krigstein) with a vision uniquely his own. This entirely new beast was the series of graphic novels and miniseries, written and drawn by Miller, collectively known as *Sin City*. *Sin City* is where Miller's heart truly lies, and stands as the best example of Miller's talent and skill as a storyteller. Start with *The Hard Goodbye*—you won't be disappointed.

The year 1986 is considered the greatest single year ever in comics due in part to this book.

# Mark Gruenwald

## Scott remembers Da Gru

It's time once more for another trip in the Way-back Machine, this time to the year 1987. Teen-aged Scott (I must've been either a sophomore or a junior in high school, I'm thinking) is on the way out the door one morning when the phone rings. My mother picks it up, speaks for a minute, and then hands me the receiver: "Phone for you. It's Mark," she says, assuming it's a friend of mine, having asked who's calling.

"Hello?"

An unfamiliar voice began: "Scott? This is Mark Gruenwald. I'm an editor at Marvel Comics."

I didn't need the explanation. At the time, Gruenwald was editing most of my favorite comics, including all three *Avengers* series, as well as writing *Captain America*, which was in the middle of what was, for me, the best storyline the series had seen in years. But why would Gruenwald at the Marvel offices in New York be calling my parents' house in California?

You might recall from an earlier chapter (page 55) that I was a full-on comic-book letterhack when I was just a fledgling teenaged fanboy. My fan letters appeared in the letters pages of all kinds of Marvel and DC books. (The morbidly curious among you can look in late-1980s issues of comics like *The Avengers*, *The West Coast Avengers*, *Captain America*, *The Incredible Hulk*, *The Flash*, *Secret Origins* and many others for examples of my far-from-deathless prose.)

"Uh, hey, Mark … what's up?" I kind of mumbled.

"So we just got your letter about the Hawkeye series, and I just wanted you to know that I've got Mark Bright in my office right now, and he's redrawing the art for the next issue, putting notches on all the arrows." I could hear someone else laughing in the background.

Notches on the … and then I remembered. I had just written a wiseass letter to the *Solo Avengers* letter column about the fact that Hawkeye must be having some difficulty firing his arrows, since there were no nocks at the ends of the shafts for the bowstring to rest in. Hey, cut me some slack—that's what passes for cleverness when you're sixteen years old, and besides, in my defense, artist Mark Bright used to draw these arrows really large in the panels—it was like Hawkeye was firing bowling pins, and you couldn't miss the fact there was no notch for Hawkeye to nock the arrow.

Gruenwald and I chatted about Marvel comics for a few more minutes, and then before I knew it, the call was over. I really don't remember much of what else was said that day—I was just stunned to be getting a call at my house from Marvel over something as petty as Hawkeye's arrows. I'm sure that's why Gruenwald made the call. Based on what I know about him from our numerous subsequent conversations, as well as everything I've read, the sheer randomness of such a phone call no doubt appealed to his wicked sense of humor.

That was how I first "met" Mark, the man who would become, for me, the face of Marvel Comics. I would get to know him better over the years through continued correspondence and our annual meetings at conventions, until his tragic and far too early death in 1996. The summer convention season always makes me think about "Da Gru," the comics he wrote, what made him a good editor and what an all-around decent fellow he was. A good man gone too soon: "Marvelous" Mark Gruenwald.

Born June 18, 1953, in Oshkosh, Wisconsin, Mark Gruenwald fell in love with comics at an early age, buying most of the early Marvels off the rack when they were first published, and forming an affection for Gardner Fox's *Justice League of America* comics that would continue throughout his life, showing itself prominently in his most acclaimed work, *Squadron Supreme* (1985). Mark graduated from the University of Wisconsin Oshkosh in 1975 with a degree in art and literature, put together a portfolio and set off for a visit to New York to break into comics. After being rebuffed by both Marvel and DC, Gruenwald decided that the only way to make this happen was to pick up and move to New York, with no job and no prospects. Taking work as a file clerk in a bank to pay the bills, Mark and fellow comics superfan Dean Mullaney began publishing a fanzine called *Omniverse*, which explored the notion of "reality" and continuity in comics, and which Mark hoped showed off his writing, editing and design skills. Clearly, the plan worked, and in 1978

Mark was hired by Marvel's then-new editor-in-chief Jim Shooter as an assistant editor.

Mark rose quickly through the ranks, becoming a full editor on many books, including *The Avengers*, *The West Coast Avengers*, *Iron Man* and *Spider-Woman*. After thriving in that position for many years, Mark was promoted to executive editor in 1988, a post he held for several years, before finally being promoted to editor-in-chief of the Marvel Heroes line in 1995 (at the time Marvel divided its publishing output into five separate imprints, each group of titles with its own editor-in-chief).

For most of this time, Mark was Marvel's resident "continuity cop," acting as the primary in-house source for information, history and current status of Marvel's characters. This no doubt led him in 1983 to create, edit and co-write *The Official Handbook of the Marvel Universe*, an exhaustively researched reference series that lists all of Marvel's characters, concepts, locations and technology from A to Z.

Mark was also active creatively throughout his time at Marvel, writing for such series as *Marvel Two-in-One*, *Hawkeye*, *D.P. 7*, *Squadron Supreme* and a lengthy, world-record run on *Captain America*, spanning some 136 issues (#307–443)—over ten years on the series. However, it was his work as an editor that had the most impact on me. From the outside looking in, it's impossible to realize what makes an editor good at his job. All I knew then was that I enjoyed the books he edited more than the rest of Marvel's line. More than that, Mark, a fan himself, realized that part of his job as editor was to connect with fans, get them excited about comics and, more important, get them excited about Marvel. For Mark, the best way to go about this was through the comic conventions, where he would go out of his way to transform the traditionally stodgy panels and discussions into things far more fun and memorable.

I remember one year at WonderCon in Oakland attending what was listed as a "Marvel Q & A Panel." (This was back when Marvel still attended the smaller conventions, a move which I think works miracles for creating lifelong fans.) As Mark came out to greet the crowd, he was holding a brown paper sack. Questions would be asked and answered, Mark revealed, but the only way to ask a question was to first receive …"The Bun of Inquisition!" Mark then dramatically reached in the bag and slowly withdrew a bran muffin, much to the excited gasps and murmurs of the audience, completely playing along with the gag. Mark then proceeded to huck the muffin around the room for the next hour and a half, hurling it in turn at each potential questioner, who would need to pluck the slowly disintegrating muffin from the air in order to ask his question. I think it was two or three questions after I had thrown it back that the muffin finally exploded in mid-air. The dejected crowd moaned at the sight, only to break into a wall-shaking roar when Mark reached back into the sack and thrust a second muffin into the air, as if pulling Excalibur from the stone. It seems like such a small thing, but in all my years at the cons, I've never seen a crowd leave a panel in a better mood.

Even the more routine panels about Marvel books were a lot more exciting with Mark in charge. Before the panel began, while the crowd was still filling the seats, Mark would get up onstage and do this bizarre maneuver that my girlfriend still refers to as "the stompy dance." He would stomp on the wooden stage with what seemed like a giant shoe, over and over and over, with his elbows jutting out at an odd angle. This insanely loud stomping noise would get the crowd more and more fired up until soon they were clapping and stomping along, worked into an absolute frenzy. By the time the guests were announced, it didn't matter who was coming out; it could have been the letterer on *Power Pack*, and the crowd would have roared as if it was Stan Lee and Jack Kirby flying in on jetpacks.

It was after Mark's surprise call to my house that we got to know each other better. The following year at WonderCon, I was looking through the preview issues at the Marvel booth when Mark approached, noticing the name on my badge, "Still checking the arrows?" It was clear he knew who I was past the single phone call—he had mentioned characters and stories I'd liked and disliked and had written to him about in numerous fan letters, some of which had been printed, and some not. Every year after that, Mark and I would meet up at WonderCon and discuss the previous year's books, what I'd liked, what I hadn't, the things he thought had worked and the things he thought could have been improved. Mark would without fail hassle me for my favorite characters: "Look, Hank Pym is staying retired, and you're the only one asking to see Stegron the Dinosaur Man again." My suggestion for a no-doubt best-selling Yellowjacket/Stegron miniseries went untaken, needless to say. One year, I stopped by the Marvel booth and Mark was immediately on the attack—"Buy any Ant-Man comics yet?"—only to mime being outdrawn, gunfight-style, when I pulled a Silver Age *Tales to Astonish* out of my bag, which I'd purchased just minutes before.

Our annual meetings continued through my college years; I'd make the trip from Santa Barbara to Oakland every spring for WonderCon. When graduation neared, I wrote to Mark and asked how the employment outlook was for an assistant editor's position. Mark replied with the blunt, but honest truth: business was bad, they were in the middle of layoffs and he wasn't even that confident about his own position. He left his office number, and we talked about it some more on the phone. Mark tried to be positive about possibilities down the road, but it was clear that Marvel wouldn't be doing any hiring any time soon.

When Marvel reorganized, it gave up its separate-imprint structure, and Mark was passed over as editor-in-chief. I thought (and hoped) that he'd head over to DC, where his old assistant Mike Carlin was in charge at the time—he'd get the chance to work on so many characters he'd never had the opportunity to write. Instead, Gruenwald and Carlin wound up working together on a project decades in the making: *DC versus Marvel Comics*, a miniseries that would pit all of Marvel and DC's heavy hitters against one another, with fans voting to decide the outcomes.

Just as *DC versus Marvel* was hitting the stands, tragedy struck, with Mark's shocking and unexpected death from a heart attack at the age of forty-three.

Before his untimely death, Mark had requested that his body be cremated, and the ashes blended with the printer's ink used in the production of a comic book. His widow Catherine and Marvel carried out the request, and in 1997, a trade paperback collection of Mark's critically acclaimed *Squadron Supreme* series was published, with the ink containing, as his wife put it in the book's foreword, "actual particles of the Gru." Although some found the request odd or macabre, I thought it perfectly in character, reflective both of his love of comics and his often completely chaotic and unpredictable sense of humor.

The summer following his death, a memorial panel was held at the San Diego Comic-Con for Mark Gruenwald. It was a packed room, probably a couple hundred people in attendance, and many of Mark's friends and fans got up to speak. I'm pretty sure I told the phone-call story.

Mark's widow, Catherine, brought us all a gift that day: video footage taken of Mark from his years at Marvel and from a local-access sketch comedy TV show that Mark and a few other Marvel cohorts did for a couple of years. We got to see some of his legendary office stunts like filling the office with crumpled paper floor-to-ceiling, or building a three-foot-tall platform beneath his desk and chair, so that he towered over all who entered; we got to see some of his equally famous quirks, like his insistence that absolutely nothing be left on the surface of one's desk (even the telephone was tucked away in a desk drawer); mostly we just got to see Mark again.

As we got ready to leave that day, Catherine had a favor to ask: we'd all seen on the video this

Da Gru is gone, but his wisdom remains, thanks to the list of *Life Lessons* handed out at Comic-Con that year.

odd, silly walk that Mark would do from time to time just to get some easy laughs, a kind of mix of a laid-back saunter and a John Cleese-style high-step. She thought Mark would like it if we all walked out of the room that way, and not tell any of the people waiting to come in for the next panel what we were doing. Sure enough, about two hundred people came lurching out of that room one at a time, and not a word was said.

Catherine passed out to all of us that day a list of life lessons that Mark had written for his column in *Marvel Age* magazine, and looking through it now, Lesson #168 strikes a bittersweet note:

> *"Someday the universe will tire of me and will break me down into the components I came from. Right now I'd mind if that happened, but when the time comes I imagine I will welcome no longer being separate from the rest of reality."*

That may be, but the rest of us are all the poorer for it.

### RECOMMENDED READING 101

#### MARK GRUENWALD

*Captain America* #332–350

*D.P. 7 Classic*, Vol. 1

*Essential Official Handbook of the Marvel Universe* – Deluxe Edition, Vol.1–3

*Hawkeye*

*Quasar* #1–60

*Squadron Supreme*

# Alan Moore

Whenever folks new to comics ask what graphic novels to pick up, we tend to recommend the same ones: *Watchmen, V for Vendetta, Swamp Thing*. It's no coincidence that these and so many more sprang from the mind of British writer Alan Moore, the "mad genius" of comics. There are countless things to say about Moore's work, but perhaps the most easily overlooked is the man's versatility. He can write anything, and do so with such subtlety and maddening effortlessness that it makes lesser writers (meaning, well, everybody else) gnash their teeth in frustration.

Moore's work on *Swamp Thing,* about a second-rate DC horror character, transformed it into an affecting, occasionally heartbreaking work of romance and suspense. His childhood affection for Marvelman, the British version of Fawcett Comics's Captain Marvel, spurred a startlingly stark and disturbing exploration of superpowers in *Miracleman. V for Vendetta* explores Moore's distrust of government and authority, taken to the ultimate degree and personified in V, probably the most cheerful and likable anarchist murderer in popular fiction. And finally, acting almost as a capstone to this period of his work is *Watchmen,* Moore and Dave Gibbons's ultimate deconstruction of the comic-book superhero, pulling in readers with a "real-world" approach, then absorbing them

in a work so intricate in its storytelling devices and layered themes that even after having read the book dozens of times, new nuances can still be discovered upon every reading.

After a bit of a fallow period, Moore roared back to life in the 1990s with scores of new projects. With artist Eddie Campbell, Moore published *From Hell*, a scratchy and chilling look at the Whitechapel murders and the theory of Jack the Ripper's identity. Working for Rob Liefeld's publishing company, Moore wallowed in his love for the Silver Age Superman in the *Supreme* series, a book that subtly mocked and analyzed the classic comics while it was at the same time paying tribute. (Moore had already written what many consider to be the best Superman story ever in "Whatever Happened to the Man of Tomorrow?" This would be the final appearance of the classic Silver Age Kal-El before John Byrne's post-*Crisis* revamp.)

Moore's output took a prodigious leap forward in 1999 with the creation of his own new comics imprint, America's Best Comics. (Published through Jim Lee's company Wildstorm, it was later purchased by DC, putting the then famously anti-DC Moore in a sticky position, which never quite settled itself to Moore's satisfaction.) After a long drought of new Alan Moore comics, suddenly new and absolutely wonderful series were hitting the shelves practically every week. *Tom Strong* channeled the best of Tarzan, Superman and Doc Savage in a brilliant mix of styles and themes. Moore's *Tomorrow Stories* put out a variety of comics archetypes, most notably Greyshirt, a thinly disguised Spirit pastiche that let Moore flex his muscles with the eight-page short story in Eisner's style. All of Moore's new interests in sorcery and the psychology of "magic" showed up in *Promethea*, and in a notion of sheer genius, Moore combined the superhero team with the storytelling style and interconnected storylines and characters of the TV cop drama in *Top 10*.

And as if all that wasn't enough, Moore took the superhero team back to the Victorian age in *The League of Extraordinary Gentlemen* (1999) uniting famed characters Allan Quatermain, Dr. Jekyll, Mina Harker, Captain Nemo and the Invisible Man in several globe-trotting adventures teeming with characters, locales and concepts from the literature of the period, so carefully and smoothly combined that the casual reader would barely notice. Moore's most recent installment of his *League* series, *Black Dossier* (2007), jumps ahead to the 1950s, as a rejuvenated Allan Quatermain and Mina Harker dodge familiar spies in a metafictional Great Britain attempting to get hold of the Black Dossier, the secret history of all the different iterations of the League that have existed over the decades. In typical Moore fashion, the book is packed with countless literary references both obvious and arcane.

Still, it's Moore and collaborator Kevin O'Neill at their best, duplicating all manner of publications from newspaper comics to government reports to Tijuana bibles, forcing readers to delve for meaning and create the history for themselves from these entirely fabricated "primary sources." A dense, engrossing read.

Moore courted controversy in 2006 with his massive work *Lost Girls*, an X-rated fairy-tale art book from Moore and his partner, Melinda Gebbie. Set in an Austrian hotel in 1914, *Lost Girls* follows the relationships of three women who begin to share their sexual histories (and later themselves) against the backdrop of a world sliding into global war. The women? Alice (a British high-society type), Wendy (a middle-class Londoner) and Dorothy (a Kansas farmgirl). If the names sound familiar, they should. Moore explores these familiar fairy tales, tapping into our affection and knowledge and casting them in a new and unsettling light, not merely to shock, but to take advantage of the weight the stories carry. At the same time, there's no denying *Lost Girls'* erotic nature, either. This is straight-out porn, with graphic depictions of sexual intercourse of just about every variation imaginable, straight, gay and otherwise. Yet Alan Moore's breathtaking craft elevates it to something more, a liberating and at the same time oddly poignant exploration of sexuality and how it's both celebrated and suppressed.

With *Lost Girls*, artist Melinda Gebbie brings the best work of her career, shifting her style and method to best fit the tone and emotional mood of each chapter, making even the most shocking acts seem quietly lyrical. As for Moore, well, what can you say? It's Alan Moore. He spins touching, poetic dialogue like thread from a wheel, all while suffusing it with meaning and import that doesn't hit you until pages later. Moore cleverly paces the story, slowly ratcheting up the sexual content with each successive volume, until the final chapters, which contain some of the most graphic and controversial material. But by this point, it's easy to look past the "taboo" material to what the story is really about: the fragility of life in an uncertain world, and the all-too-human need to look to another for fleeting moments of pleasure.

Any one of these books would be enough to cement a writer's reputation. The fact that they're all the work of a single man is staggering.

---

### RECOMMENDED READING 101

#### ALAN MOORE

*From Hell* by Alan Moore and Eddie Campbell

*The League of Extraordinary Gentlemen* by Alan Moore and Kevin O'Neill

*Lost Girls* by Alan Moore and Melinda Gebbie

*Promethea*, Books 1–5 by Alan Moore and J.H. Williams III

*Superman: Whatever Happened to the Man of Tomorrow?* by Alan Moore, Curt Swan and George Pérez

*Tom Strong* by Alan Moore and Chris Sprouse

*Top 10: The Forty-Niners* by Alan Moore and Gene Ha

*V for Vendetta* by Alan Moore and David Lloyd

*Watchmen* by Alan Moore and Dave Gibbons

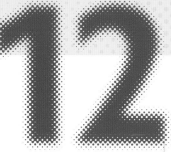

# Neil Gaiman

Neil Gaiman has made a name for himself as one of the most critically acclaimed creators of comic books, a writer whose landmark *The Sandman* series revitalized the notion of comic books as literature, and who has since crossed over into prose novels, television and film with unprecedented success.

Following the great success of Alan Moore on *Swamp Thing*, Neil Gaiman found his way to DC Comics via the publisher's new talent search program in Great Britain. Gaiman had already published some notable comics work, such as Eclipse's *Miracleman,* which he took over from Moore, and the graphic novels *Violent Cases, Signal to Noise* and *Mr. Punch* with collaborator Dave McKean. DC gave him a list of dormant properties to tackle, with the hopes he could breathe new life into them as Moore had done with *Swamp Thing*. Gaiman's

---

**RECOMMENDED READING 101**

### NEIL GAIMAN

*The Absolute Sandman*, Vol. 1-4

*Death: The High Cost of Living* by Neil Gaiman and artist Chris Bachalo

*Stardust* by Neil Gaiman and Andy Kubert

---

first project, *Black Orchid*, again with Dave McKean, was positively received but hardly a sensation. It was Gaiman's next attempt that catapulted him from little-known British newcomer to comics' #1 writer: *The Sandman*.

There had been previous Sandman characters at DC before: a 1940s cloaked mystery man (later turned standard tights-wearing superguy) and a psychedelic hero created in the 1970s by Joe Simon and Jack Kirby. However, Gaiman was given strict marching orders by his new editors: keep the name, but make everything else new. Left to his own devices, Gaiman first came up with his protagonist, Lord Morpheus, a.k.a. the immortal Lord of Dreams (who, by the way, is almost never called "The Sandman" in the work itself). Next he developed his own mythology—the Endless—Morpheus's brothers and sisters. The Endless are anthropomorphic representations of mankind's fears, hopes and driving forces: Destiny, Death, Destruction, Despair, Delight and Delirium.

Made up of ten graphic-novel collections, *Sandman* takes the reader though Morpheus's interactions with humanity, some minor and some major. Gaiman varies the tone of his stories widely, from a hunt for rogue nightmares in "The Doll's House" to a bidding war for Hell itself in "Season of Mists." Along the way, we find out about Morpheus's past over the centuries, his tragic love affairs with mortal women and the vendettas among his own kin that would eventually become his undoing. But in a larger metatextual sense, what *Sandman* is about is the very nature of storytelling, how we create stories for ourselves in our own lives to inspire or delude ourselves, and how it happens at the most primal level when we dream.

The popularity of *Sandman* prompted DC to create a separate imprint for its dark fantasy/horror books called Vertigo, whose launch was inaugurated by another series of Gaiman's, *Death: The High Cost of Living*, a solo miniseries starring Morpheus's older sister, Death. Probably the most popular character in Gaiman's *Sandman*, Death takes the form of a plucky, lovable sixteen-year-old girl with Goth-like eye makeup and an ankh around her neck, and goes about her duties of escorting mortals to the afterlife not by the glowering point of the scythe, but with a friendly slip through the arm. In one of the most heartbreaking moments in the series, we see a mortal visited by Death struggling with the unfairness of the situation. "Is that all? Is that all I get?" she asks.

"You get what everyone gets," replies Death, evenly but not unsympathetically. "You get a lifetime."

*The Sandman* was an anomaly at DC because it had a heavy female readership, many of whom were not habitual comics readers. The success of *Sandman* in collected graphic novel format certainly helps continually cultivate new readership, and has also prompted DC to heavily market its other comics in the collected format at mass media outlets and bookstores.

Gaiman elected to end his series with issue #75, building *The Sandman* to a grand crescendo with the death and rebirth of its title character. Since its finale, Gaiman has only dabbled in comics sporadically, with the most high-profile work being *1602*, a transplantation of Marvel's cast of superheroic characters to Elizabethan England. Most of Gaiman's time these days is spent on novels, such as *American Gods* and *Anansi Boys*, and film, such as the adaptation of his and Charles Vess's graphic novel *Stardust* and the Gaiman-scripted CGI-rendered *Beowulf*. However, from time to time Gaiman decides to grace the comics world with his presence, and it's always a welcome treat.

Chris and *Comic Books 101* cover artist Gabriel Rodriguez got to channel Gaiman in their comic book adaptation of the Gaiman/Avary *Beowulf* movie.

# 13 Grant Morrison

Like Neil Gaiman, Grant Morrison was another young writer offered work by DC after its talent-recruiting tour of the United Kingdom in the late 1980s. He was assigned *Animal Man* (1988) as a four-issue miniseries with artist Chas Truog, but by issue #2 DC had made the decision to make it an ongoing series. The first four-issue story arc merely set up the status quo for the new series and revived the character, but with the news that the series would continue, Morrison began setting in place his long-range plans for the book: to explore both his own beliefs and doubts about the animal-rights movement, as well as the very nature of fiction and the relationship between author and creation. In the first issue following the initial four-issue storyline, Morrison tells a heartbreaking single-issue allegory, "The Coyote Gospel," that turns out to be the road map for the next two years' worth of stories. This kind of narrative foresight was unheard of at the time, and even now is rarely done to best effect.

Over the course of his run, Morrison explores the very nature of fictionality by putting his title character, Buddy Baker, through all sorts of trials, hardships and eventually tragedies. In the final issue of his run (#26,

Morrison occasionally goes the writer/artist route, but only in the form of Comic Con sketches.

1990), "Animal Man" Buddy and his creator Grant Morrison have a twenty-two-page heart-to-heart about the nature of Buddy's reality, and the limits and frailties Morrison has felt as his writer. It's at once ludicrous and compelling, yet doesn't at all feel self-indulgent, perhaps because it so perfectly caps off all of Buddy's frustrations at not being in control of his own life, contrasted with Morrison's frustrations with not doing a better job creating Buddy's life. The series continued after Morrison left, but was never as compelling as those first twenty-six issues. By breaking down the wall between creator and creation, and between character and reader, Morrison created one of the most fully realized and identifiable characters in comics. Buddy Baker may have been a puppet, but unlike the rest of us, he was at least given a glance at the fellow pulling the strings.

Morrison was given a chance to redefine DC's trademark book *Justice League of America* with the debut of *JLA* #1 (January 1997). He returned to the book's original concept, uniting the biggest guns in the DC arsenal of characters with a fast-paced, supercharged approach to storytelling. Morrison's approach to the series can best be described as *power plotting*: he crams many ideas and concepts into a storyline (the amount lesser writers might use for two or three story arcs), then

ANIMAL MAN™ © DC COMICS. FROM THE COLLECTION OF SCOTT TIPTON.
ART BY GRANT MORRISON.

moves the story forward at breakneck speed, carrying the reader along with a whirlwind sense of feet-off-the-floor excitement. Accentuating the process was *JLA* artist Howard Porter, whose modern, fluid style gave the JLA a vitality they'd lacked for years. Between Morrison's scripts and Porter's images, this JLA seemed all-new to readers, though Morrison managed to keep the book steeped slightly in a Silver Age sensibility with a 21st-century sheen. In addition, Morrison returned the series to its epic Silver Age proportions, pitting the League against world-shattering threats that none of them could handle alone.

Morrison had a lot of characterization to establish in this first storyline, and he did a marvelous job. Superman and Wonder Woman stand out as the team's pillars of strength, while J'onn J'onzz remains the heart of the team. Aquaman is portrayed as the distracted monarch unhappy to be constantly called away from his people, while the Flash and Green Lantern's love-hate relationship (mostly hate early on) serves as enjoyable comic relief. And the new Green Lantern Kyle Rayner's constant nervousness as he slowly grows out of his role as the team's rookie turns into one of the most satisfying character bits (his portrayal here would be the reason many fans would finally turn the corner on accepting Kyle as the new Green Lantern).

A prolific writer, Morrison has turned out scores of comic-book series for Marvel, DC and DC's boutique imprint Vertigo, everything from the avant-garde epic *The Invisibles* to his redefining runs on *New X-Men* to all-new innovative postmodern science fiction *Seaguy* and *WE3*. One thing is certain: if it's a Grant Morrison comic, it'll be like nothing else you've read.

A prolific writer, Morrison has turned out scores of comic-book series for Marvel, DC and DC's boutique imprint Vertigo, everything from avant-garde epics like *The Invisibles* to his redefining runs on *New X-Men* to all-new innovative postmodern science fiction such as *Seaguy* and *We3*. One thing's for certain, though: if it's a Grant Morrison comic, it'll be like nothing else you've read.

*SCOTT SAYS*

The first summer after Grant Morrison's *JLA* hit it big, he attended the San Diego Comic-Con, and I remember being in a packed panel where someone asked him what that weird noise was Batman was making now. Morrison demonstrated the noise, a guttural kind of breathy grunt. Why was he doing that, another fan asked. Morrison's response? "It just seemed like an odd, scary thing for Batman to do. Come on, everyone do it with me!" The crowd played along, and the room rang out with a resounding grunt. Morrison: "Someone just walked into the back of the room and said to himself, 'Aaaah! It's 300 Batmen!'"

# 14 Mark Waid

There are writers who happen to write comic books, and there are comic-book writers. Mark Waid is a *comic-book writer*. And that is meant in the best sense of the term.

Born in Hueytown, Alabama, Mark Waid broke into the comics biz as a fanzine editor, writing and editing Fantagraphics Books' *Amazing Heroes* magazine, a kind of 1980s precursor to *Wizard*. Within a couple of years, he'd gotten his foot in the door at DC Comics, where he served as an editor on series like *Legion of Super-Heroes* and *Secret Origins*. It wasn't until he left the company's full-time employ to go freelance that Waid really made a name for himself, though, beginning in 1992 with his critically acclaimed and commercially successful eight-year run on DC's *The Flash*.

Waid's best-known and most successful work is the 1996 DC Comics graphic novel *Kingdom Come*, which features Waid's script

and the gorgeous painted art of Alex Ross. The book, set in the not-too-distant future, pits a middle-aged Superman and Wonder Woman versus their rebellious, destructive superheroic descendants, while Lex Luthor and a cabal of villains plot to turn the strife to their advantage, with Batman and a cadre of his own vigilantes acting as the wild card. While the book's subtext is clear—it contrasts the traditional heroics of the classic DC superheroes against the more bloodthirsty, younger, Image-style super-types popular throughout the 1990s—the book is more than just an excuse for allegory. Waid provides some of the best characterizations of Superman, Batman and Wonder Woman to see print in more than twenty years.

Also highly recommended are Waid's stellar run on *Fantastic Four*, and his sci-fi thriller *Empire* with artist Barry Kitson. Oh, and if you ever run into Waid at a convention, ask him what Clark Kent's Social Security number is. We're not sure what's scarier, the fact that this bit of information actually exists, or the fact that Mark Waid knows it off the top of his head. And the really annoying thing is, he won't tell us.

---

**RECOMMENDED READING 101**

*MARK WAID*

*Captain America: Man Without a Country* by Mark Waid and Ron Garney

*Empire* by Mark Waid and Barry Kitson

*Fantastic Four*, Vol. 1: *Imaginauts* by Mark Waid and Mike Wieringo

*52, Vol. 1-4* by Morrison, Johns, Rucka, Waid and Giffen

*The Flash: Terminal Velocity*

*JLA: Year One* by Mark Waid and Barry Kitson

*Kingdom Come* by Mark Waid and Alex Ross

# PART VII

# HOORAY FOR HOLLYWOOD

*Wherein paper gives way to celluloid; and the best, and way too much of the worst, examples of comic-book adaptations are explained. Supermen and Bat-men are covered in great detail, and the filmed and animated exploits of nearly every comic-book hero, villain and supporting cast are cited.*

# Superman

## It's a bird, it's a plane... it's box office

As one might imagine, the superhero with the most expansive show-biz career would have to be the one that started it all, Superman.

### RADIO DAYS

The first to play the Man of Steel was Bud Collyer, a journeyman radio announcer and actor in radio dramas who took on the dual role of Clark Kent and Superman in *The Adventures of Superman* for the Mutual radio network in 1940, only two years after Superman's debut. Collyer was the originator of the distinctive sound for Clark's and Superman's voices, his Kent a mid-range tenor voice, then shifting to a gravelly baritone for Superman: "This looks like a job for Superman!" Sometimes the shift was too distinct and Superman's voice was so deep that it was flat and inflectionless. Still, Collyer's performance on the radio show was a popular one, and a lucrative one for Collyer, who remained in the role on the radio for more than ten years before turning the role over to another actor, Michael Fitzmaurice, for the series' final year in 1951. Collyer became so identified with the role that for years, any vocal performance of Superman seemed to go to him by default. And this despite the fact that for years, Collyer received no credit for the part. However, they dared not replace him. On those occasions when Collyer would leave for vacation, the radio producers would find ways to explain his absences and focus on the supporting cast. In fact, Kryptonite was created on the radio show for just such a reason, allowing another actor to whimper out Superman's Kryptonite-induced moans of pain while Collyer was off sunning himself on a beach somewhere.

### THE BIG SCREEN

In 1941, the Fleischer Studios's *Superman* theatrical animated shorts distributed by Paramount Pictures utilized Collyer's vocal talents for all seventeen cartoons. Lavishly animated with a budget far beyond most animation at the time, these cartoons still hold up as achievements in animation and as one of the best animated versions of the character to date. Cartoons such as *The Mechanical Monsters*, which featured Superman duking it out with an army of flame-throwing robots, are simply stunning to this day, particularly a sequence in which Superman protects Lois Lane from molten lava by shielding her with his cape. The Fleischer *Superman* cartoons are now available on DVD, and well worth your cash.

Superman went live action with two fifteen-part theatrical serials, *Superman* (1948) and *Atom Man vs. Superman* (1950), both starring Kirk Alyn as Superman. Alyn was fresh-faced and innocent-looking in 1948, and while his Superman suit was obviously padded to give him a bit more muscle mass, he cut a striking figure as Superman, particularly with his trademark jet-black hair and spitcurl. Alyn's Clark Kent was less impressive, a little blah. Although one could make the argument that the mild-mannered Kent should be a little blah, his distinctly different-from-Superman characterization of Kent wasn't that appealing.

Audiences were also disappointed in Kirk Alyn's flying. That is, they didn't get to see any. In a budget-conscious move, rather than rigging the actor with wires when Alyn as Superman leapt into the air to take flight, his figure would shift to an animated cartoon superimposed onto the real-world landscape. It's an odd-looking result—not necessarily bad, just a little off-putting. Lois was played by Noel Neill, later to reprise the role on television. *Atom Man* was notable mostly for the inclusion of Lex Luthor, played by Lyle Talbot. Pretty standard fare, neither remarkable nor awful.

## THE SMALL SCREEN

Superman really hit it big in 1952 with the *Adventures of Superman* television series, starring George Reeves as Clark Kent/Superman, Phyllis Coates and Noel Neill as Lois, Jack Larson as Jimmy Olsen and John Hamilton as Perry White. The show quickly cemented the image of Superman in the public eye, making him even more of a household word.

*Adventures in Superman*'s biggest asset was its star, George Reeves, whose easy, confident

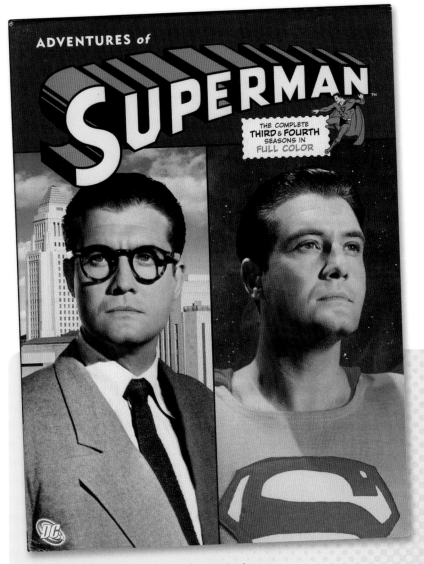

George Reeves's Clark Kent was on screen far more than Superman because of budget constraints for special effects.

charm as Clark Kent went against the "mild-mannered coward" take from the comic books, and made an instant connection with viewers. Reeves was a charming presence on camera, coming off as instantly likable either as Clark or Superman, and he brought a real physicality to the role that Kirk Alyn had lacked. More than anything, George Reeves exuded confidence. His Superman really looked as if he enjoyed being Superman. He'd be flying around with a big cheese-eating grin on his face, or making with an almost dismissive smirk as the bullets bounced off his chest (just before performing the de rigueur snatch of the revolver and crushing it in his hand). Watch as he busts through a brick wall—he's practically giddy.

As enjoyable as Reeves's Superman was, his Clark Kent was the real star of the show. No longer a nebbishy milksop and Lois Lane's doormat, Reeves's Kent was a hard-boiled investigative reporter, quick with a quip and every bit a match for Lois. Picture Reeves's Kent behind his desk at the Daily Planet, feet up on the desk and his fedora rakishly cocked back on his head, winking to the camera. Even in the staid 1950s, George Reeves made Superman cool.

The series remained a success as long as it was on the air—104 episodes—and a seventh season was about to go into production in 1959 when the shocking news broke of George Reeves's death by gunshot wound, declared a suicide by the LAPD. Although the common story is that Reeves was despondent over being typecast as Superman, there's plenty of circumstantial evidence to the contrary. However, it's unlikely any answers will ever be forthcoming at this late date. There are only two defining performances of Superman, and Reeves's is one of them. Fortunately, we have his legacy of work to enjoy on DVD.

More than two decades after his debut in the role, Bud Collyer reprised the role for a series of Saturday-morning cartoons for Filmation: *The New Adventures of Superman* (1966), *The Superman/Aquaman Hour of Adventure* (1967) and *The Batman/Superman Hour* (1968). By the 1960s, Collyer's already gruff Superman voice had become even more gravelly, but he remained the go-to man for the job until his death in 1969.

From 1973 through 1985, Danny Dark provided the distinctive rich baritone for Superman on various *Super Friends* cartoon series. Dark spent most of his career as an announcer, his lengthy stint as the "official voice" of NBC throughout the late 1970s and 1980s being his highest-profile gig other than *Super Friends*. Danny Dark's performance of Superman had a reliable, paternalistic quality that gave the character a sense of utter dependability and stability, even when faced with some of the most nonsensical and downright goofy plotlines. Dark passed away from a pulmonary hemorrhage in 2004, but for millions of kids growing up in the 1970s and countless new fans still watching on video, he's still what Superman sounds like.

## THE MOVIES

When *Superman: The Movie* premiered in 1978, it was a triumph creatively and commercially. Directed by Richard Donner, the film deftly handles the stark, sterile world of Krypton, the Midwestern plains of Clark Kent's childhood, and the big-city buzz of Metropolis. Christopher Reeve is note-perfect as Superman, with his nebbishly Clark Kent a joy to watch, as is Margot Kidder's wiseass Lois Lane turning to mush around Superman. Gene Hackman is both suitably villainous and laugh-out-loud funny as Lex Luthor, although his need to surround himself with dopey assistants is a bit overplayed, and his character suffers for it somewhat. However, the movie's success can almost entirely be laid at the feet of Reeve, who was the absolute best, the personification of what Superman should be, and whose performance still stands as the benchmark to measure all Superman performances, either before or since.

The Julliard-trained Reeve landed the part after Donner and the producers came to the realization that the superstars of the day like James Caan and Robert Redford (both of whom were considered for the role) simply wouldn't be believable in the part, not because they weren't good enough actors, but because the audience wouldn't be able to make the necessary disconnect to buy them as a guy flying around in a cape and tights. The decision to go with an unknown was the single biggest component in the success of the movie. Reeve's sincere, grounded and heartfelt performance served as an anchor for both the fantastic feats of super-powered derring-do and the lighter, comedic moments of Gene Hackman and Ned Beatty. Reeve plays a slightly restrained Superman—polite, courteous, friendly, yet always reserved—as if he's all too aware of the power at his disposal and his responsibility to use it wisely. Yet when pushed to the brink, Reeve's Superman is steely and intimidating, as seen in his exchanges with Luthor in *Superman* and General Zod in *Superman* II.

Some have criticized Reeve's Clark Kent as being too nerdy and clumsy, but his performance as the powerless, mortal Superman in *Superman II* validates his Kent, highlighting the lengths to which Superman goes to protect his identity and sublimating his true self to a ludicrous and embarrassing degree, all for the greater good. And for sheer dramatic gravitas, the moment in *Superman* when a heartbroken Kal-El cradles the lifeless body of Lois Lane in his arms—show us better acting than that in a more "serious" movie, because we'd like to see it.

The other strength of Reeve's performance, like George Reeves's (no relation between the two men, by the way), is his physicality in the role. Not only is Reeve in good enough condition to always look great in the none-too-forgiving costume, but his willingness to commit completely to the part, particularly in the films' breakthrough flying scenes, cements his place as the most convincing screen Superman. When Reeve angles his body to bank during flight or extends a foot for a gentle landing, it's difficult not to be convinced. To borrow a catchphrase, if you believe a man can fly, it's only because Christopher Reeve makes you believe.

*Superman II* (1980) is just as good as the original, with Richard Lester coming on board to direct the sequences that hadn't already been filmed by Donner in the gargantuan shooting schedule of the first film. The stuff that remained to be shot was crucial: the enormous fight sequences between Superman and General Zod, Ursa and Non, the three Kryptonian criminals who have come to Earth looking for a fight. And boy, they get one, in a fantastic sequence set in downtown Metropolis that still holds up nearly thirty years later. Terence Stamp's performance as General Zod is compelling. A lesser actor might have broken the intensity for a moment somewhere, and allowed a hint of self-deprecating humor or irony to sneak in, but not Stamp. He just sells it, every moment he's on camera. "Now, son of Jor-El: Kneel before Zod!" We love this movie.

As for *Superman III* (1983) and *Superman IV: The Quest For Peace* (1987), well, the less said the better. *Superman III*, with a bewildering emphasis on Richard Pryor, is notable only for two things: Annette O'Toole's sweet performance as Lana Lang and a great sequence in which Superman is split into good and evil versions of himself by synthetic Kryptonite, and engages in a knuckleduster of a junkyard brawl. As for *Superman IV*, here's all you need to know: Jon Cryer as Lenny Luthor. Avoid it like the plague.

## NEW ADVENTURES

The year 1988 saw a brand-new Saturday-morning animated *Superman* on television, following the lead of the newly revised comic books from DC, complete with the new billionaire version of Lex Luthor. The CBS series starring Beau Weaver in the role of Clark Kent/Superman lasted only one season and didn't make much of a splash.

Also in 1988 came the premiere of *Superboy*, a new live-action syndicated series from the Salkinds, the producers of the *Superman* films. Taking on the role of young Kal-El was John Haymes Newton in the series' first season, followed by Gerard Christopher in seasons two through four. The series began atrociously, with poor scripts, substandard visual effects and a limp, unmotivated performance by Newton, who never showed that charismatic spark that Reeves, Reeve or even Alyn had. The series improved dramatically in its second season, thanks to a transfusion of new talent in the writing room, many of whom were longtime comic-book writers such as Cary Bates, Mike Carlin and Andy Helfer. Also showing up more often were supervillains, as opposed to the crime bosses and thugs from the series' first season. Most responsible for the series' turnaround was new Superboy Gerard Christopher, brought in as a replacement for Newton, who held out for more money. Christopher seemed to take the role more seriously, his Clark Kent was more likable and approachable, and he had that ineffable quality as Superboy that Newton lacked—Christopher carried himself like a Superman.

Superman returned to television in 1993 with the ABC premiere of *Lois & Clark: The New Adventures of Superman*, which rethought the concept as a romantic comedy, with a little superheroic action sprinkled on top to keep the kids and fanboys interested. The series premiered to strong success, thanks primarily to the charisma and chemistry of its leads, Dean Cain as Clark/Superman and Teri Hatcher as Lois Lane. While the acting was appealing, the producers couldn't seem to figure out what kind of show they wanted it to be. It varied wildly from week to week, from semi-serious romance to boneheaded juvenile kids' programming. Cain made an excellent Clark Kent, and his college athlete's physique allowed him to pull off the Super-suit, but his Superman lacked a certain something. The show ran for four seasons, and only got worse, culminating in Lois and Clark's wedding being crashed by *Designing Women*'s Delta Burke as the evil Wedding Destroyer. We'd tell you more about this, but it just makes us sad.

While *Lois and Clark* was stinking it up over on ABC, a far superior version of Superman was airing on the WB. Starting in 1996, *Superman: The Animated Series* was produced by the same first-rate crew as the outstanding *Batman* animated series. The Man of Steel was voiced by Tim Daly, best known from his starring role on the sitcom *Wings*. Much like the series' producers, Daly seemed to take George Reeves as a model for his performance—he tended to play Clark Kent as an assertive, take-charge reporter, without even a hint of mild-mannered-

ness. Daly's Superman was right on the money, combining George Reeves's toughness with Christopher Reeve's sincerity. It's a great performance, one that Daly improved over the course of the series. Dana Delaney brought both toughness and charm to her portrayal of Lois Lane, while Clancy Brown delivered a career-defining vocal performance as Lex Luthor. The series itself was overall a triumph, the best translation of Superman's entire mythology to either film or television. It gets overlooked simply because it followed the groundbreaking *Batman* series, but it's as much of a gem in its own right. The producers wisely buttressed Superman's weaker rogues gallery with Jack Kirby's Fourth World characters, utilizing Darkseid as a frequent opponent for Superman, and one who could really bring the menace.

In 2001, two new actors took on the role of Superman in different series. Providing vocals only was George Newbern, who would voice the Man of Steel for the next five years on Cartoon Network's *Justice League* and *Justice League Unlimited*. Newbern got a bad rap from fans of the *Superman* series early on, unfavorably comparing his performance to Daly's, but the blame can be more accurately placed at the feet of the producers, who had difficulties finding ways to use Superman in a team dynamic. As the series matured, Newbern brought a tougher edge to the character than even Daly had, while still retaining Daly's humanity. One standout episode is "For the Man Who Has Everything" (adapting Alan Moore's classic story), in which Newbern gets to play both the devastation of losing the home and family he's always dreamed of, and the white-hot rage of getting his hands on the evil bastard who put him through it.

Also debuting in 2001 was the WB series *Smallville*, starring Tom Welling as a teenage Clark Kent and Michael Rosenbaum as a young Lex Luthor and focusing on their slow, unavoidable slide from friends to enemies. Although Welling has never donned the cape and tights (and according to the series' producers, never will), he anchors the series with strength and likability. The show struggled a bit initially with the overuse of the Kryptonite plot device ("shy/angry/horny classmate of Clark's is exposed to Kryptonite and becomes invisible/pyrokinetic/vampire"), but improved dramatically in its second season, and has since settled into a successful if creatively inconsistent run. Its success has been aided by an appealing cast, including Kristin Kreuk as Lana Lang, Allison Mack as Clark's pal Chloe Sullivan and series-anchoring performances by John Schneider and Annette O'Toole as Jonathan and Martha Kent.

## THE RETURN

Superman made his long-awaited return to the big screen in 2006 with *Superman Returns*, directed by Bryan Singer, starring Kate Bosworth as Lois Lane and Kevin Spacey as Lex Luthor, and introducing Brandon Routh as this generation's Clark Kent/Superman. The film is extremely faithful to Richard Donner's vision of Superman, picking up where the first film left off—if anything, it's too worshipful of Donner's film, right down to Luthor's obsession with real estate and insistence on hiring incompetent henchmen. Although there are sequences in the film that are breathtaking (particularly when Superman halts a plummeting airliner mere inches above a Metropolis baseball stadium), Singer's insistence on trying to re-create Donner's film only highlights what Singer's film lacks: Christopher Reeve's strong, charismatic performance. Routh's performance as Kent is decent enough, although it's clear he is trying to replicate Reeve. His Superman simply lacks the approachable quality that Reeve brought to the part, instead coming across as cool and distant. Spacey's Luthor is serviceable, although played far too much for laughs, and Kate Bosworth's Lois doesn't work at all. She brings none of the charm or flintiness that Margot Kidder imbued in the character, and she simply looks far too young for the part. The other problem with the film is a thematic one: Singer's puzzling decision to introduce the character of Jason, the out-of-wedlock son of Superman and Lois Lane, supposedly born while Superman was off-planet. While the moment at the end of the film in which Superman repeats Jor-El's oath of fatherhood to his own son is a touching one, it's simply too drastic a change for many viewers to accept Superman's having a son that he refuses to raise, and it creates a serious complication for future films.

While *Superman Returns* is a worthy effort, we can't help but think that the character (and the actors) may have been better served with a fresher take on the material.

# Batman

## *Same bat-time, same bat-channel*

Although Batman was already quite popular in comic books (and even newspaper strips for a short time in the mid-1940s), it was remarkably early in his career that he made the jump to the silver screen, in the Columbia serial *Batman* in 1943, just four years after his comic-book debut. You might be wondering why you've never seen this on TV or video—it's not that it's not very good (although it's really not)—it's just a little racist. Starring Lewis Wilson as Batman and Douglas Croft as Robin, *Batman* pits the Dynamic Duo against the evil Dr. Daka, a stereotypical fiendish Japanese spy. Dr. Daka is played by J. Carrol Naish, a Caucasian actor in yellowface. Even though it was wartime, the film's references to "shifty-eyed Japs" are very uncomfortable today.

The 1943 *Batman* serial was the first source to actually give a name to the Batcave, and created some impressive-looking sets, especially for the typical low budgets provided for Saturday-morning serials. Still, the acting was rather blah, with Lewis Wilson's Batman coming across a bit snobbish and Douglas Croft delivering an absolutely hateable Robin.

Columbia tried again in 1949 with another serial, *Batman and Robin*, this time starring Robert Lowery as Batman and Johnny Duncan as Robin. Although this one had Batman and Robin facing off against the Wizard, a

fairly standard hooded mastermind-type often found in the serials, at least it didn't have horribly racist overtones. *Batman and Robin* made an effort to stay closer to the source material, with appearances by the Bat-Signal and Vicki Vale, and Commissioner Gordon played by serial veteran Lyle Talbot.

In between the film appearances, Batman and Robin also made their debut on the radio, America's sole mass-media system of the day, exposing the characters to a far larger audience than the serial did. On a 1945 episode of *The Adventures of Superman*, one of the more popular radio programs, Superman discovers an unconscious boy in a rowboat, wearing a red tunic and a yellow cape. With Robin on the scene and Batman not far behind, soon Superman, Batman and Robin team up against the evil Zoltan. Following that first appearance, Batman and Robin would periodically return to take over the program for a week or two, whenever Superman actor Bud Collyer needed a vacation, filling in for the ailing Superman. There were several attempts to give Batman his own radio program, but it never happened.

## CAMPING IT UP

After the 1949 serial, Batman remained ensconced in the four-color world of comics until the mid-1960s. As the legend goes,

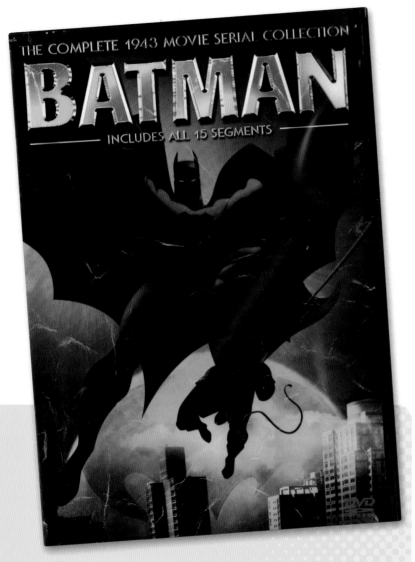

THE COMPLETE 1943 MOVIE SERIAL COLLECTION
BATMAN
INCLUDES ALL 15 SEGMENTS

Luckily, Batman's filmed exploits would only get better than this initial 1940s effort. And then worse, and then better again.

*Playboy* publisher Hugh Hefner had taken to showing some of the 1940s serials for "Movie Night" at the Playboy Mansion in Chicago, and the *Batman* serials were a favorite. One of these screenings was attended by an ABC executive, who then acquired the television rights to the character from National Comics. The project was handed off to producer William Dozier, who embraced the cliffhanger-serial origins, devising the 1966 series *Batman* as an unprecedented twice-weekly program, allowing for a cliffhanger every week. Also held over from the serial inspiration was the over-the-top narration, which was provided by Dozier himself.

While the show was at times wickedly funny and campy, thanks to the tongue-in-cheek scripts provided by writers such as Lorenzo Semple Jr. and Stanley Ralph Ross, the show's success can be chalked up to two factors: the production design and the casting. The Batcave was one of the most fantastic sets ever created for a television series. Throw in the various villain's lairs, the bright, garish costumes (another key to the series success: color TVs were a relatively new arrival in 1966, and there wasn't anything on TV more colorful than *Batman*) and, of course, the fabulous George Barris-designed Batmobile, and you had a show that looked and sounded like nothing else on television.

Of course, all this would've been moot without the right people inside the costumes. Anchoring the series was Adam West, who wisely opted for a more understated portrayal of Batman, only chewing the scenery when it was really called for and otherwise maintaining a deadpan approach that made his lines all the funnier. Though West wasn't called to play Bruce Wayne that much in the series, when he did, it was with a droll smoothness that fit the character well. Joining West was neophyte Burt Ward, who brought an emphatic enthusiasm to the role of Robin, one that didn't call for much besides the ability to wear the outfit and not look horribly out of shape.

The Batman and Robin parts were cast with solid, if unremarkable, actors intended to serve as the baseline for the show's real stars: the villains. In a bravura casting coup, the parts of Batman's four most significant villains were each filled by actors who would forever define the roles, and in turn be forever identified with them. The first to appear was the Riddler, played by comedian and impressionist Frank Gorshin. A popular nightclub act and character actor in film, Gorshin was catapulted into stardom by the part. His Riddler was a manic, hyperactive antagonist, constantly chortling and skittering about the scene, and occasionally letting loose his trademark Riddler laugh, instantly identifiable to this day.

In an interesting side note, Gorshin disliked the closely fitting Riddler tights so much that on some days he would just refuse to wear them, necessitating the creation of a second outfit for the Riddler, a natty green sport jacket, tie and derby combo that became just as closely identified with the character, appearing in *Batman* comic books, cartoons and toys

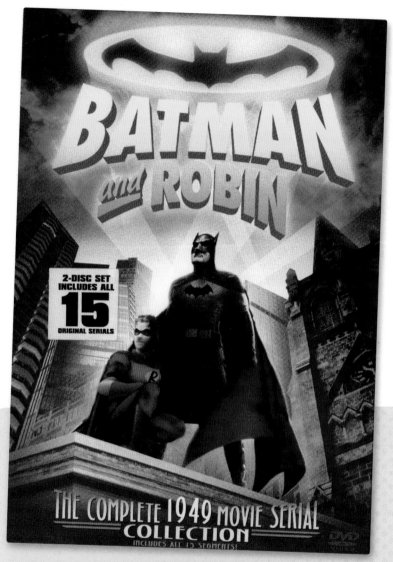

The Dynamic Duo returned to theaters in 1949, matching wits for fifteen chapters with the mysterious Wizard.

for decades to come. (John Astin made a single appearance as the Riddler, but he lacked the frantic giddiness that Gorshin brought to the role.)

Appearing most frequently was Burgess Meredith's Penguin. The Penguin worked far better on screen than he ever did in the comics, thanks to Meredith's charisma. The actor's waddling and squawking character was a favorite with audiences, and the villain returned to the program again and again.

The Joker also showed up quite often, played with zeal by Cesar Romero. Romero's Joker was also a standout, gleefully chewing the scenery and bounding about the room as the Clown Prince of Crime. Somehow, the Joker's dyed-white moustache didn't even register as out of the ordinary. While the Joker's laugh still came in second to the Riddler's, Romero's booming chortle and incessant chuckling served the character well.

Finally, there was Julie Newmar, who absolutely owned the screen as Catwoman. Wearing a skintight black outfit that was probably illegal in some states, Newmar purred, pouted and flirted her way through the series. When film commitments forced Newmar to drop out of the role in the third season, she was replaced by Eartha Kitt. Though Kitt was attractive, she had neither Newmar's charm nor sense of humor in the part.

There were other characters from the comics who showed up in the series, such as Mr. Freeze and the Mad Hatter, but the Joker, the Riddler, the Penguin and Catwoman were the most popular, and made the most appearances. When the show's popularity shot through the roof and being a Bat-Villain was suddenly the "in-thing" to do in Hollywood, all manner of goofy villains were devised to suit whatever celebrity was slated to appear. Some of these turned out to be great—for example, Victor Buono's hilarious turn as King Tut and Vincent Price's Egghead. Others were just plain atrocious such as Milton Berle's mind-numbingly bad Louie the Lilac, a flower-obsessed crime boss with the insipid and meaningless catch-phrase, "It's lilac time, Batman. Lilac time." Wow.

The cast of ABC's *Batman* television series hit the silver screen in 1966, but it was the quartet of villains and all-new Bat vehicles that stole the show.

At the height of the show's popularity between the first and second seasons, a theatrical feature was released, 1966's *Batman*, pitting Batman and Robin against the Joker, the Penguin, the Riddler and Catwoman. All involved resumed their roles, with the exception of Julie Newmar, who bowed out because of a back injury and was replaced by former Miss America Lee Meriwether. The feature, designed to help sell the TV series to overseas markets, made use of a heightened budget to introduce fabulous prop vehicles such as the Batcycle, the Batboat and the Batcopter, all of which would be utilized in stock footage throughout the series' run. One of the movie's high points is a hilarious sequence filmed on the Santa Barbara pier, in which Batman desperately tries to get rid of a bomb with a slowly burning fuse, and is foiled at every turn, by families, nuns, ducks and even a marching band, prompting an exasperated Batman to grumble, "Some days you just can't get rid of a bomb..."

When ratings for *Batman* began to fall at the end of the second season, panicked producers cut the show back to once a week, and introduced Yvonne Craig as Batgirl in an effort to increase the show's sex appeal. Even with the addition of Batgirl, the third season suffered a drop in quality thanks to a run of uninspiring, lame villains, such as Lord Ffogg, evil feminist Nora Clavicle and Minerva, Queen of Diamonds. Still, the season was not a total loss, as we did get to see Batman face off against the Joker in a surfing contest in the episode "Surf's Up! Joker's Under!" By the end of the third season, ABC wanted out, and the show was canceled. NBC was interested in picking up the series, but before a deal could be met, ABC execs had already ordered the sets demolished, and NBC balked at the $800,000 cost of rebuilding the Batcave.

Batman returned to television in animation the following year with *The Batman-Superman Hour* cartoon on CBS, but the Filmation-produced series was nothing special. Batman's next significant TV appearance came in 1973, with Batman and Robin's starring roles in the ABC Saturday-morning cartoon *Super Friends*, along with Superman, Wonder Woman and Aquaman. Throughout most of the show's thirteen-year run, Batman and Robin were played by Olan Soule and Casey Kasem, although the last two seasons in 1984 and 1985 featured none other than Adam West as the Caped Crusader.

In an unusual bit of programming, while the Hanna-Barbera-produced *Super Friends* was running on ABC in 1977, CBS aired its own all-new Batman Saturday-morning cartoon, *The New Adventures of Batman*, again produced by Filmation. This time, Adam West and Burt Ward returned to the roles of Batman and Robin, but that's pretty much the only redeeming quality to this mess of a cartoon. It featured not only the addition of Bat-Mite as comedy relief, but also some of the more insipid villains Batman has ever faced, including Moonman, Professor Bubbles and—get this—Sweet Tooth, a candy-obsessed villain who fiendishly replaces Gotham City's water supply with chocolate syrup. Where's Louie the Lilac when you need him?

## BAT-MANIA

Bat-mania returned in a big way in 1989 with the release of Tim Burton's long-awaited feature film version, *Batman*. Starring Michael Keaton as Batman and Jack Nicholson as the Joker, the film at long last shattered the common public perception of Batman as a goofy, Batusi-dancing Adam West, and opened the door for more serious versions of Batman in the mass media. As for the movie itself, the good outweighs the bad.

Despite the initial fan uproar over the casting, Keaton's distracted, haunted portrayal of Bruce Wayne resonated well, and anyone would look like Batman in the sculpted rubber suit he lurched around in. Jack Nicholson's Joker was also a standout, equal parts hilarious charm and creepy menace—the scene in which the Joker murders his former boss is quite effective and chilling. Even Kim Basinger isn't bad as Vicki Vale, although she doesn't have a whole lot to do besides look pretty and scream a lot. The film looks amazing, thanks to Burton's signature style and direction and the production designs of Anton Furst. The biggest problem is the script, which was the victim of a writer's strike during production. The strike prompted a new writer to come in and rewrite the ending, which is a mess. Precisely why Alfred would let Vicki Vale into the Batcave is still a mystery, and revealing that the Joker killed Bruce Wayne's parents is just plain lame. Still, *Batman* hits a lot more than it misses, and was the first time the Batman material was treated seriously outside of the comics.

Burton and Keaton returned to the character in 1992 with *Batman Returns*, an even darker look at the Caped Crusader that pitted him against Catwoman, as portrayed by Michelle Pfeiffer, and a new grotesque version of the Penguin, played by Danny DeVito. Muddying things up further is a third villain, Gotham magnate Max Shreck, as played by Christopher Walken. Pfeiffer's Catwoman is spot-on brilliant, and the scenes between her and Keaton's Batman (as well as the romantic moments between Pfeiffer's Selina Kyle and Keaton's Bruce Wayne) make up the movie's high points. Burton's vision of the Penguin as a sewer-dwelling flippered mutant doesn't quite work, and one can't help but wonder what DeVito might have done with the character if he'd been allowed to play it as conceived by Bob Kane and Bill Finger. Overall, *Batman Returns* improved on the first in both script and direction, and even misgivings about the new Penguin can't detract from what is still the best of the four 1990s Batman films.

## THE ANIMATED SERIES

Also premiering in 1992 was Warner Bros.' *Batman: The Animated Series*, which stands to this day as the single best version of the character in any medium: comics, TV, movies, you name it. Before 1992, action-adventure animation was all but dead on American television. Following the success of its new comedy series *Tiny Toon Adventures*, Warner Animation President Jean MacCurdy announced that they were looking to develop a new *Batman* animated series and that anyone with an idea was welcome to make a pitch. *Tiny Toons* storyboard artist Bruce Timm and background painter Eric Radomski were chosen to put together a sample reel, and their two-minute short netted them the jobs as the producers of the new series. Writers Alan Burnett and Paul Dini were brought in to spearhead the scripting of the series, sharing Timm's vision of how the character should be portrayed: dark, serious and brooding.

But it wasn't just the stories that were groundbreaking. The character design, primarily the work of Bruce Timm, along with artists Lynne Naylor, Kevin Nowlan and Mike Mignola, eschewed the detail-heavy, ultra-real style favored by adventure cartoons in the past, in favor of a cartoonier approach, for lack of a better word. The art combined the barrel chests and square jaws of the Fleischer Studios *Superman* cartoons of the 1940s with the clean linework of Alex Toth (the influence of whose Space Ghost design is clearly apparent). The influence of Batman artists such as Bob Kane, Dick Sprang, Frank Miller and David Mazzucchelli also is evident.

Furthermore, the entire series was given a moody, timeless feel with 1940s architecture, wardrobe and roadsters co-existing with late 1990s-technology. The backgrounds, designed by Ted Blackman and based on Eric Radomski's vision, were painted on black paper, lending the entire series a noir-ish darkness appropriate to their vision of the Dark Knight.

The acting on the series was top-drawer, as well. Rather than going to the same recycled group of cartoon voice actors working every Saturday-morning series at the time, series voice director Andrea Romano opened the auditions to the best actors available, and instructed them to play it straight, as if they were performing a film or stage role. The cast for *Batman: The Animated Series* was one of the most talented casts ever assembled for an animated series—many of the actors could have easily stepped into their parts in a live-action feature-film version and performed splendidly. In addition, the score for the series, provided by Shirley Walker and her team of composers, provided lush, operatic soundtracks granting each episode a soaring, larger-than-life feel.

Kevin Conroy as Batman gave a nuanced, textured performance, in which he wrung intimidation, anger and pathos out of as few lines as possible. Conroy deftly delineated between Batman, Bruce Wayne and Bruce Wayne's public persona, altering his voice's pitch and timbre to make them each identifiable, yet recognizable as the same character.

As in the comics, however, Batman is only as good as his villains, and *Batman: The Animated Series* did a marvelous job translating Batman's rogues' gallery for animation. In many cases, the show's villains were so superior to earlier versions that they supplanted them in the public consciousness, as well as in the source-material comic books.

You can't have a Batman series without the Joker, and *Batman: The Animated Series* provided one of the most well-rounded and satisfying portrayals of the Joker in any medium, comics included. As realized here, the Joker was both funny and terrifying, capable of being motivated by egotism as well as sheer insanity. The Joker design seemed most inspired by Bob Kane's original artwork, but what made the character come alive was his voice, provided by Luke Skywalker himself, *Star Wars'* Mark Hamill. The part was originally given to Tim Curry, but the producers recast because they didn't feel that Curry, though sufficiently threatening, provided the necessary madcap levity and humor for the part. Enter Hamill, who had already played a supporting role in an earlier episode, but wished to play one of the trademark villains. One audition later, including Hamill's unforgettable rendition of the Joker's laugh, and the part was his. Hamill's Joker could foam at the mouth in an insane rant one moment, then instantly switch gears into a witty charmer.

As of 1996, *Batman: The Animated Series* had been out of production for two years, but still remained extremely popular in reruns. A variety of factors (including the show's continued popularity and a new film on the horizon) combined to encourage Warner Bros. to order the production of a new series of episodes. Rather than simply going back to the formula and cranking out new episodes in the same style as before, the producers took the opportunity to rethink the series from the bottom up, throwing out what hadn't worked in the past, introducing new characters and relationships, and re-designing nearly the entire show. The biggest change was that the WB Network didn't share FOX's reticence of putting a child in danger, so Dick Grayson was immediately changed to Nightwing, and a new, much younger Robin was introduced in Tim Drake. With both the new Robin and Batgirl (now privy to Batman's secrets and a full-time member of his team) appearing in almost every episode, and the distant, alienated Nightwing making occasional appearances, Batman's days as a loner were over. This didn't mean that Batman lost any of his grim, scary appeal—just the opposite. With Robin and Batgirl around, Batman talked even less than he did in the first series, and was darker and scarier than ever.

The new series, eventually named *The New Batman Adventures*, was set three years after the events of *Batman: The Animated Series*, during which time Bruce Wayne and Dick Grayson had a falling out and Grayson left Gotham to travel the globe, eventually returning to Gotham to embark on a solo crime-fighting career as Nightwing (with former Robin actor Lorin Lester making a surprisingly smooth transition to the more mature Nightwing character). In Grayson's absence, Barbara Gordon, whose identity as Batgirl had long been deduced by Batman, was entrusted with Bruce Wayne's secrets and replaced Grayson as Batman's partner.

As for the new Robin, thirteen-year-old Tim Drake worked as a character in a way the college-age Dick Grayson never quite did in *Batman: The Animated Series*. He provided a spark of humor and vitality to the show—aided by the charming voice work of Matt Valencia—and humanized Batman through his protectiveness and concern for the boy. The series' new take on Batgirl was also a great improvement, spotlighting her as a fully competent and formidable counterpart to Batman. She never needed "rescuing" and was fully capable of kicking ass alongside the Caped Crusader, while having a lot of fun doing it. Veteran voice artist Tara Strong provided Batgirl's kickier, more spunky voice. Some episodes alluded to a soured relationship between Batgirl and Nightwing, but never pigeonholed her in the category of "Nightwing's girlfriend." Batgirl was as strong and integral a part of the team as anyone, and because of that, her character was always a welcome presence.

Just as the characters and relationships were being remodeled, so too were the character designs. While developing the *Superman* animated series, Bruce Timm refined his style, making his characters sleeker, more streamlined and a touch more angular. Timm and art director Glen Murakami carried this new design theory to the Batman universe, giving all the *Batman: The Animated Series* characters the new treatment, some more drastically than others. While not everyone loved the new design scheme for *The New Batman Adventures*, no one could argue that the production was in high gear. The new animation was tighter and more lavish than ever (especially for network television), and the scripts were outstanding, with not a stinker in the series' twenty-seven-episode run.

The *Batman* movie series continued in 1995 without Tim Burton and Michael Keaton, though it was not a smooth transition. Joel Schumacher directed *Batman Forever*, featuring Val Kilmer in his sole turn in the Batsuit. Kilmer's portrayal was muted, as if he had been trying to mimic what Keaton had done, but could not channel that manicness behind the eyes that Keaton does so well.

Also introduced in *Batman Forever* was Chris O'Donnell as Robin. Although the movie keeps pretty close to the character's comic-book origins, the fact that Dick Grayson is a grown man when Bruce Wayne takes him in is dumb at best and troubling at worst. The Batman/Robin relationship has always been that of surrogate father/son, which is why Robin by definition must be a child. Even worse, both Jim Carrey (as the Riddler) and Tommy Lee Jones (as Two-Face) have their overacting meters cranked up to eleven, as they carry out a criminal plot to suck the brains out of Gotham with some "brain machine" devised by the Riddler. Whatever, man. While Carrey's overacting is to be expected (and we maintain that Frank Gorshin, even at his age, would've been a far better choice for the part), Tommy Lee Jones's performance is truly awful. Rather than researching and understanding the character, who's meant to be coolly psychotic, Jones tries to out-Jack Jack Nicholson's performance as the Joker, giggling, butt-shaking and all. As for leading lady Nicole Kidman, she has even less to do than Kim Basinger.

However, *Batman Forever* would look like *Citizen Kane* in comparison to Schumacher's thankfully final Batman film, *Batman and Robin* (1997). Where to start?

The lingering shots of Batman and Robin's rear ends in the opening sequence let you know just what you're in for, and the nipples on the sculpted Batsuits don't help. George Clooney has repeatedly credited himself for killing the Bat-franchise, but it really wasn't his fault. Between the horrible script by Akiva Goldsman and the completely misguided and juvenile direction from Schumacher, Clooney was doomed from the start. Arnold Schwarzenegger spouts off one awful cold-related pun after another as Mr. Freeze, when he's not shuffling around in an unintentionally comical oversized "freeze suit." Uma Thurman's Poison Ivy is also atrocious, but again, it's not really the fault of the actors. With a good script and a talented director, this same cast could have created a first-rate *Batman* movie.

There's just so much to hate about the movie. Batman pulls out a credit card at one point that reads "Batman Forever" on it. Alfred comes down with a terminal illness, so he transfers his brain into the Batcomputer (complete with "Max Headroom"-style animation,

which was about ten years out of style) and then encourages his niece to put on a Batsuit and go fight criminals alongside Batman, even though she has no training nor experience. As for Alicia Silverstone as Batgirl, it's no good. Silverstone is passably entertaining in comedies, but here she pouts and scrunches her face through action sequences, and mumbles her inane dialogue with all the conviction of a high school play. *Batman & Robin* is cinematic Ebola. Avoid it at all costs.

## BEGINNING AND BEYOND

While the films floundered, Batman continued to thrive in animation, thanks to the caretaking of producers Bruce Timm, Alan Burnett and Paul Dini. Starting in 1999, viewers were treated to a look at Batman's dystopian future in the criminally underrated series *Batman Beyond*, which featured teenage Terry McGinnis taking up the cape and cowl some forty years in the future, with the assistance of his crotchety mentor, an elderly and still intimidating Bruce Wayne. Smartly avoiding the easiest route of creating updated "future" versions of Batman's rogues' gallery, *Beyond*'s producers instead created a whole new mythology for their Batman that subtly builds upon the old without strip-mining it. When *Beyond* finished up, Timm turned his attention in 2001 to a wider look at the DC Universe with *Justice League* and *Justice League Unlimited*, both of which heavily featured Batman. But even before *Justice League Unlimited* came to an end, an entirely new Bat-series had already made its debut.

Premiering in 2004, *The Batman* was completely unrelated to the earlier Batman series and its descendants, instead featuring a younger Batman (voiced by Rino Romano) and a more anime-influenced design. While the series is clearly intended for a younger audience, with less sophisticated stories and dialogue, it improved steadily over the course of its four-year broadcast run, maturing into a fine series. There was also a direct-to-video film, *The Batman vs. Dracula* (2005), which is much better than it sounds.

The Caped Crusader made his triumphant return to the silver screen in 2005 with *Batman Begins*, directed by Christopher Nolan. Christian Bale as Batman brought a physicality and sense of menace to the character that had never been seen, while retaining some of Keaton's intensity. Jettisoning the previous four films entirely, *Batman Begins* finally brings a proper version of Batman's origin to the screen, with David S. Goyer's script deftly interweaving elements of Denny O'Neil's "The Demon's Head" stories and Frank Miller's *Batman: Year One*. It also smartly avoided any villains that had ever been seen in film, instead featuring immortal assassin Ra's al Ghul and the master of fear known as the Scarecrow, played with aplomb by Liam Neeson and Cillian Murphy, respectively. Throw in Gary Oldman's wry and subtle performance as not-yet-commissioner Gordon and Michael Caine's delightfully sardonic Alfred, and you have pretty much the perfect Batman movie.

## THE DARK KNIGHT

That is, until Nolan and Bale struck again in the *The Dark Knight*, anchored by Heath Ledger's spellbinding performance as the Joker, perhaps the best portrayal of the character ever. However, it's unfortunate that Ledger's performance somewhat overshadows the equally impressive work done by Aaron Eckhart as District Attorney Harvey Dent and his tortured alter ego Two-Face. Really, this film is Eckhart's more than anyone's, because it's his character that undergoes the most change, and his tragedy that is central to the film.

Almost everyone gets his moment in the spotlight here, whether it's Batman struggling with how to deal with copycat vigilantes and finally getting to do a bit of actual detective work, or Gary Oldman's Gordon struggling as what seems like the only honest cop in Gotham. And there, constantly circling, is Ledger's Joker, both repellent and undeniably magnetic, leaving the viewer deathly afraid of what he'll do next yet unable to look away.

This is a movie *about* things, about the choices we make and how they define us, about what a man is willing to give up for the greater good, and whether or not he's able to live with it. Every character in the film is met with a moral dilemma, and one way or another, they all bear the scars. All except for the Joker, who explains his scars away differently as the situation requires, and laughs his way through life free of moral repercussions, leaving only bodies in his wake.

# Movies

## *You oughtta be in pictures*

Movies and comic books go hand in hand. All the way back to the 1930s, comic-book artists have looked to film for inspiration, and as succeeding generations who grew up reading comics have gone on to work in cinema, they've been inspired by the four-color exploits from their childhood. It was only a matter of time before the comics themselves were translated into movies, and as you'll soon discover, with varying degrees of success.

Your humble narrators might not love every comic-based movie to be released, but we're duty-bound to see 'em all.

### 30 DAYS OF NIGHT

David Slade's directorial effort on *30 Days of Night* accomplished a lot: it gave actor Josh Hartnett a role where his laconic, low-key delivery enhanced the role of Eben; it maintained the stark, washed-out look and feel of Ben Templesmith's graphic novel art; and best of all, it restored some of the horrific luster that big-screen vampires had lost in recent years. The vamps here, as in the graphic novel, are monstrous things, single-minded, feral and terrifying. Slade's movie is an admirable and truly frightening flick, one that deserves more credit for remaining so loyal to its source material.

### 300

Perhaps the most literal comic-book translation ever made, *300* (2006) is practically a line-for-line, panel-for-panel adaptation of Frank Miller's graphic novel about the legendary Spartan sacrifice at the Hot Gates, brought to the screen in loving, gruesome detail by director Zack Snyder. Gerard Butler brought humor and a super-size dose of testosterone to the role of King Leonidas. Not for those with weak stomachs, but brutal and satisfying.

### AMERICAN SPLENDOR

Much like Harvey Pekar's life itself, the film *American Splendor* (2003) defied conventions and exceeded expectations by turning an independent cartoonist's small, rather grouchy and mundane autobiographical tales into an award-winning movie. The film version of Pekar's comic series stars Paul Giamatti as Pekar, and also features Pekar as himself, commenting on the movie version of his character. This worked much better than it might sound, and it resulted in accolades from the Sundance Film

Festival and the Writer's Guild of America. A quietly intriguing and well-acted affair.

## AVENGERS
Released direct-to-DVD in 2006, *Ultimate Avengers* and its sequel try to have it both ways, adapting Mark Millar and Bryan Hitch's *Avengers* revamp *The Ultimates* for animation, while excising some of the more controversial elements of the book, including much of the sexuality and violence. What resulted was a project that's decent if not inspired, but ultimately pleased no one. It's not enough like classic *Avengers* for *Avengers* fans, and not enough like *The Ultimates* for *Ultimates* fans.

## BLADE
Unlikely as it seems, it was *Blade*, an R-rated adaptation of a second-string horror character, that kicked off Marvel's current run of success at the box office. Released in 1998, *Blade* starred Wesley Snipes as the title character, a half-human, half-vampire hybrid devoted to eradicating vamps from the face of the earth. Co-starring Kris Kristofferson as Blade's mentor, Whistler, and Stephen Dorff as the evil Deacon Frost, *Blade* was a solid and satisfying action piece as directed by Stephen Norrington. However, it was surpassed by its 2002 sequel, *Blade II*, directed by Guillermo del Toro, offering a sharper, wittier script, more visually inspired action sequences and a strong performance by Ron Perlman. Sadly, the same can't be said for the final installment, *Blade: Trinity*, written and directed by David

Goyer, who had scripted the previous *Blade* films, as well. Snipes's Blade takes a back seat to two new vampire hunters portrayed by Ryan Reynolds and Jessica Biel. While not a terrible movie, it lacks the mood of the first film and the vitality of the second. The entire trilogy is fun and definitely worth watching, but if you've got time for only one, make it *Blade II*.

## CAPTAIN AMERICA
Cap's career in film has been a decidedly mixed bag. Actually, it hasn't been that mixed; it's been pretty much all bad. Cap was in movie theaters as early as 1944, thanks to the fifteen-episode Republic Saturday-morning serial *Captain America*. Starring Dick Purcell, the serial pitted a shieldless Captain America (who was really crusading District Attorney Grant Gardner) against the villainy of the Scarab, who was plotting to destroy the city with a sound-vibration device. Pretty routine Republic cliffhanger stuff. Nothing terrible, but certainly not up to the standards of Republic's earlier effort, the outstanding *Adventures of Captain Marvel*. The Republic *Captain America* is available on VHS, but it's really only for the hard-core fan.

As bad as the serial was, it was still just Saturday-afternoon kiddie fare. The 1990 *Captain America* film, however, has no such excuse. Directed by Albert Pyun from an atrocious script by Stephen Tolkin, the film is awful in every category. At the time, Pyun and Tolkin professed in interviews their total lack of interest in the history of the character, and boasted of having never read a *Captain America* comic. Believe us, it shows. Cap is in costume for maybe twenty-five minutes out of the entire excruciating two-hours-plus running time. Pyun, who had previously directed such gems as *The Sword and the Sorcerer* and the abysmal Kathy Ireland vehicle *Alien From L.A.*, couldn't even get a good performance out of stalwart character actors Ned Beatty and Ronny Cox. Actor Matt Salinger, J.D.'s son, is stiff and uncharismatic, showing neither Steve Rogers's all-American charm or Captain America's gritty determination. We won't even discuss Scott Paulin's horrendous performance as the Red Skull; even through what looks like pounds of latex makeup, he's dull and uninspired.

## CAPTAIN MARVEL

In 1941, *The Adventures of Captain Marvel* graced Saturday-morning theater screens for twelve weeks. The Republic serial, starring Tom Tyler as Captain Marvel, is considered by many to be one of the best examples of the action serial genre. You can still find this on VHS in video stores if you look hard enough.

## CATWOMAN

For most moviegoers, the definitive big-screen Catwoman is Michelle Pfeiffer, the insanely sexy bad girl Selina Kyle from Tim Burton's 1992 film *Batman Returns*. With a skintight vinyl catsuit, a bullwhip and a withering glare, Pfeiffer's Catwoman can drive you crazy one moment and break your heart the next. Definitely the highlight of the film.

Not a highlight was the 2004 attempt to give Catwoman her own film. *Catwoman*, directed by uni-named French director Pitof and starred Halle Berry, who earned a Golden Raspberry Award for Worst Actress for her performance. However, she's far from the only thing wrong with this movie. An incomprehensible plot, horrible origin for Catwoman and Sharon Stone's performance as an evil cosmetics magnate all contribute to the stink. Avoid at all costs.

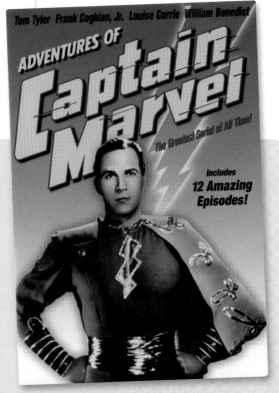

The 1940s Captain Marvel serials: you will almost believe a man can fly.

ADVENTURES OF CAPTAIN MARVEL © 1942 REPUBLIC ENTERTAINMENT, INC.

## CONSTANTINE

Keanu Reeves took on the role of John Constantine in *Constantine*, Francis Lawrence's 2005 adaptation of the *Hellblazer* comics from DC's Vertigo imprint. Fans of the comic were aghast at the notion of Reeves playing the blond, sardonic, British title character, and the end result is a somewhat mediocre mystical thriller that didn't really please anyone. It's neither a must-see nor an all-time worst, but might be worth your time if you catch it on cable.

## DAREDEVIL

*Daredevil* hit theaters in 2003. This overblown and occasionally unintentionally funny adaptation by director Mark Steven Johnson starred Ben Affleck as Matt Murdock/Daredevil, Jennifer Garner as Murdock's ninja love interest Elektra, Colin Farrell as the murderous assassin Bullseye and Michael Clarke Duncan as crime boss the Kingpin. Well-intentioned and far more faithful to the comics than one might expect, the movie suffered from a slightly too angsty, melodramatic script and an at-the-time overexposed star (Affleck), who may not have been the best choice for the brooding, intense Matt Murdock. At times, it stretches the suspension of disbelief, but it's not the worst movie you'll ever see.

## DOCTOR STRANGE

The only appearance for Doc Strange so far has been the 2007 direct-to-DVD animated feature *Doctor Strange: The Sorcerer Supreme*, directed by *Batman: The Animated Series* alum Frank Paur. An extended version of Strange's origin story, the movie does a fair job of capturing the feel of the comics, but lacks both Stan Lee's trademark rhyming couplets for Strange's spells and the trippy, psychedelic look of the original Steve Ditko artwork. Maybe the biggest disappointment is Dormammu, the Ditko-designed Doctor Strange villain, who loses his trademark flaming-headed look in favor of a sort of fiery horned skeleton.

## ELEKTRA

Not satisfied to let DC claim the "worst comic-book movie ever" crown with *Catwoman*, Marvel rallied in a big way in 2005 with *Elektra*, its spin-off of the Ben Affleck *Daredevil* film, with Jennifer Garner reprising her role as Elektra Natchios. The film takes its cue from much of the Frank Miller comic-book run, involving the sensei Stick (played by onetime General Zod Terence Stamp) and the ninja organization known as the Hand. Bad script, bad performances, bad fight scenes, just bad all around.

## FANTASTIC FOUR

As much as the never-released 1994 *Fantastic Four* movie has been pilloried by the fan press over the years, it may actually be the more faithful and better-acted adaptation of Stan Lee and Jack Kirby's most famous comic-book creations.

In 1992, German producer Bernd Eichinger held the production rights to the property. The scuttlebutt in Hollywood was that Chris Columbus, fresh from the success of the *Home Alone* movies, wanted to make *Fantastic Four* his next project and was waiting for the rights to lapse. So he wouldn't lose his option, Eichinger called in famed B-movie schlockmeister Roger Corman to produce the film. The movie was quickly filmed and in the can, only to never again see the light of day.

The producers of Columbus's version bought up Corman's film so his low-budget version couldn't be released before theirs. Eventually Columbus lost interest in the project, and *Fantastic Four* was locked away to languish in limbo for nearly a decade.

Directed by Oley Sassone and written by Craig J. Nevius and Kevin Rock, *The Fantastic Four* (1994) is a surprisingly decent little piece of escapism. Not to say there aren't problems—there are problems by the bucketload. The dialogue has more than a few real groaners, the plot is needlessly padded out with a dull B-story and a secondary villain, and the special effects are occasionally low-rent beyond belief. But there are more than a few things to like here, too, not the least of which are the engaging performances by the four leads, who do their best to elevate the occasionally cheesy dialogue and chintzy-looking props with real emotion and heart, succeeding more often than not. The relationship between Reed and Sue is believable and kinda sweet, and Michael Bailey Smith's limited screen time as Ben Grimm goes a long way toward investing the Thing with his necessary humanity, allowing the puppeteers to do the rest. Even the score is very effective, conveying both the action-adventure derring-do and the nostalgic, family feel the story needs.

In 2005, the Fantastic Four finally received the big-budget, big-screen release it deserved, and it resulted in a film that deserved to be much, much better. *Fantastic Four* takes much of the simple charm of the characters and their origin and needlessly mucks it up. The film is almost uniformly miscast, with the exception of Ben Grimm (Michael Chiklis) and Johnny Storm (Chris Evans). Though the two have a playful energy, even the mighty Thing can only carry so much of a bad load. At least *FF* creator Stan Lee gets in a good cameo as the team's ear-wiggling mailman, Willy Lumpkin.

The 2007 sequel, *Fantastic Four: Rise of the Silver Surfer*, doesn't necessarily improve upon the flaws of the first, but it has a modicum more charm. Whether this is because the film's now-jokey, all-ages tone is less jarring or because the CGI-constructed Silver Surfer actually adds some dramatic weight to the picture is for you to decide. It's not anywhere near the epic Fantastic Four movie the comic deserves, but at least it's short and not any more embarrassing than the first.

### GHOST RIDER

For years, actor Nicolas Cage, an avowed comics fan, looked for the right movie to satisfy his comic book jones. He was attached to many projects that never materialized (Nic Cage as Superman? Disaster averted), but ended up in one that he shouldn't have: *Ghost Rider* (2007). After Cage waited so long for a comics movie, *Ghost Rider* stands as proof that the comics gods have a wicked sense of humor. Director Mark Steven Johnson somehow earned another crack at a Marvel comics movie after *Daredevil* and delivered on the public's low expectations. Cage's arch sense of humor—the few times his visage isn't buried under flaming special effects—helps redeem the movie in places, but overall, the movie is a muddled, largely plodding mess. Also, Peter Fonda appears as the demonic Mephisto, which is exactly as bad as it sounds.

## GHOST WORLD

Terry Zwigoff's acclaimed 2001 film *Ghost World* is everything most comic-book movies are not. It's a quiet film, with nary a costume or special effect in sight. Based on indie cartoonist Daniel Clowes's blackly humorous graphic novel tale of two teenage disaffected teenage girls and the older recluse they torture and then come to understand, the film is a faithful, funny and touching adaptation.

## HELLBOY

Guillermo del Toro did a masterful job adapting Mike Mignola's signature character in the 2004 release *Hellboy*. Starring Ron Perlman as the titular demonic monster-hunter, the movie manages to introduce audiences to the main character and establish a surprisingly touching romance between Perlman's Hellboy and Selma Blair's firestarter Liz Sherman, all while executing a rollicking action movie. Del Toro did a great job of capturing the mood, the heart and the look of Mike Mignola's stories while retaining his own uniquely ornate visual style. A fantastic movie, yet del Toro and Perlman managed to surpass it in its 2008 sequel, *Hellboy II: The Golden Army*.

## HOWARD THE DUCK

One of the most legendary movie flops of all time, *Howard the Duck* ignores nearly everything that made the Marvel comic book a cultural sensation in the 1970s. Where as the comics are smart and satirical, the 1986 film is dull and mindless, with unfunny quip after unfunny quip out of Howard's rubbery beak. And therein lies the biggest problem of all: Howard himself. Whereas the comics allow the reader a certain suspension of disbelief regarding a talking duck in a world of men, on film there is no getting around the fact that you're looking at a tiny man in a duck suit—and not even a particularly good duck suit at that. We haven't seen this movie in twenty years, yet it's still irreparably burned into our brains.

## HULK

Highly anticipated as Marvel's follow-up to the runaway successes of *X-Men* and *Spider-Man*, Ang Lee's 2003 film *Hulk*, though somewhat commercially successful, is widely viewed as a misfire. Almost a psychological drama disguised as a superhero movie, the film devotes far too much time to Bruce Banner's damaged childhood and the backstory of his father, played by Nick Nolte, and not nearly enough to what audiences had come to see: Bruce Banner changing into the Hulk and smashing stuff up.

Complicating matters is that the Hulk, rendered on screen entirely by computer graphics, never quite seems real to the viewer, and he's not compelling enough a character to overlook his obvious fakiness. Compounded with a long running time and head-scratching climax that involves the Hulk fighting a cloud, the result is a whole lot of angry moviegoers. And you wouldn't like them when they're angry.

Happily, the character was redeemed with Louis Leterrier's *The Incredible Hulk* (2008). With a standout cast including Ed Norton, Liv Tyler, William Hurt and Tim Roth, the film is an extremely entertaining mix of the comic books and the fondly remembered 1970s television series. As for the Hulk himself, he's much more lifelike than the previous version, and doesn't look digitally "dropped in" among his flesh-and-blood co-stars. He feels more like a real character on screen, and better able to convey emotion. This CGI Hulk also performs much better in the action scenes, which are far better executed here than in the last film, and also a lot more fun, with the army bringing out some slightly sci-fi-tinged weaponry against the Hulk, sonic cannons and the like. Norton is the perfect choice to play Bruce Banner, and he portrays both Banner's withdrawn intensity and tortured soul elegantly.

Best of all, this film actually has an antagonist in Tim Roth's Abomination, and the resulting fight scene is a doozy, a super-slugfest reminiscent of the big Superman vs. General Zod fight in *Superman II*, only with much less comedy and played with a lot more brutality. Everything you'd want in a *Hulk* movie is here.

## IRON MAN

Iron Man first got the feature treatment in 2007 with the direct-to-video DVD release *The Invincible Iron Man*, directed by Frank Paur. It's not a bad translation of the character, but it places far too much focus on one of Iron Man's villains, the Mandarin, considering he never actually shows up in the movie. There's also the inclusion of a father-son dynamic that winds up weakening Tony Stark's character, and far too much mystical mumbo-jumbo that doesn't fit the tone of what Iron Man is about.

Fortunately, Jon Favreau's *Iron Man* (2008) does just about everything right. It's a great movie for everyone, whether you're a long-time *Iron Man* fan or someone who's never read a comic book. Much of the credit goes to Favreau, who knows how to get the best out of his actors—there's not a single scene that seems forced or doesn't ring true. Favreau clearly did his research, deftly weaving elements from four decades' worth of Iron Man comics into a film that feels more like Iron Man than any Iron Man comic we've ever read.

As great as everything else in the movie is (and it is pretty great), this movie lives or dies by its star. If you don't believe in Tony Stark, then all of the high-tech SFX wizardry is just going to feel like a big video game. Robert Downey Jr.'s Stark is charismatic, charming, funny and conflicted, and you can't take your eyes off him. For the first time in one of these big-budget super-movies, you're not just counting the minutes until the protagonist climbs back into his superhero suit. Bravo.

## JUSTICE LEAGUE: THE NEW FRONTIER

Darwyn Cooke's outstanding 2003 series *DC: The New Frontier* was adapted to a direct-to-DVD feature *Justice League: The New Frontier* in 2008, with similarly outstanding results. Directed by Dave Bullock and scripted by animation vet Stan Berkowitz, it manages to retain most of the story's important sequences and even cleverly alludes to the material that had to be eliminated for space. Set in the late 1950s and early 1960s, *New Frontier* is Cooke's love letter to the Silver Age heroes of DC Comics, and Bullock and Berkowitz manage to keep every drop of that affection on the screen. Sensitive, subtle voice work from actors David Boreanaz, Kyle MacLachlan, Lucy Lawless and Miguel Ferrer completes the package.

## THE LEAGUE OF EXTRAORDINARY GENTLEMEN

If you've never read the astounding and brilliant comics by Alan Moore and Kevin O'Neill, you might not understand why fans were so unhappy with Stephen Norrington's 2003 film *The League of Extraordinary Gentlemen* (sometimes called *LXG*). Other than the basic concept—translating the "superhero team" idea to famous literary characters—the two barely have anything in common. This makes some sense, though. Moore and O'Neill's dense, allusion-filled and deliberately paced masterpiece would be a hard sell for summer blockbuster audiences. *The League* film is a fun, fast-moving action-adventure gem, with Sean Connery chewing up the scenery as aging adventurer Allan Quatermain. The filmmakers do get extra points for achieving Kevin O'Neill's design concept for Mr. Hyde in live-action. Approach it with an open mind, and you'll be surprised how enjoyable it is.

## THE PHANTOM

Criminally underseen by audiences and under-rated by critics, *The Phantom* (1996) is not only a rollicking adventure flick in the tradition of the Indiana Jones movies, it's also a smart and loyal translation of Lee Falk's long-running newspaper-strip and comic-book character. Directed by Simon Wincer and scripted by Jeffrey Boam, *The Phantom* mixes 1930s-period style with some excellent stunt work in its engaging action sequences and an absolutely charming cast—Billy Zane as the Phantom, Patrick McGoohan as his ghostly father, Catherine Zeta-Jones as air pirate Sala and Treat Williams positively stealing the show as the heavy tycoon Xander Drax. It's also beautifully shot, with the jungles of Thailand filling in for the Phantom's fictional African homeland of Bangalla. One of the best movies nobody ever saw.

## THE PUNISHER

Marvel's resident vigilante, the Punisher, has made his way to the big screen twice so far, with a bit more success the second time around. Dolph Lundgren plays Frank Castle in 1989's *The Punisher*, a low-budget B-movie co-starring Louis Gossett Jr. Short of the title and the character's name, there's not much to link the movie with the comics. Even the Punisher's skull T-shirt was considered "too comic-booky" by the producers.

A more faithful translation hit theaters in 2004, starring Thomas Jane as the Punisher and John Travolta as mob boss Howard Saint. Directed by Jonathan Hensleigh, the film takes its cues from such *Punisher* stories as "Year One" and "Welcome Back, Frank," and does a much better job of capturing the anarchic, vengeful spirit of the comics at their best.

## THE ROCKETEER

It didn't take long for Dave Stevens's nostalgic adventure yarn *The Rocketeer* to gain the attention of Hollywood. Eventually, Disney turned the project over to Joe Johnston to direct, with Stevens attached as a producer. Johnston, a career visual effects guy, had only directed one film before this, the effects-heavy *Honey, I Shrunk the Kids*, but he delivered big-time, deftly handling the proper mix of action, comedy and drama that the project needed. The script by Danny Bilson and Paul De Meo (best known for the 1990 *Flash* CBS TV series) was also spot-on, retaining all of the charm of Stevens's original work while adding a more cohesive plot and a much-needed villain in the form of movie star and Nazi sympathizer Neville Sinclair (portrayed with aplomb by Timothy Dalton, doing his best Errol Flynn impression).

In addition to a shining cast, the movie looks great and perfectly captures the period. The visual effects for the Rocketeer in flight are very good, especially for the pre-digital era of special effects in 1991. The air-show sequence, in which Cliff uses the rocket pack for the first time, to rescue Malcolm, is a near-perfect translation of the comic-book sequence.

The Rocketeer costume is also a thing of beauty, exactly replicating Dave Stevens's design. Putting the final touch on things is James Horner's stirring score, a piece of music so satisfying that to this day it's still used as a temp score for all kinds of movie trailers. This is a fantastic, fun film, and it's a shame that practically no one saw it. Check out the DVD, and you won't be disappointed.

## SIN CITY

Frank Miller's series of noir thrillers comes to life in garish, bloody black and white, thanks to Miller and his co-director Robert Rodriguez. The 2005 film opened to rave reviews and surprisingly good box office, thanks not only to the strength of the source material (slavishly followed by Rodriguez) but also to the film's singular look: stark, high-contrast black and white with flashes of brilliant color. Of course, it didn't hurt that *Sin City* also boasted an all-star cast. Bruce Willis, Clive Owen, Jessica Alba, Rosario Dawson and Mickey Rourke all did their part to bring Miller's cast of tough guys, dames and hoodlums to life. Another of the few note-perfect translations from comics to cinema.

## SPAWN

So far, Spawn is the only one of the Image Comics characters to make it to the big screen. Todd McFarlane's *Spawn* hit theaters in 1997, starring Michael Jai White as the title character,

John Leguizamo as the demonic Clown, and Martin Sheen as Jason Wynn, Spawn's former boss and the man behind his untimely demise. Directed by Mark A.Z. Dippé, the film is a fairly faithful adaptation of the original McFarlane comics. However, much like the comics themselves, the film hasn't aged well, and feels very much like a product of its time. All but forgotten against the more recent spate of high-profile comic-book blockbusters, *Spawn* is nevertheless notable for being one of the first films to adhere so faithfully to the look and feel of the comic-book source material.

## SPIDER-MAN

After years and years of rumors, promises, cancellations and disappointment, Marvel's trademark character finally hit the silver screen in 2002, in Sam Raimi's *Spider-Man*, starring Tobey Maguire as Peter Parker/Spider-Man, Kirsten Dunst as Mary Jane Watson and Willem Dafoe as Norman Osborn/the Green Goblin. A longtime Spidey fan, Raimi understood that a good Spider-Man movie would combine a proper mixture of angst, action and laughs, along with a healthy dose of the classic Spidey motivation: guilt. The only missteps in the first *Spider-Man* film are the slightly overlong origin sequence and the decision to dress the Green Goblin in an uninspired armored suit and expressionless mask, instead of the outlandish and much creepier costume from the comics. With just a few makeup applications, Dafoe could have made a truly frightening Green Goblin straight out of the Ditko and Romita comic books.

Director Raimi gets just about everything right in *Spider-Man 2* (2004), with the returning Maguire and Dunst shining in their roles as the star-crossed lovers Pete and Mary Jane, and Alfred Molina pulling out one of the best super-villain performances yet as Doctor Octopus.

Unfortunately, *Spider-Man 3* (2007) didn't reach anywhere near those creative heights, despite the return of Raimi and pretty much the entire cast. For one thing, the movie tries to tell too many stories, juggling the arrival of Spider-Man's alien black costume with the introduction of the Sandman, and the eventual birth of Venom, along with a romantic triangle involving Pete, Mary Jane and new love interest Gwen Stacy. Combine all that with too much ill-timed comedy and *three separate* musical sequences, and the end result is an unfocused disappointment, especially considering the extremely high quality of the previous two films. It's still an enjoyable movie, and certainly better than most comic-book movies, but when you compare it to the brilliance of its predecessors, you can't help feeling a little unsatisfied.

## SUPERGIRL

An attempt to cash in on the success of the Christopher Reeve *Superman* films, Jeannot Szwarc's *Supergirl* (1984) is a prime example of how not to handle your franchise. To wit, if you can't convince your Superman to appear in your Superman spinoff film, then don't make it. Christopher Reeve's glaring absence really prevents the film from gaining any traction. After all, if Kara Zor-El really is Superman's cousin, why can't she get a visit from her famous blood relative, much less some help against Faye Dunaway's witch Selena? Though Marc McClure is brought in as Jimmy Olsen in an attempt to create some connection to the *Superman* films, and Helen Slater is appealing enough as Kara, without Superman, the film feels second-rate. A seriously hammy Peter O'Toole doesn't help matters, either.

## V FOR VENDETTA

Alan Moore and David Lloyd's brilliant tale of alternate-future anarchy was successfully adapted by director James McTeigue in 2006. With a script written by the Wachowski brothers, much of Moore and Lloyd's work makes it to the screen intact, with the glaring exceptions of the Hollywood-style bombastic ending and the excision of Moore's brilliant monologue from the middle of the book. Natalie Portman does perhaps some of the best acting of her career as Evey, and the brutal and shocking sequence involving her detention and torture by the British government appears verbatim as it did in the comic, along with its shocking climax. It's not the book, but it's a fair enough approximation to be worth your time.

## X-MEN

The big-budget blockbuster that cemented Marvel's place as King of the Comic-Book Movies, Bryan Singer's *X-Men* hit theaters in 2000, and received critical acclaim and box-office success with its well-balanced mix

of action and social commentary. A cleverly chosen mix of established "serious" actors and unknowns fills out the cast, including Patrick Stewart as Professor Xavier, Ian McKellen as Magneto and Halle Berry as Storm. However, it was new discovery Hugh Jackman whom audiences fell in love with. His portrayal of Wolverine is universally acclaimed as just about perfect.

Lightning struck again in 2003 with the release of *X2*, which reunited the cast and director Singer, and introduced Alan Cumming as Nightcrawler, in another very well-received performance. *X2* sets both the X-Men and Magneto against anti-mutant military scientist William Stryker (played by Brian Cox), and wisely keeps the focus strongly on Jackman's Wolverine once more, for a sequel that manages to surpass its predecessor.

And then it all went wrong. For the third movie, Brett Ratner took over as director and delivered a film, *X-Men: The Last Stand* (2006), that few can stand. Gone is any allegory or bit of symbolism, and in its place is a botched version of one of the most beloved *X-Men* comic runs of all time, "The Dark Phoenix Saga." Ratner's film mashed that storyline with elements from a more recent *X-Men* story arc written by Joss Whedon and ended up neutering both tales. New characters fell off, old characters seem bored, and an overwhelming sense of chaos and indifference reign. *The Godfather III* of this particular film series.

# Television

## Video made the comic-book star

As the insatiable machine that is the entertainment industry marches on year after year, it's always looking for new raw material to feed the beast, so naturally, all kinds of comic-book properties have found their way to television adaptations. Some have been animated, some live-action, some excellent and some have been just awful. Let's look at a few of the highlights and lowlights.

### AQUAMAN

Aquaman shared the spotlight with Superman in 1967 in Filmation's *The Superman/Aquaman Hour of Adventure*, which aired Saturday mornings on CBS. Along with new animated adventures of the Man of Steel and the King of the Sea, viewers were treated to cartoons featuring Green Lantern, the Atom, Hawkman, the Justice League of America and the Teen Titans. When Superman got the boot the following year, *Aquaman* remained in a half-hour format featuring his army of guest stars. Though Aquaman and Aqualad riding around on giant seahorses has a certain goofy charm today, it doesn't hold up to repeat viewings.

### AVENGERS

Marvel's Avengers haven't had much success in translations to other media. Aside from a few fleeting guest appearances in the second season of the syndicated *Fantastic Four* animated series, the Avengers have made only one leap to television, in the 1999 Fox animated series *The Avengers: United They Stand*. The absence of Captain America, Iron Man and Thor hurt the show, as did the bizarre use of Power Rangers-style "battle armor," worn by all of the characters and donned during interminable "armoring-up" sequences. Still, just the sheer novelty of seeing characters like Ant-Man, the Wasp, Wonder Man, the Vision and the Falcon on TV every Saturday morning made the series worth watching. Passable if not terribly exciting.

### CAPTAIN AMERICA

Captain America first hit the small screen in 1966. The *Marvel Super Heroes* cartoon series from Grantray-Lawrence featured barely animated cutouts taken directly from the original Marvel comics. Of all these cartoons, Cap's theme song seems to have stuck with viewers the most: "*When Captain America throws his mighty shield... All those who chose to oppose his shield must yield...*" Undeniably catchy.

Following the 1977 television success of *The Incredible Hulk*, CBS quickly churned out the pilot TV movie *Captain America* in 1978 hoping to strike gold again. Starring the mannequin-like Reb Brown, the TV movie was, to say the least, less than satisfying. Cap's redesigned costume looked absolutely hideous (he was given his traditional outfit in the movie's closing moments), and his transparent shield that doubled as the windshield of his motorcycle was a neat idea that looked silly in practice. The ratings were good enough to warrant a second TV movie, *Captain America II: Death Too Soon*. The second telefilm involved a plot to infect America with an aging drug, and featured a clearly slumming Christopher Lee as its villain. These movies are memorable mostly for the scenes of Cap on his motorcycle blasting out of the back of his cool 1970s-style Chevy van. We suspect that's where most of the budget went.

## DOCTOR STRANGE

Unlike many of his Marvel cohorts, Doctor Strange hasn't had a lot of luck making it big outside of comics. His first TV appearance was in the 1978 CBS TV movie *Dr. Strange*. It came in the wake of the successes of *The Incredible Hulk* and *Spider-Man* TV projects, and was intended to act as a pilot for a series to follow. However, the movie was broadcast at the same time as the ratings smash *Roots*, so almost no one saw it. Not that it would've mattered much. The film, written and directed by Philip DeGuere, was pretty mediocre fare, featuring Peter Hooten as a rookie and somewhat befuddled Stephen Strange pitted against (and fending off the advances of) sorceress Morgan le Fey, played by *Arrested Development*'s Jessica Walter.

## FANTASTIC FOUR

Stan Lee and Jack Kirby's seminal Marvel comic has found itself the target of adaptation on numerous occasions over the last four decades.

In 1967, Hanna-Barbera produced *Fantastic Four*, a remarkably faithful adaptation of the Lee/Kirby comics that aired for three years on ABC. The animation is pretty good by H-B standards, the scripts are reasonably intelligent and the voice acting is a little stodgy but effective. It's one of the better adventure cartoons of its day, and it boasts a finger-snapping, jazzy little theme song. It's a shame it's not available on DVD.

In 1978, *The New Fantastic Four*, produced by DePatie-Freleng, aired on NBC. Rights to the Human Torch were elsewhere, so he was replaced by the remarkably annoying H.E.R.B.I.E. the Robot. Despite Jack Kirby's presence on staff as a storyboard artist, this was a real stinker. Only thirteen episodes were produced, and that's thirteen too many if you ask us.

In 1994, *Fantastic Four* aired as part of the syndicated *Marvel Action Hour* animated series. The series ran for two years, and the first year was not good at all, with bone-stupid scripts, terrible characterizations and some of the worst attempts at comedy relief ever. When Galactus arrives on Earth to consume it, he's actually licking his lips as if he's sitting down for lunch at Arby's. It was so bad, in fact, that the entire production team was replaced by all-new creatives who acted as if the first season never took place, a good choice. The second season was as good as the first was bad, with superior animation, vastly improved acting and suspenseful, intelligent scripts that featured plenty of action and guest stars galore, everyone from the Avengers to the Hulk to Ghost Rider.

In 2006, following the FF's successful feature film debut, Cartoon Network premiered *Fantastic Four: World's Greatest Heroes*, a French-produced animated series with a modern, slightly anime-styled feel. While the scripts were heavily comics-influenced and featured plenty of cameos from other Marvel characters, the series failed to catch on with young viewers and was never embraced by older fans. A shame, because as the series progressed through its twenty-six episodes, it steadily improved. Definitely worth checking out on DVD.

## THE FLASH

Aside from his supporting appearances on shows such as *Super Friends* and *Justice League*, the Flash's sole foray into show biz was with *The Flash*, his 1990 live-action television series that aired on CBS. Produced as a reaction to the smash success of the *Batman* movie, the series showed a heavy Tim Burton influence, from the title character's oversculpted muscle suit to the Danny Elfman score. Unfortunately, it had none of the *Batman* movie's vitality or innovation. Starring John Wesley Shipp as Barry Allen and Amanda Pays as scientist Tina McGee, the series had none of the wild, manic action or colorful visuals you might expect of

a Flash TV show. Instead, Flash mostly found himself fighting dull thugs and mobsters, with one or two overly produced special-effects sequences each episode. The producers tried to liven things up with supervillains once or twice, the most successful being Mark Hamill's two appearances as the Trickster, but overall audiences were bored and the series ended after twenty-two episodes.

## INCREDIBLE HULK

Of all the Marvel characters, the Hulk has had the most success in TV translations. The Hulk's first appearance on the small screen came in the original 1966 *Marvel Super Heroes* animated series from Grantray-Lawrence, the barely animated moving cutouts of Silver Age Marvel comic books that are mostly remembered for the wacky theme songs. Come on, sing it if you know it:

> *Doc Bruce Banner,*
> *Belted by gamma rays,*
> *Turned into the Hulk.*
> *Ain't he unglamo-rays!*

The Hulk had much better luck with his next TV project, the 1978 CBS dramatic series *The Incredible Hulk*. Executive producer Kenneth Johnson kept the most important aspects of the *Hulk* comics—Banner's struggle with his transformations into the Hulk (played by Mr. Universe Lou Ferrigno) and his search for a cure—and discarded the rest, transplanting the newly renamed David Banner into a premise much like that of the TV classic *The Fugitive*. Every week, Bill Bixby's Banner would make his way to a new town, searching for a cure for his condition and taking odd jobs along the way to survive, while always being pursued by investigative reporter Jack McGee, played by Jack Colvin. Sure, the show was predictable, but it was a *good* predictable. Bixby, Colvin and Ferrigno were appealing and committed to the material, and the action sequences were decent considering the show's budget and when it was produced. The show ran for five seasons, ending in 1982—a very respectable run for a 1970s action drama. The two-hour premiere movie was released on DVD in conjunction with the release of the first film. Check it out.

*The Incredible Hulk* (1982) animated series aired Saturday mornings on NBC in conjunction with *Spider-Man and His Amazing Friends,* and was produced by Marvel's then-new animation division. The series was based on serious old-school *Hulk,* featuring scientist Bruce Banner working at the missile base with fellow scientist Betty Ross, under the watchful eye of "Thunderbolt" Ross and the still-rodent-like Glenn Talbot. Rick Jones was also around, sporting quite the mullet and an enormous cowboy hat. The series only ran thirteen episodes and was nothing special.

Bixby and Ferrigno returned in 1988 in the first of three made-for-TV movies for NBC, *The Incredible Hulk Returns*. The first of these stinkers featured Thor, Marvel's resident god of thunder. The script played pretty fast and loose with the Thor canon, introducing Don Blake as a former colleague of Bixby's David Banner, who had discovered the hammer of Thor, which allowed him to mystically summon Thor himself, who was more of a hapless Viking goofball with a penchant for brawling and boozing than any sort of noble thunder god. Those of you bent on punishing yourselves can pick this loser up on video.

The Hulk and Daredevil teamed up the next year in *The Trial of the Incredible Hulk* (in which the Hulk is never put on trial and the only courtroom scene is a dream sequence). It's memorable mostly for the horrendous Daredevil costume Rex Smith sported—all black with a blindfold over his eyes. OK, we get it. He's blind. The Bixby/Ferrigno snoozer also featured John Rhys-Davies as a bearded Kingpin, and *Daredevil* creator Stan Lee as the memorable Guy in Jury Box.

Finally, *The Death of the Incredible Hulk* (1990) featured exactly that. The final shot of the film shows the Hulk's dead body after a midair fall from a helicopter. Another film, *The Rebirth of the Incredible Hulk,* was in the works, but Bill Bixby's passing in 1993 permanently shelved the project. This one is available on DVD, too, albeit not something we recommend.

The most recent *Incredible Hulk* animated series premiered in 1996 as part of UPN's short-lived Sunday morning animation block. This series was produced by the same folks who put together the vastly improved second seasons of the syndicated *Fantastic Four* and *Iron Man* series, and the quality shows.

Aspects from all the *Hulk* comics made their way into the series, including Rick Jones, the gray Hulk, Mr. Fixit and the John Byrne "Hulk separation" storyline. The show featured lots of Marvel guest stars as well, including She-Hulk, Thor, Iron Man, Doctor Strange, Ghost Rider, the Thing and Mr. Fantastic. The voice talent was above par, with Neal McDonough playing Bruce Banner and Lou Ferrigno returning to the role of the Hulk, speaking in the part for the first time. The show ran two seasons for twenty-one episodes, and is well worth checking out on video.

## IRON MAN

Like Captain America, the Hulk and a few others, Iron Man was part of the 1966 *Marvel Super Heroes* animation package from Grantray-Lawrence. As discussed before, these are good for some yuks, and the stories are faithful retellings, but they barely qualify as animation.

Iron Man returned to television in 1994 as part of the syndicated *Marvel Action Hour*. Just like its sister series, *Fantastic Four*, the first season of *Iron Man* was horrendous. Iron Man is saddled with a second-rate Avengers-knockoff superhero team featuring War Machine, Spider-Woman, Hawkeye, the Scarlet Witch and Century. The scripts are juvenile and unfunny—they all seem to feature the Mandarin week after agonizing week—and the voice acting, with the notable exception of Robert Hays as Tony Stark/Iron Man, is well below par. Like *Fantastic Four*, however, in a rare move for television, producers noticed

and took action, replacing the entire creative team, and recasting the whole show with the exception of Hays.

As a result, the second season is much better, with smarter, less formulaic scripts, better animation and improved acting. There is a well-done adaptation of the "Armor Wars" storyline from the comics, and most important, the Mandarin (who for some reason is colored a lovely shade of green in the series) doesn't appear in every stinking episode.

## JUSTICE LEAGUE OF AMERICA

The Justice League premiered on television back in 1967, in three segments of *The Superman/Aquaman Hour of Adventure*, and consisted of a lineup of characters who also appeared in solo cartoons on the same series: Superman, Aquaman, Green Lantern, Hawkman and the Atom. (Batman, whose television rights were tied up elsewhere at the time, was notably absent.) These are quaint but fun little cartoons, enjoyable mostly for their camp value.

Most television viewers of a certain generation think of the Justice League under another, more innocent name: *Super Friends*. Premiering on ABC in 1973 and produced by Hanna-Barbera, *Super Friends* featured Superman, Batman, Robin, Aquaman and Wonder Woman, alongside teen superhero trainees/comic relief Wendy, Marvin and Wonderdog. The series mostly pit the JLA (although they were seldom called by the name) against natural disasters, aliens, mad scientists and, occasionally, natural disasters caused by aliens or mad scientists. The emphasis tended to be on cooperation and settling disputes peacefully. Although laudable, this doesn't make for the most exciting show.

The series returned with a slight revamp in 1977 with *The All-New Super Friends Hour*, notable mostly for the introduction of Wendy's and Marvin's replacements: Zan and Jayna, the Wonder Twins. Alien teenagers accompanied by their space monkey Gleek, Zan and Jayna could transform into water or animals, respectively. While an obvious attempt to add kids to the series to capture young viewers, at least Zan and Jayna were more interesting than their predecessors, who mostly just stood around and got kidnapped a lot.

However, the version of *Super Friends* most fondly remembered is *Challenge of the Super Friends* (1978). After several seasons of mealy-mouthed socially conscious *Superfriends* cartoons, the programming executives at ABC inexplicably grew a spine and assigned *Super Friends* producers to create a cartoon show more like the comics, with real villains and real threats. Under the supervision of story editor Jeffrey Scott, out were the cloying teen heroes Wendy and Marvin and the Wonder Twins, and in were an all-star cast of DC's best superheroes and supervillains.

Hanging out in the Hall of Justice were Superman, Batman, Robin, Wonder Woman, Aquaman, the Flash, Green Lantern and Hawkman, with newly created heroes Black Vulcan, Apache Chief and Samurai (included to add a little much-needed ethnicity to the team). What really makes the show work is the Legion of Doom, who are the true stars of the show: Lex Luthor, Brainiac, Bizarro, Toyman, the Riddler, Cheetah, Giganta, Captain Cold, the Scarecrow, Black Manta, Sinestro, Solomon Grundy and Gorilla Grodd. A pretty strong lineup. Every episode opens with the Legion putting their newest scheme into action, and ends with their escape. They're motivated, proactive and work well as a team, and more often than not, the Super Friends win out by sheer happenstance as opposed to any measurable superiority of skill or desire.

After one season of *Challenge*, *Super Friends* went back to its less interesting "Wonder Twins" style until the series got another retool in 1984 with *Super Friends: The Legendary Super Powers Show*, which added new superhero Firestorm to the mix, and again in 1985 with *The Super Powers Team: Galactic Guardians*, which introduced Cyborg, from DC's *The New Teen Titans* comic. Both of these series were largely intended as promotional tools for the "Super Powers" action-figure line from Kenner, but the redesigned series had a crackle and vitality that had been lacking since the Legion of Doom disappeared. *Galactic Guardians* is also noteworthy for the first television appearance of Jack Kirby's classic villain Darkseid.

In 2001, the Warner Animation production team behind the outstanding *Batman* and *Superman* animated series tackled the JLA with *Justice League*, airing on Cartoon Network. *Justice League* featured a classic lineup of Superman, Batman, Wonder Woman, the Flash, the Martian Manhunter, Green Lantern and Hawkgirl, the best and most faithful translation of DC's characters to date. Though the first season was slightly uneven—the production team had to figure out how to utilize so many protagonists and how to best use Superman in a team dynamic so he didn't appear too weak—the second season was rock solid, culminating in "Starcrossed," a smashing three-episode finale that pitted the Justice League against a full-on alien invasion force, with devastating results for both the planet and the League. Highly recommended.

Just when it seemed the good times were over, the series was back, slightly retooled as *Justice League Unlimited* (2004), which assembled nearly every DC superhero under the Justice League banner. Despite the new cast of dozens, the series managed to tell season-long, suspenseful stories without neglecting the core characters that had made the series popular in the first place. *JLU*'s two seasons each had a central arc. The first, an ambitious political thriller that dealt with the notions of power and responsibility, and the second a back-to-basics supervillain brawl that elicited fond memories of the old Legion of Doom days. Even better than the first *JL* series.

## SHAZAM!

SHAZAM! hit the small screen in 1974 when CBS began airing Filmation's live-action Saturday-morning series, starring Michael Gray as Billy Batson and Jackson Bostwick as Captain Marvel (later John Davey). To be honest, we haven't seen the show since the seventies and remember being spellbound by it, but it would look pretty silly now. We remember Billy traveling the country in an RV with an old guy named Mentor, but that's about it.

In 1981, *The Kid Superpower Hour With Shazam!*, a Saturday-morning cartoon version by Filmation, aired on NBC. It was probably the most faithful translation of Captain Marvel, with appearances from the whole Marvel Family. The series is noteworthy for some of the early animation scripts of Paul Dini, who would later revolutionize Batman as part of the award-winning *Batman: The Animated Series* team. These were briefly available on video, but are long out of production.

## SILVER SURFER

The Surfer has occasionally appeared on television over the years, primarily in the various *Fantastic Four* animated series. There was one appearance in the 1967 ABC Saturday morning series, and several in the 1994 syndicated series. As discussed earlier, the first season of the 1994 *FF* series was horrendous, and the Galactus/Surfer episodes were no exception. The second-season appearances were better. "When Calls Galactus" makes use of an excellent John Byrne story involving Galactus and his new herald Terrax, while "Doomsday" adapts the classic Lee/Kirby story about Doctor Doom stealing the Surfer's Power Cosmic.

The Silver Surfer got his own animated series in 1998 on Fox. The scripts, shepherded by head writer Larry Brody, were intelligent and faithful to the source material while taking the characters in new directions. The animation was also first-rate, utilizing a combination of traditional cel animation for the primary characters, with a distinct Kirby influence, and 3-D CGI effects for Galactus and the outer-space imagery. *The Silver Surfer* series was hampered by production delays, which kept it from finding a steady audience. Eventually disagreements between Marvel and the production house Saban Entertainment caused the cancellation of the series, and problems between Fox and Marvel stemming from Marvel's then-precarious financial situation resulted in the series' being pulled from all repeats, rebroadcasts and any video release. We're hopeful the series will find its way through the legal morass and hit DVD—it deserves more viewers than it got.

## SPIDER-MAN

Marvel's trademark character, Spider-Man, burst onto TV screens in 1967 on ABC. *Spider-Man* became an instant TV sensation, with an insidiously catchy theme song that carved itself in the minds of generations of viewers. The score was cool, jazzy, and head-bopping, but the animation was at best average, and often worse than that, with certain web-swinging sequences repeated ad nauseum to save money. Frequently the only thing that salvaged the mediocre scripts was the hilarious delivery and timing of the voice actors.

The first twenty episodes of the series, produced by Grantray-Lawrence, have a sleek, streamlined design, particularly in the character models for Peter Parker and J. Jonah Jameson. Some shots look to be directly lifted from the original Steve Ditko artwork, particularly in close-ups of the Green Goblin. As for the stories themselves, they're faithful to the comics, utilizing many of Spidey's classic villains. Even when they venture out into new villains and threats, the tone of the series stays close to the comic's sensibilities.

When Krantz Films took over in the second and third seasons, under the supervision of Ralph Bakshi, the show's mood became

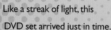
Like a streak of light, this DVD set arrived just in time.

SPIDER-MAN: THE '67 COLLECTION © BUENA VISTA HOME ENTERTAINMENT, INC.

darker. Most of the episodes put Spidey in completely out-of-character battles with monsters, aliens, demons or subterranean cave dwellers, and sloppy action sequences and sometimes bewildering character poses made Peter Parker look more constipated than concerned. Furthermore, it was obvious that animation bits were reused to pad out the episodes, sometimes breaking out into the opening theme song in the middle of the episode over yet another web-slinging montage. Still, even when it's bad, it's pretty good, the kind of quaint cartoon show that's dated but still satisfies.

Spidey returned to the airwaves in 1978, in live-action prime time, with the CBS TV movie *The Amazing Spider-Man*, followed by a weekly series in 1978. The series starred Nicholas Hammond as Peter Parker/Spider-Man and Robert F. Simon as J. Jonah Jameson and ran for fourteen episodes before being canceled despite decent ratings. It was just as well; other than the two or three brief appearances per episode of Spidey climbing up a skyscraper (often the same reused stock footage) or throwing an improbably woven webbed net over a couple of bad guys, there wasn't much difference between this and any other mediocre action/cop series airing at the time. The technology simply wasn't there to portray either Spider-Man's powers or any supervillains in any sort of realistic fashion.

The wallcrawler returned to animation in 1981 with two separate series, the syndicated *Spider-Man* and the more popular *Spider-Man*

*and His Amazing Friends*, which aired Saturday mornings on NBC. The latter featured Spidey teaming up with fellow teen heroes Iceman and Firestar, and is more fondly remembered than it deserves to be.

Following the success of *Batman: The Animated Series*, Fox brought Spidey back to animation in 1994 with *Spider-Man: The Animated Series*. While it struggled with a troubled production in its early episodes, it premiered to a generally positive reception and strong ratings, lasting for five seasons and a respectable sixty-five episodes. With all kinds of Spider-Man villains making their first appearance on television, from big leaguers like Venom and the Hobgoblin to third-stringers like the Rocket Racer and the Spot, the series provied the most thorough translation of the Spidey mythology to TV. After it ended in 1998, an attempt was made the following year to carry over its success to a new series, *Spider-Man Unlimited*, which catapulted Spidey to a weird parallel Earth. Audiences weren't buying it, and the series was cancelled after thirteen episodes.

In an attempt to ride the wave of Sam Raimi's film version of the webslinger, MTV aired *Spider-Man: The New Animated Series* in 2003, which roughly followed the continuity of the film. However, with its poor scripts, uninspired character designs and murky, stiff CGI animation, it too failed to catch on and quickly vanished after thirteen installments.

The most recent adaptation of Spider-Man to animation premiered in 2008, with *The*

*Spectacular Spider-Man* on the CW Network. A nice mix of the classic comics, the movies and the "Ultimate" revision books, *The Spectacular Spider-Man* sets its stage in Peter Parker's high school days, not long after Pete's debut as Spider-Man. The series switches things up in its supporting cast, featuring Gwen Stacy and Harry Osborne as Pete's high school buddies and Eddie Brock as Dr. Curt Connors's college-age lab assistant. It also features a contemporary, less frail Aunt May and a virtually unchanged J. Jonah Jameson, who seems to survive intact whatever media *Spider-Man* is translated into. The scripts are engaging and intelligent, if slightly kiddie-directed, and the character designs by Sean "Cheeks" Galloway give the series a modern, vibrant look without straying too far into anime territory.

One of the most welcome sights? In the show's title sequence, right up front: "Created by Stan Lee & Steve Ditko." Nice.

### THE TICK

Ben Edlund's absurdist gem *The Tick* made its animated premiere in Fox's Saturday morning television lineup in September 1994. That rare example of an adaptation that actually exceeds its source material both in execution and intent, *The Tick* was a hilarious send-up of the superhero genre, chronicling the adventures of its endlessly cheerful and super-strong protagonist The Tick and his nebbishy mothman sidekick Arthur as they protect The City from fiends like Chairface Chippendale, an urbane supervillain with a chair for a head. The real strength of the series lay in its hilarious scripting by Edlund, and Townsend Coleman's outrageously over-the-top performance as the Tick didn't hurt, either. Fox tried again with a live-action sitcom version in 2001, but it failed to capture that same spark and only lasted nine episodes.

### TEEN TITANS

Although the Titans had premiered on television in 1967 with their brief, three-episode stint on *The Superman/Aquaman Hour of Adventure*, it wasn't until 2003 that they really received the spotlight in their hit animated series *Teen Titans* on Cartoon Network. Heavily anime-influenced, the show took its lead from the 1980s Marv Wolfman/George Pérez comics run, featuring Robin, Cyborg, Beast Boy, Starfire and Raven. While it took some criticism from fans of the previous Warner Animation series because of its clear and obvious targeting of younger viewers and exaggerated Japanese style, *Teen Titans* was a clever, fun translation of the comics for an all-new audience. And it was a strong commercial success, airing for five seasons and sixty-five episodes.

### WONDER WOMAN

Wonder Woman's biggest bit of mass-media exposure was her hit 1970s TV series, starring Lynda Carter as Diana Prince/Wonder Woman. Premiering in 1975 as a pilot movie entitled *The New Original Wonder Woman* (to avoid confusion with an earlier and unsuccessful 1974 attempt entitled simply *Wonder Woman*, starring a blonde Cathy Lee Crosby) the ABC TV movie scored high enough ratings to warrant a weekly series, which first aired April 21, 1976.

The series' initial run, on ABC from 1976 to 1977, was a period piece, with Wonder Woman in World War II fighting Nazis and the like. In 1977, the series moved to CBS and modernized the plot away from the war. The immortal Diana returns to Paradise Island for thirty years, until she meets Steve Trevor Jr., who just happens to look exactly like his father, Steve Trevor Sr. (Lyle Waggoner in both roles). She decides to return to Man's World and work with Steve Jr. at the spy agency IADC. While the first season had more of a comic-book flavor, between the World War II setting and

Wonder Woman doing battle with foes such as Fausta, the Nazi Wonder Woman and Gargantua, the last two seasons were more typical of 1970s TV. In other words, Wonder Woman fights a lot of goons sporting black turtlenecks under brown sport blazers.

THE COMPLETE ★ 1 FIRST SEASON
*Wonder Woman*

Lynda Carter's embodiment of the title character was enough to make you overlook the show's many faults and keep coming back for more.

The main reason for the show's success was the tall, charming and drop-dead gorgeous Lynda Carter. Carter's charisma carried the show because, let's face it, people weren't tuning in for the spellbinding plots. Unlike the Adam West *Batman* series, which was silly, but with a self-reflexive wink to the audience, the ABC *Wonder Woman* was just goofy, with bad scripts, bad acting, and poor production values. Any show that expects you to take Lyle Waggoner seriously as a leading man has its work cut out for it. So why does it work? Lovely Lynda Carter sells it—smiling, running, jumping, and kicking ass. With anyone else, it never would have worked.

### X-MEN

The X-Men made a few guest appearances in the 1980s *Spider-Man and His Amazing Friends* series, and even had a pilot for their own show in 1989, *Pryde of the X-Men*, which aired numerous times in syndication but never generated a full series order. It wasn't until 1992 that the X-Men broke wide open in a blockbuster way, with the premiere of *X-Men* on the Fox Network. A smash hit upon its premiere and a ratings champion for the next six years, *X-Men* was based primarily on the team roster of the mid-1990s—Cyclops, Beast, Rogue, Storm, Jean Grey, Jubilee, Gambit, Wolverine

and Professor Xavier. However, this didn't stop the series' writers from adapting nearly every significant storyline from the X-Men's comic-book history, from "Rise of the Phoenix," to "The Dark Phoenix Saga" to "Days of Future Past," with dozens of X-characters making guest appearances over the course of its seventy-six episode run. Not only that, the writers of *X-Men* weren't afraid to make their audience pay attention, with frequent four- and five-episode storylines, as well as long-running story arcs that spanned the course of a season. The *X-Men* series cemented the characters' perception within the pop-culture zeitgeist as something everyone should know about, and most definitely paved the way for Bryan Singer's blockbuster films. Shamefully, there's no complete box set of the series available on DVD. For a series this influential, it's a must.

The success of Singer's film spawned another animated series, *X-Men: Evolution* (2000), which focused more on the characters as teenagers and the notion of Xavier's School, as opposed to the more adult versions on the previous series. *X-Men: Evolution* was popular and successful in its own right, airing on the WB for four seasons and fifty-two episodes. While it doesn't have the depth and scope of the original Fox *X-Men* series, it still stands on it own merits and is well worth watching.

*Origins of Marvel Comics* by Stan Lee

*Son of Origins of Marvel Comics* by Stan Lee

*Bring on the Bad Guys* by Stan Lee

*The Superhero Women* by Stan Lee

*The World Encyclopedia of Comics* by Maurice Horn

*The Great Comic Book Heroes* by Jules Feiffer

*Marvel: Five Fabulous Decades of the World's Greatest Comics* by Les Daniels

*DC Comics: Sixty Years of the World's Favorite Comic Book Heroes* by Les Daniels

*Superman: The Complete History* by Les Daniels

*Batman: The Complete History* by Les Daniels

*Wonder Woman: The Complete History* by Les Daniels

*Comics: Between the Panels* by Mike Richardson and Steve Duin

*Kirby: King of Comics* by Mark Evanier

*Comics and Sequential Art* by Will Eisner

*Understanding Comics* by Scott McCloud

*Tales to Astonish: Jack Kirby, Stan Lee, and the American Comic Book Revolution* by Ronin Ro

*The Ten-Cent Plague: The Great Comic-Book Scare and How It Changed America* by David Hajdu

*Will Eisner's Shop Talk* by Will Eisner

*Seal of Approval: The History of the Comics Code* by Amy Kiste Nyberg

*Superheroes and Philosophy* edited by Tom and Matt Morris

*The Comic Book Heroes* by Gerard Jones and Will Jacobs

*The Marvel Vault* by Roy Thomas and Peter Sanderson

*Excelsior! The Amazing Life of Stan Lee* by Stan Lee and George Mair

*A Smithsonian Book of Comic-Book Comics* by J. Michael Barrier and Martin T. Williams

*The Smithsonian Collection of Newspaper Comics* edited by Bill Blackbeard and Martin Williams

*The Comic-Book Book* edited by Don Thompson and Dick Lupoff

*Writing for Comics with Peter David* by Peter David

*The Comic Book Makers* by Joe Simon and Jim Simon

Probably not the first black man I'd ever seen, but certainly the first one I remember. It had to be 1940; I was born in '34, so I was no older than six or seven. If I could remember what month it was—though it *was* the summertime, absolutely—I'd know down to the pinpoint.

My mom and dad were taking a breather from me, as they tried to do *every* summer, and this time they didn't shanghai me off to some goddamn Camp HaHa or its ilk: they sent me to my Uncle Martin and Aunt Maxine in Shelby, North Carolina, (1939 and 1940 were the years of the legendary New York World's Fair). The day before this day I am about to recount, I bought, or was given, what I've always stored in the memory bank as the first comic book I ever owned. It was the 1940 *New York World's Fair Comics*, published by DC at 15¢, a very heavy cost in the barely-post-Depression days of summer, 1940. This comic book with its cardboard covers featured Superman and Batman and

Sandman and a full 96 pages of the sort of stuff a kid in those days, pre-*American Idol*, pre-gangsta, pre-iPod, even pre-television or the Internet, found mesmerizing.

It was my McGuffey's Primer, my Joseph Campbell, my Will & Ariel Durant Story of Civilization. I am convinced no smug, self-absorbed, arrogant Xboxer wallowing in today's BritneyParisR.Kelly mudhole can have the faintest perturbation of soulful cognition as to what I'm positing here. On that summer day of which I will write, in Shelby, North Carolina, with the sun undoing the horizon and the whirring insects filling the space around me with conflicting soundtracks, I wandered with *World's Fair* in hand, into an enormous stand of sugar cane. I was a very *little* kid: the sugar cane field may *not*, in fact, have been so enormous. But I, for my part, was not enormous. I was great in expectations and wonder; but not high enough to see the tops of the stalks around me.

And I came through to a large clearing and there, all around that circle, were black men. Giant black men, shining in the sunlight. They glimmered and glittered with their own sweat, and they wielded huge blades, and they swung and swung to the wash and wind from their godlike strokes. And down came the sugar cane, whistling down in small crashing and chittering sounds, a million scarab husk sounds as the crew moved in a stately, methodical way.

One great Nubian chieftain glanced over from his labors, and saw me. He may not have been the first black man I'd ever seen (Painesville, Ohio *must* have had such a population *before* I attended junior high, years later, and saw black kids my age), but he is the first gentleman of color I remember.

He grinned at me. From 'way up there, his head brushing the sky, he didn't just smile, he grinned. Wide friendly hi-kid sort of smile. And I walked over to him, and he said, "Whachoo doin' out here, son?" and I told him "Nuthin'," because I was six or seven, and at six or seven the answer to any question from an adult as to what you were up to was (and still is) "nuthin'." And we chatted for a few words, and this living icon from mythology asked me if I'd ever tasted the sweet taste of a sugar cane stalk; and I said nuh-uh. So he swept that mighty blade twice across a pipe of cane, and handed me a length about the size of a *shakuhachi*—which, as you know, is a long Japanese tubular flute—more of a contrabass transverse than, say, a piccolo or a zuffolo. And he advised me to go out into the sun and enjoy my treat. So I did.

Oh, and just as an askance, I know you'll have noted that somewhere a few paragraphs back I slipped somewhichway into *faux*-Bradbury. I will not apologize. I read Ray long before he and I became chums, but if one is writing about being a country lad on a hot summer's day, one cannot do better than to emulate the Once and Future King of Mars. Now, back to our thrilling story.

I went out there, and I lay down on my side bowered among the flowers and the grass, and I sucked on that impossible wand of sugar cane, and I read my 1940 *New York World's Fair Comics*, and it was one of the most perfect days of my life. And here's what is the nicest part: I *knew* I was having one of the best days of my life, even then, even six or seven years of age. *That*, my friends, is a small miracle of self-awareness. I hope you've had a few of those; so rare, so spiffy.

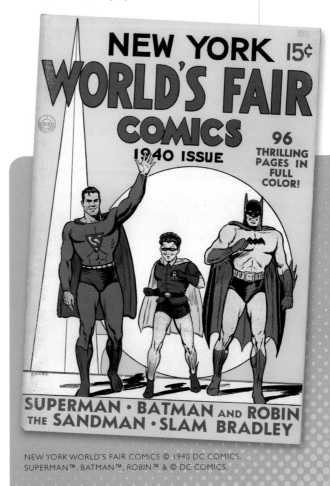

NEW YORK WORLD'S FAIR COMICS © 1940 DC COMICS. SUPERMAN™, BATMAN™, ROBIN™ & © DC COMICS.

There is a shot near the end of Kurosawa's *Stray Dog*, in which the young police detective played by the great Toshiro Mifune has run to ground the desperate and tragic young thief who stole his revolver: and they flee out into a vast flowering field, and all you can see for some time are the beaten-down paths of their passage. Years after that summer afternoon in Shelby, North Carolina, I saw *Stray Dog* for the first time, and as I sat in the theater, it was the *nostalgia* of smelling the perfume my mother wore when she lifted me from the crib; it was the memory of the first pomegranate seeds that exploded on my tongue in some far place I cannot name;

it was going back sans time machine, to that astonishing idyll.

And remembered it again, in 1993, I'm almost sixty years old, and I remember that day, and it comes back to me *another* thought I had, lying there agape at Zatara and Sandman and Batman in my 15¢ cardboard-cover window on the world. There are dreams to be had as a child which, if realized in adult terms, mean you have made a success of your life. If you loved to play cowboy, and you grow up owning a cattle ranch, you're a success. If you liked playing doctor or nurse, and you wind up a brain surgeon, you are a success: I wanted to have my own comic book.

Lying there, like Mifune's Officer Murakami; like Bradbury's young Douglas Spaulding, imbiber of dandelion wine; like the spawn of Siegel and Shuster I've been, and never knew it, I hungered for a kind of adult success that included my own comic book, my very own, with my name on it.

Along about 1992 or '93—in a tangential anecdote too long and interesting to be told in *précis* here—but I've told it in detail in one of my books—my friend Mike Richardson of Dark Horse Comics said yes to an endeavor to be titled *Harlan Ellison's Dream Corridor*. And for the next decade-and-a-half (with abysses here and there, through no one's dilatory behavior but mine own) we put together such wonderful comic books you wouldn't believe! I worked with three sensational editors, Anina Bennett, Bob Schreck, and the glorious Diana Schutz. We published the last pages ever done by Curt Swan and Doug Wildey. My

HARLAN ELLISON'S DREAM CORRIDOR : © 1996 THE KILIMANJARO CORPORATION.

stories were adapted by Big Names like Len Wein and Tony Isabella and Mark Waid, Mike Gilbert and Steve Niles. We were in at the beginning of Mike Deodato the Younger, Teddy Kristiansen, Gene Ha, David Lapham. Hundreds of writers, letterers, colorists, great pencillers like Gene Colan and gallery artists like Michael Whelan, Steve Hickman, Leo & Diane Dillon. The list goes on and on. I will have to omit dozens. But that's acceptable, at this reading, because this is the answer to the question that was asked of me, "What was your favorite Creative Time on a title?"

It was the *Dream Corridor*.

It was the sweet fulfillment of the sweet dreams a six- or seven-year-old kid had while supine under the North Carolina sun, thousands of miles from Painesville, Ohio, hungering to exist as an equal in the grandiloquent world of Superman and Sandman and Will Eisner and Julie Schwartz, even if (at that childhood moment) he had only met two of them.

That non-spandex comic, at its bestselling number, never came anywhere close to the tsunamis of last month's *Spider-Man* or *Star Wars* or *Batgirl*, frankly broke my heart. It was such a nice comic. So good, so smart, so interesting, all Eric Shanower interstitial. And apart from the few thousands who loved it, across fifteen years, it is slightly less case-hardened steel forged in the memories of comic-book geeks than, say, *Brother Power, the Geek*. Yet, on sum, the best I had in me, and the sweet dreams memorialized. You could look'm up.

Harlan as one of his current favorite comic characters: Wormwood, Gentleman Corpse.

## SCOTT TIPTON

**Scott Tipton**, founder and editor-in-chief of Comics101.com, writes the weekly column of the same name, the site's most popular and highly trafficked destination. In recent years, Scott has crossed over from comics historian to comics creator, writing such series as *Doomed*, *Angel: Auld Lang Syne*, *Klingons: Blood Will Tell* and *Star Trek: Mirror Images* for IDW Publishing. Scott currently serves as editorial services manager for a Santa Monica ad agency, and communications director for a Sherman Oaks-based toy company. He lives in Los Angeles, California, with his high school sweetheart, Jenny, and more comic books and action figures than a grown man has any right to have.

### THE FIRST ISSUE I EVER READ
I think it was an issue of *Spidey Super Stories*, the 1970s *Electric Company* tie-in kiddie book, with Spidey and guest-star Iceman helping to save Easy Reader from some super-villain, maybe the Beetle.

### THE BEST CREATIVE TIME ON A TITLE
*Justice League International*, the first two or three years. After the Justice League books had been unremarkable for years with characters like Vibe and Gypsy shoved into the limelight, here was a League book with big guns like Batman, J'onn J'onnz, Captain Marvel and Green Lantern again. With the addition of great new characters like Blue Beetle and Booster Gold, every issue was exciting, and at the same time rip-roaringly funny.

### THE BEST COVER
*Animal Man* #5 (1988). The sight of Buddy Baker symbolically crucified while an unseen Chuck Jones-like hand continues to paint him in is a startling one, and it perfectly conveyed both the contents of the issue and the thematic design for the remaining two years of Grant Morrison's expertly planned storyline. Pure genius, and gorgeously executed by Brian Bolland.

### THE BEST STORYLINE
*Starman* by James Robinson, Tony Harris and Peter Snejbjerg. Robinson introduces us to Jack Knight, a young man thrust into the family business of being a superhero, and over the course of a little more than eighty issues, we watch him resent it, learn to love it, become really good at it, and then decide to walk away. Beautifully written and drawn.

### THE GOOFIEST STORYLINE
*Batman* #92 (June 1955), the first appearance of Ace the Bat-Hound. Even when I read it as a child in *Batman: From the 30s to the 70s*, I recall thinking, "Wow. Batman puts a mask on his dog. That's really weird."

**Chris Ryall** has been the publisher and editor-in-chief of IDW Publishing since 2004. He is also an Eagle- and Eisner Award-nominated comic book writer of such series as Clive Barker's *The Great and Secret Show*, *Zombies vs. Robots*, *Groom Lake*, *Doomed*, *George A. Romero's Land of the Dead* and dozens of others. Chris also served as chief content provider and editor-in-chief for filmmaker Kevin Smith's Web venture where Comics 101 got its start; a corporate speechwriter for American Honda; a creative executive with Dick Clark Communications; and an advertising copywriter. He lives in San Diego, California, with his wife, Julie, and daughter, Lucy.

## THE FIRST ISSUE I EVER READ

*Fantastic Four* #130 (January 1973). I was five years old; the comic belonged to my neighbor. The cover image was a Jim Steranko gem showing a giant, stretchy arm, a guy made of rocks and a villain made of sand. Did I mention I was five and therefore powerless before those kinds of visuals? I made off with the comic and was started on the path before I even fully knew how to read.

## THE BEST CREATIVE TIME ON A TITLE

Chris Claremont and John Byrne on *The Uncanny X-Men*. There were so many other great teams before and after that time, but as an impressionable teen, reading their clever, beautifully illustrated and ultimately tragic storylines changed what I'd come to expect from a comic.

## THE BEST COVER

*The Amazing Spider-Man* #39 (August 1966). John Romita's depiction of the cackling Green Goblin capturing Spider-Man in civilian guise—but with identity clearly revealed—has resonated since I first spied it in my older brother's collection as a kid. This one proved much harder to boost than that first *Fantastic Four* issue, so it still holds the top spot on my wish list. Spidey's arch-nemesis attacking him where he lived? That was chilling stuff and perfectly captured by Romita's linework, which was all the more impressive because it was his first issue as regular artist on the title.

## THE BEST STORYLINE

*Daredevil*'s "Born Again" storyline (1986) by Frank Miller and David Mazzucchelli. Only this team and this storyline could supplant Miller's first run on *Daredevil* in my head. The brilliant, mature but fully accessible superhero storytelling earns it this spot, but Mazzucchelli's art elevates it to comics godhood. Even without ninjas.

## THE GOOFIEST STORYLINE/ISSUE

*Secret Wars II* (1985). Goofy doesn't have to be bad, but in this case, it definitely is. When a perm-haired, godlike character being taught how to void his bladder by Spider-Man and then celebrating the feeling afterward is the most—and only—memorable part of a much-ballyhooed miniseries sequel, you know something has gone seriously awry.

# Look for these exciting titles!

These and other fine **IMPACT** books are available at your local art & craft retailer, bookstore or online supplier, or visit our website at www.impact-books.com.

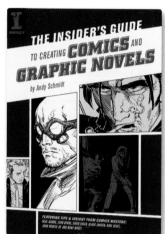

The volume of artistry and memorable characters in this one-of-a-kind guide is staggering, and entices both avid collectors and casual fans. Readers will find comic books from various genres, produced between 1930 and the present, each represented by its cover and background details including publisher, imprint year, series and issue numbers, intriguing story notes and why it was chosen for the book.

ISBN 13: 978-0-89689-921-6
ISBN 10: 0-89689-921-7
HARDCOVER, 272 PAGES, #Z3599

In this unprecedented, behind-the-scenes guide, former Marvel editor and current IDW senior editor Andy Schmidt and his superstar industry friends give you the inside track on creating engaging, professional-looking comic books. Written for upcoming creative stars and comic-book enthusiasts, *The Insider's Guide* covers the entire creative process from beginning to end.

ISBN 13: 978-1-60061-022-6
ISBN 10: 1-60061-022-6
PAPERBACK, 176 PAGES, #Z1306

This second edition of Peter David's hit book is a must-have for all comics, fantasy and science fiction fans who want to write their own comics or improve their storytelling techniques. The revised content features a new introduction by the author, dozens of specific writing issues in Q+A format from David's fans, and an all-new chapter by Andy Schmidt on how to break in to the comics business.

ISBN 13: 978-1-60061-687-7
ISBN 10: 1-60061-687-9
PAPERBACK, 192 PAGES, #Z4812